A Behavior Analytic View of Child Development

APPLIED CLINICAL PSYCHOLOGY

Series Editors:
Alan S. Bellack
University of Maryland at Baltimore, Baltimore, Maryland
Michel Hersen
Nova Southeastern University, Fort Lauderdale, Florida

Current volumes in this Series

BEHAVIOR ANALYSIS AND TREATMENT
  Edited by Ron Van Houten and Saul Axelrod

A BEHAVIOR ANALYTIC VIEW OF CHILD DEVELOPMENT
  Henry D. Schlinger, Jr.

CASEBOOK OF THE BRIEF PSYCHOTHERAPIES
  Edited by Richard A. Wells and Vincent J. Giannetti

CLINICAL PSYCHOLOGY SINCE 1917
Science, Practice, and Organization
  Donald K. Routh

ETHNIC VALIDITY, ECOLOGY, AND PSYCHOTHERAPY
A Psychosocial Competence Model
  Forrest B. Tyler, Deborah Ridley Brome, and Janice E. Williams

FUNDAMENTALS OF BEHAVIOR ANALYTIC RESEARCH
  Alan Poling, Laura L. Methot, and Mark G. LeSage

GUIDEBOOK FOR CLINICAL PSYCHOLOGY INTERNS
  Edited by Gary K. Zammit and James W. Hull

PERSPECTIVES AND PROMISES OF CLINICAL PSYCHOLOGY
  Edited by Anke Ehlers, Wolfgang Fiegenbaum, Irmela Florin, and
  Jürgen Margraf

SEXUAL BEHAVIOR
Problems and Management
  Nathaniel McConaghy

SOURCEBOOK OF ADULT ASSESSMENT STRATEGIES
  Nicola S. Schutte and John M. Malouff

THERAPEUTIC CHANGE
An Object Relations Perspective
  Sidney J. Blatt and Richard Q. Ford

A Continuation Order Plan is available for this series. A continuation order will bring delivery of each new volume immediately upon publication. Volumes are billed only upon actual shipment. For further information please contact the publisher.

A Behavior Analytic View of Child Development

HENRY D. SCHLINGER, JR.
Western New England College
Springfield, Massachusetts

Plenum Press • New York and London

Library of Congress Cataloging-in-Publication Data

Schlinger, Henry D.
    A behavior analytic view of child development / Henry D.
  Schlinger, Jr.
        p.   cm. -- (Applied clinical psychology)
    Includes bibliographical references and index.
    ISBN 0-306-45059-3
    1. Clinical child psychology. 2. Child development.
  3. Developmental psychology.   I. Title. II. Series.
  RJ503.3.S35   1995
  305.23'1--dc20   95-23848
                                                            CIP

RJ
503.3
.S35
1995

ISBN 0-306-45059-3

© 1995 Plenum Press, New York
A Division of Plenum Publishing Corporation
233 Spring Street, New York, N. Y. 10013

10 9 8 7 6 5 4 3 2 1

Printed in the United States of America

To my parents, Henry and Norma Schlinger,
who always encouraged me

Preface

The cover story of a *Life* magazine was titled, "Babies Are Smarter Than You Think" (July 1993). The cover went on to say, "They can add before they can count. They can understand a hundred words before they can speak. And, at three months, their powers of memory are far greater than we ever imagined." These ways of talking about human infants are intended to capture the attention of readers, and they usually do. Developmental psychologists often talk about infant behavior in similar ways. Serious scientists might write such descriptions off as little more than the popularization of psychology or, as it is often termed, "pop psychology."

The research cited in the *Life* article represents a sample of developmental research in which the interpretations of the results exceed what the results themselves support. Developmental researchers usually study the relationship between infant behavior and various events in the environment. But when they talk about what is going on, they refer to such unobservable constructs as the infant's "mind," "memory," and "understanding." Among other "powers," infants are said to "grasp simple mathematics" and to "have a rudimentary knowledge of the way the world works."

The problem with talking about infants in these ways is that, although we are told what things infants are likely to do in particular situations, and even when in their lives they are likely to do them, we are told nothing about *how* the behavior comes about, that is, the processes responsible for the observed behavior. Lacking adequate scientific explanations, developmental researchers frequently use ordinary language to describe behavior. Consider, for example, that before infants are able to say "telephone," they are able to point to or look at one when the parent says, "Where's the telephone?" That most infants demonstrate such behavior is indisputable, but when asked to explain such observations, developmental researchers are likely to say that it is because infants "understand" words before they can speak. While such an explanation may sound good, scientists and logicians recognize it as being circular. The researchers have only labeled the phenomenon "understanding" and then used that label as the explanation. The behavior of pointing to objects remains unexplained in the sense that researchers cannot identify the independent variables responsible for the behavior. So they infer unobservable and untestable events such as "understanding," "memory," and "mind" as explanations. Describing behavioral relations using mentalistic or cognitive language is not problematic per se. Mentalistic and cognitive language does organize and describe the content of everyday behavior pretty well. The problem, however, is that such language does not readily specify the variables that can be manipulated in an attempt to discover the processes by which the behavior comes about. Moreover, mentalistic language may actually lead researchers to try to study the mental or cognitive processes they assume underlie behavior.

In the past several decades, the field of developmental psychology has generated a vast amount of research. Despite this growth, the field remains theoretically fractionated; that is, very little of its research is united by a common orientation. Not surprisingly, textbooks in the field reflect this state of affairs. Although many developmental textbooks are written from a generally cognitive perspective, none adopts a unitary theoretical approach. On the contrary, textbooks in developmental psychology reveal a field populated by many different explanations and theories. It is also not unusual to find numerous instances of contradictory evidence for the same phenomenon. Developmental psychologists have provided valuable information about child behavioral development. Unfortunately, such information lacks a strong unifying theoretical background and fails to impart practical knowledge that can enable psychologists to reliably change behavior in natural settings.

Although many theoretical systems within developmental psychology are inadequate for the scientific understanding of the subject matter, much of the research is valuable and worthy of consideration. Therefore, we needn't throw the baby out with the bathwater. Instead, we ought to ask whether it is possible to make sense of this accumulation of apparently unrelated data according to a single, unifying theory.

There are some psychologists, behavior analysts, who take a natural science approach to psychology. For them the subject matter of developmental psychology consists of the behavioral changes that are observed over time in the life of an individual largely as a function of his or her interaction with objective, environmental events. Over the years, there have been some attempts by behavior analysts to offer a behavior analysis of development (e.g., Bijou, 1976; Bijou & Baer, 1961, 1978). Behavior analysts, however, have not by and large addressed the extensive research in the area conducted mainly by psychologists who are not behavior analysts (c.f. Gewirtz, 1972a, 1972b; Gewirtz & Pelaez-Nogueras, 1990, 1991b). Since much of the existing research in developmental psychology suggests a strong environmental component to behavioral development, behavior analysts are in a prime position to study the processes responsible for this development.

Although behavior analysis is necessary for the understanding of behavioral development, its treatment in most developmental textbooks is inadequate. It is relegated either to being an almost historical marker in developmental psychology, or it is never credited with being able to explain anything more than trivial behavior. Some textbooks offer rather lengthy sections on learning in which the principles of respondent (i.e., classical) and operant conditioning are detailed; however, subsequent discussions of behavioral changes attributed to learning rarely refer back to these principles. In many textbooks, the discussion of learning, not to mention behavior analysis, is almost nonexistent. Finally, many standard textbooks omit the significant empirical and theoretical contributions of behavior analysts to the scientific understanding of behavioral development. At the very least, this omission does a disservice to students of developmental psychology by depriving them of valuable information concerning development.

The purpose of *A Behavior Analytic View of Child Development* is twofold. First, I want to introduce behavior analysis to the reader. It is frequently said that behavior analysis is antitheoretical or that it is at best a collection of unrelated, trivial facts. I hope this book disproves both ideas. Moreover, I intend to show that behavior analysis has a strong claim to "theory" in the natural science sense of the term. Second, I want to show how behavior analysis can be used fruitfully to interpret existing research in developmental psychology, thus offering the field a more unified theoretical approach. Although this book is intended primarily as an explication of behavior analysis as it relates to child behavioral development, throughout, I consistently contrast the behavior analytic approach with a more traditional psychological approach to similar problems. This should help the reader make comparisons between the two approaches.

The book is composed of two major sections. The first three chapters deal with the concept of theory in developmental psychology. In Chapter 1, science is defined and several criteria for evaluating scientific theories are discussed. In Chapter 2, the main features of traditional approaches in developmental psychology are presented—largely as structural theories based frequently on normative, correlational data. Chapter 3 introduces behavior analysis as it will be used throughout the book to interpret developmental research. Chapters 4 through 10 comprise the second major section. Here, behavior analysis is used to interpret research in the development of infant memory (Chapter 4), motor development (Chapter 5), perceptual development (Chapter 6), cognitive development (Chapter 7), language development (Chapter 8), the development of attachment relations (Chapter 9), and the development of prosocial behavior (Chapter 10).

Although this book could be used as a primary text in courses on infant or child development, it would be equally valuable as a supplemental text, especially if the instructor is using one of the standard textbooks in child development. In such cases, I see the present book serving as a theoretical anchor for students.

Finally, several technical points need to be mentioned. First, throughout the book I reference standard textbooks in developmental psychology. These books were not selected according to any special criteria; they simply represent random sampling from various publishers. Although some may criticize the practice of referencing secondary sources, my intention is to present mainstream developmental psychology as it is likely to be introduced to students in the field. Second, I use the term "theory" frequently to describe both behavior analytic and nonbehavior analytic approaches. When the term is used for behavior analysis, I mean it in the scientific sense as described in Chapter 1. Next, I use the term "cognitive" to describe most theoretical approaches other than behavior analysis. I do this because all of these approaches have in common the practice of studying observable behavioral relations and then either reifying them as hypothetical internal events or processes or inferring such events and processes as explanations of those relations.

Throughout the book I analyze the language of traditional developmental psychology. I do this because how we talk about our subject matter determines, to varying degrees, what we do about it. For instance, if developmental psychologists talk about hypothetical cognitive events as explanations of behavior, that may determine the kinds of research methods they use to study the behavior, or the kinds of strategies they might employ in applied settings. A behavior analysis of the traditional language of developmental psychology may help to elucidate more objective controlling variables and to suggest more scientific ways of studying the behavior.

I would like to acknowledge several people who helped during various stages in the writing of this book. First, I want to thank all those at Plenum for their help, including, but not limited to, Mariclaire Cloutier, Robin Cook, and Herman Makler. I especially want to thank Eliot Werner for his encouragement, support, assistance, and patience from the beginning of the project. I also want to thank the staff of D'Amour Library at Western New England College, especially Lucy Brunelle and Suzanne Garber, for their help in acquiring interlibrary loan materials. I want to thank Dennis Kolodziejski and Dave Palmer for reading and commenting on earlier drafts of individual chapters. I am especially grateful to Ed Morris for taking the time to review the entire manuscript and for his many helpful suggestions for improving both its style and substance. His knowledge of both behavior analysis and developmental psychology, as well as his editorial expertise, made him an ideal reviewer. Finally, I want to thank my loving wife, Julie Riggott, for reading and reviewing the manuscript twice. Her keen eye for grammatical mistakes and inconsistencies has resulted in a greatly improved product.

HENRY D. SCHLINGER, JR.

Contents

1. SCIENCE 1

Defining Scientific Theory 1
Fact versus Theory in Science 2
Scientific Laws 4
Scientific Theory 4
   Scientific Prediction 5
   Scientific Interpretation 7
Criteria for Evaluating Scientific Theories 8
   Generality (or Inclusiveness) 9
   Testability 9
   External Validity (or Accuracy) 10
   Fruitfulness (or Utility) 10
   Simplicity (or Parsimony) 11
Scientific Understanding 11
Summary 13

2. DEVELOPMENTAL PSYCHOLOGY 15

The Concept of Behavior in Developmental Psychology 15
Structural Approaches to Behavior 16
   Structural Approaches and Explanations of Behavior 18
Research and Theory in Developmental Psychology 20
   Correlational Research 20
Problems with a Structural Approach to Behavior Change 24
Developmental Theory Assessed 26
Summary 29

3. BEHAVIOR ANALYSIS 31

A Little History: Are Theories (of Learning) Necessary? 31
Skinner on Theory in Science 32

Basic Units in Behavior Analysis 33
The Environment 35
    The Traditional View of the Environment 35
    A Behavior Analytic View of the Environment 36
Locus of Control 37
The Role of Inference in Behavior Analysis 38
A Behavior Analytic Taxonomy 39
    Stimulus Functions 39
A Behavior Analytic View of Development 41
    The Concept of Development 41
    Genes, Brain, and Behavioral Plasticity 42
    Proximate and Ultimate Causation 43
Applying a Behavior Analytic Interpretation 44
    Cognitive and Behavior Analytic Approaches to Behavior 45
Summary 46

4. THE DEVELOPMENT OF MEMORY 49

The Concept of Memory in Developmental Psychology 50
Research on Infant Memory 51
    Visual Recognition Memory 51
    Experiments Using Operant Conditioning Procedures 57
Cognitive and Behavior Analytic Views of Memory 65
Summary 66

5. MOTOR DEVELOPMENT 67

Basic Concepts in Motor Development 68
Maturation and Experience in Motor Development 68
Rhythmical Stereotypies and Reflexes 70
    Rhythmical Stereotypies 70
    Reflexes 74
Structural Categories of Motor Development 76
    Body Control 76
    Manual Control 85
Voluntary (versus Involuntary) Control 90
Cognitive and Behavior Analytic Views of Motor Development .. 92
Summary 94

6. PERCEPTUAL DEVELOPMENT 95

Sensation and Perception 95
Visual Perceptual Behavior 96

Depth Perception 97
A Behavior Analytic View of Depth-Appropriate Responding .. 108
Object Perception 109
A Behavior Analytic View of Object-Appropriate Behavior 114
Summary 119

7. COGNITIVE DEVELOPMENT 121

Piagetian Concepts 122
Organization and Adaptation 122
Psychological Structures 124
The Sensorimotor Period of Cognitive Development 125
The Substages of Sensorimotor Development 125
Imitation and Object Permanence 136
Piaget's View of Imitation 137
Imitation in Infancy 139
The Role of Learning in Infant Imitation 140
Search Behavior and Object Permanence 142
Summary 148

8. LANGUAGE DEVELOPMENT 151

Speech Perception 152
Categorical Perceptual Behavior in Infants 153
The Development of Prespeech 155
Crying 156
The First Languagelike Sounds 157
The Development of Speech 161
Structural versus Behavior Analytic Views 161
Single-Word Production 162
Multiple-Word Production 169
One-Word Period 169
Two-Word Period 171
Grammar and The Production of Sentences 171
Rule-Governed Morphology 172
Speed of Acquisition 174
Language Universals 175
The Nature and Nurture of Language 177
Criticisms of Chomsky's Argument for a Universal Grammar .. 177
The Treatment of Behavior Analytic Views of Language in
    Developmental Textbooks 178
The Role of Reinforcement in the Acquisition of Language 179
The Child as Passive Recipient of the Environment 181

Language as Inherently Generative (Creative) 182
Summary 182

9. SOCIAL AND EMOTIONAL DEVELOPMENT I: ATTACHMENT
   RELATIONS 185

Defining Attachment 186
Interpreting Bowlby's Theory of Attachment 187
   Bowlby's Evolutionary–Ethological Perspective 187
Attachment Behaviors 189
   Signaling Behavior 190
   Approach Behaviors 196
Proximity-Establishing and Proximity-Maintaining Behaviors 196
   Attachment Behaviors in Precocial Animals: Imprinting 197
   Attachment Behaviors in Altricial Animals 199
Development of "Fearful" Behaviors 200
   Separation Anxiety 201
   Stranger Anxiety 204
A Behavior Analysis of Social–Emotional Development 206
   Social Reinforcement 207
   Social Discriminative Stimuli 208
Summary 212

10. SOCIAL AND EMOTIONAL DEVELOPMENT II: MORAL BEHAVIOR   215

Views of Moral Development 216
   A Traditional View of Moral Development 217
   A Behavior Analytic View of Moral Development 218
The Development of Prosocial Behavior 218
   The Problem of Definition 218
   Formal Categories of Prosocial Behavior 220
Empathy 230
   Defining Empathy 231
   The Origins of Empathic Responding and Prosocial Behavior .. 239
Summary 242

REFERENCES 243

INDEX 259

1

Science

The first part of this chapter discusses theory in science and distinguishes it from the ordinary conception of theory as simply a guess or opinion. The chapter also points out that scientific theories are not separate from scientific facts but, rather, that they are broad generalizations of those facts. The chapter then introduces several criteria used to evaluate the merit of scientific theories. Finally, scientific "understanding" is briefly discussed.

DEFINING SCIENTIFIC THEORY

Most definitions of theory in developmental psychology textbooks are not unlike the one offered by Santrock (1988), who writes that "theories are general beliefs that help us to explain the data or facts we have observed and to make predictions" (p. 24). This definition of theory may be valid, but it is not precise and may be open to misinterpretation. For example, it is easy to come away thinking that scientific theory is separate from scientific fact, when nothing could be farther from the truth. Moreover, Santrock's definition of theory does not indicate where the "general beliefs" come from. Are they just someone's opinions or guesses? Finally, although Santrock's definition is correct that theories permit prediction, it doesn't say what can be predicted or where the predictions come from.

If one looks up the word "theory" in the dictionary, it becomes easier to understand why there might be some confusion as to its meaning; that is, why the term is used differently in different contexts or by different authors. For example, the *Oxford English Dictionary* (1989) states that "theory" is:

> A scheme or system of ideas or statements held as an explanation or account of a group of facts or phenomena; a hypothesis that has been confirmed or established by observation or experiment, and is propounded or accepted as accounting for the known facts; a statement of what are held to be the general laws, principles, or causes of something known or observed. (p. 902)

1

While this definition seems to possess the essential ingredients of what many scientists hold theory to be, it still leaves unanswered questions about the origin of the "ideas or statements" that function as explanations, as well as the nature of the facts to be explained. Before I offer a working definition of scientific theory, let me briefly try to dispel some of the misconceptions of scientific theory, a few of which I have already mentioned.

Fact versus Theory in Science

First we must clarify what is usually meant when scientists speak of scientific facts. Scientific discovery begins with empirical observations. Those observations are called scientific facts when the empirical events upon which they are based are ordered by scientists into functional relations. A *functional relation* is a type of relation between at least two variables (A and B) such that the value of A determines the value of B. All things being equal, B is said to be a function of A. When scientists have discovered a functional relation between two events, they are said to have discovered a rudimentary scientific fact. So, scientific facts are not simply casual observations, but rather observations that possess a reliable, repeatable order among them. The natural sciences (e.g., physics, chemistry, and biology) are noteworthy for the number of scientific facts they possess; the field of psychology possesses few.

The nature of the relationship between fact and theory also needs clarification. Suppose that in a discussion of evolution by natural selection a teacher mentions the idea of common descent; that is, that all species are related to each other. Then a student asks, "Is that fact, or is it just theory?" In the student's question, the word "guess" or "opinion" could easily be substituted for the word "theory" without losing any of the meaning. When the word "theory" is used in science, however, it means something quite different from conjecture. In the natural sciences, theory is derived from scientific facts. In a loose sense, theory is a way of making sense of the facts; a scientific theory begins to take shape when the facts are ordered by scientists according to common features. Specifically, "scientific analysis involves ordering observations at several levels of specificity" (Poling, Schlinger, Starin, and Blakely, 1990, p. 32).

To understand better these different levels of scientific observations, let us consider the principle or law of reinforcement as an example of theory development. Suppose we place a food-deprived rat in a standard operant conditioning chamber and arrange food to be delivered if the rat presses a metal lever, which extends from one of the walls of the chamber. If we maintain this contingency between pressing the lever and food delivery, lever pressing will soon occur with a frequency greater than before the contingency was imposed. The process of following some behavior, such as lever pressing, with a stimulus, such as food, which results in an increase in the frequency of the behavior under similar conditions is termed "reinforcement." (According to more recent conceptions of reinforcement, it is the change in the probability of the behavior of eating, relative to other behaviors, rather than the presentation of food, that should be considered the reinforcer [Premack, 1965; Timberlake & Allison, 1974]). Now, suppose that we discontinue delivering food after the rat presses the lever. This will cause the frequency of the behavior to decline to preconditioning levels. This process of discontinuing reinforcement with a resulting decrease in the frequency of some behavior is termed "extinction."

If we are able to repeat this observation (i.e., reinforcement and extinction) many times with this rat we will have discovered a functional relation between lever pressing and food delivery. All things being equal, we can say that lever pressing is a function of the food as a consequence. So, what can we conclude about our discovery? As Bijou and Baer (1978) stated, we can sum up these observations in a general statement. In this particular case it would be: When food immediately follows the behavior of pressing a lever by a hungry laboratory rat, the frequency of lever pressing will increase.

Are we ready yet with a theory or even a law of reinforcement? No. We need to answer some other questions before we can venture a more general conclusion. For example, we might want to know whether the same results can be obtained with other rats. Perhaps our rat was somehow unique. So we repeat the demonstration with several other rats. Maybe the nature of food as a consequence was unique or the specific nature of the response was special. So, we repeat our demonstration using delivery of water to thirsty rats, heat onset to cold rats, etc., and, moreover, we select other types of responses for conditioning. After demonstrations with different types of rats and reinforcers and responses, our summary statement now reads: When certain consequences immediately follow behavior in *laboratory rats*, the frequency of the behavior will increase. This represents a much broader generalization of the data. In fact, our level of observation has now become a little less specific and might be said to represent functional relations between classes of variables specifically, classes of behavior and classes of consequences. The term "reinforcement" is no longer used for the relation between food and lever pressing in one rat, but rather for consequences and behavior in rats in general. But maybe rats as a species are somehow unique and the process we call reinforcement only works for them.

Are we now ready to make a more general statement about other species? No. Our next step is to try to replicate our demonstration with other species, including humans, with different responses followed by different consequences. Now suppose that we accomplish this with essentially the same results each time. Our summary statement now looks like this: Under certain conditions, certain consequences immediately following behavior will produce an increase in the frequency of the behavior. The main point for the present discussion of the relation between fact and theory is that as scientific facts accumulate and are grouped and ordered, certain generalizations emerge that will eventually make up the theory. Although our last generalization may not yet properly be considered a theory, it is closer to being considered a scientific law, which is the next level of specificity.

SCIENTIFIC LAWS

In the present context, a law is the next level of specificity in the ordering of scientific observations. According to McCain and Segal (1988), scientific laws are "descriptions of relatively constant relationships between certain kinds of phenomena," which "may be in sentence form or symbolic form, such as an equation.... [I]t is the reproducibility of phenomena that leads one to accept the relationship as a law" (p. 51). The Law of Effect (or reinforcement) is an example. The Law of Effect states that behavior is a function of its consequences. That this relationship between behavior and its consequences is so reproducible strengthens its description as a scientific law. Of course, scientific laws depend on other variables. For example, the Law of Effect depends on motivational operations, such as food deprivation or painful stimulation, the context in which the behavior occurs, and the health of the organism, not to mention the species to which the organism belongs. Thus, perhaps the most accurate statement of the Law of Effect is as follows: *All things being equal*, behavior is a function of its consequences. This brings us to the last, and highest, level of specificity that we will consider, that of theory.

SCIENTIFIC THEORY

The discussion so far implies that each level of specificity of ordered observations is in some way related to the previous level; that is, each level is an empirical generalization based on the previous level. Individual functional relations are ordered into functional relations between classes of variables, or scientific facts. Functional relations between classes of variables are ordered into more general statements called scientific laws, which are ordered into even more general statements called theories. The purpose of theory in science "is to describe and explain observable and observed events and to predict what will be observed under certain specified conditions" (McCain & Segal, 1988, p. 96). But before we can describe (potentially) observable events, we must have already described observed events; and this is done at the three lower levels of specificity: individual functional relations, functional relations between classes, and laws. Moreover, before we can predict what will happen under specified conditions, we must have already observed what happened under similar specified conditions, usually through experimentation. The point is that theory in science is an induction, or generalization, of the basic facts of the particular science. By the time it becomes general enough to be called a theory, it has already been tested under many varied conditions and its limiting conditions and qualifications have been incorporated. This conception of scientific theory is grounded in, developed from, and, therefore, inextricably tied to scientific facts and laws. Thus, the scientific conception of theory is at odds with the ordinary view that theory is an educated guess or hypothesis that precedes the discovery of facts and the development of laws.

Webster's Seventh New Collegiate Dictionary (1965) provides an acceptable definition of theory as used by scientists: (1) "the analysis of a set of facts in their relation to one another"; (2) "the general or abstract principles of a body of fact," or a "science"; (3) "a plausible or scientifically acceptable general principle or body of principles offered to explain phenomena." To paraphrase, scientific theory includes some already established body of fact, abstract principles derived therefrom, and the use of such principles to explain new facts. This description of theory assumes that scientists already possess a set of facts (functional relations between classes of variables). The theory emerges when scientists abstract from those sets of facts certain commonalities that seem to be more universally true. Those commonalities are summarized in the form of statements (or equations) and become the "abstract principles" (or laws). Thus, to complete our example, the "Law of Effect" becomes "Reinforcement Theory" when "it goes beyond facts to suggest that an observed generality is probably more general than the cases observed so far" (Bijou & Baer, 1978, p. 8). The commonality or "observed generality" that we call the Law of Effect is that behavioral consequences are an important determinant of behavior. This scientific law is now ready to be tested by predicting what will happen under certain conditions.

Scientific Prediction

Recall that, according to McCain and Segal (1988), one of the purposes of a scientific theory is to make predictions about what *will be* observed under certain circumstances. Prediction, control, and understanding are the major goals of the natural sciences. The word "control," in this sense, means control of the subject matter, which in turn means discovering functional relations between the (independent and dependent) variables that make up the science. In other words, when one variable, known as the *independent variable*, is manipulated or altered in a systematic way, systematic changes in the other variable, known as the *dependent variable*, are observed. This type of control is most readily seen in the laboratory, and it is no coincidence that the basic laboratory sciences, physics, chemistry, and biology, have been so successful in discovering functional relations and, thus, in attaining control over their subject matter. The relation between prediction and control is an intimate one. Once scientists have achieved a certain amount of control over their subject matter, that is, over "observed events," they can then make predictions about what will happen under conditions that are like those they have already observed (experimentally). Hence, prediction in science follows from control.

The kind of prediction frequently found in developmental psychology shouldn't be confused with scientific prediction. One of the most common research tools in developmental psychology is the correlational method in which the degree of correspondence between two or more existing variables in a population is calculated. For example, the correspondence (or correlation) between height and weight in a given population can be calculated. The typical result is that height and weight are positively correlated, which means that as height increases in the population weight does also. In developmental psychology, children's ages are frequently correlated with changes in their behavior. The resulting data are called *normative*, which means that the result of the correlational research is a statistic that represents the average age, or norm, at which a particular change takes place. Once research like this is carried out, researchers may then make predictions about the "average" child. For example, Berndt (1992) has pointed out that decades of research have established the average age at which children will reach the major milestones in motor development. We know, for instance, that infants will sit without support at between 5 and 6 months of age. We know this because researchers have studied thousands of children and recorded the ages at which they sat without support, and then calculated correlations from these observations. Based on their results, they can predict that another child who hasn't been studied will sit without support by approximately 6 months. While such information is not without important value, it must not be confused with scientific prediction which is based on controlled experimentation between independent and dependent variables. (We will talk more about correlational research methods and their drawbacks in chapter 2.)

What about the scientific prediction of natural events, that is, those outside the control of the laboratory? When a scientist offers a prediction about some natural event, the prediction is based on what scientists have discovered in the laboratory where the variables can be precisely controlled and measured. Thus, the prediction is based on an ideal situation. For example, suppose that you and a physicist friend are watching leaves falling from a tree. To test how much your friend really knows, you ask her to predict exactly where a certain leaf will fall and, moreover, the course it will take to get there. When your friend declines by saying that she is unable to predict either event with much accuracy, do you question her education and training as a physicist? Do you wonder how, if the science of physics can't predict something as simple as where a leaf will fall, it can predict more complex events in nature like the formation of stars?

Actually, your friend could predict where the leaf would fall, if she knew all of the variables that affected the fall, such as the weight of the leaf, the current wind velocity, etc. Those are the kinds of variables that can be controlled in the laboratory and, under such controlled conditions, your friend could predict with a high probability where the leaf would fall. With such knowledge, scientists can design machines (e.g., airplanes) that will land exactly where they want them to.

Consider a similar example in psychology. You are asked to consult with a teacher in a special education classroom. Upon entering the classroom, the teachers says, "You're a psychologist and you claim to know about behavior. So if you're so smart, predict what Timmy will do next." Of course, you are unable to do so. In fact, the teacher and the other children could more accurately predict what Timmy will do than you could, even though you are the scientist. Is there something wrong with your behavioral science? Of course not. In fact, you could predict Timmy's behavior, if you knew something about his particular history, including what behaviors he normally engages in under different conditions, what events function as reinforcers or punishers for him, and the relative rates of reinforcement for all of his behaviors. The more you know about these relationships for Timmy, the better you will be able to predict what his behavior will be under similar conditions. With such knowledge, you could design a behavioral program that could increase the probability of certain behaviors occurring at specific times.

Scientific Interpretation

Scientific interpretation is related to prediction. It is difficult for scientists to predict some events in nature with the same level of accuracy as in the laboratory. But this doesn't mean that they aren't able to understand those events. Scientific understanding follows from control and prediction. In one sense, we understand something if we can make it happen, that is, if we can control it. Scientific understanding of this sort, however, is achieved with only a relatively small subset of the phenomena that make up the scientific subject matter, namely those that can be observed and measured under controlled conditions. But scientists can obviously tell us about events they have not been able to study in the laboratory. Therefore, a critical ingredient in science is interpretation, the extrapolation of knowledge and understanding from the laboratory to events outside it. According to *Webster's New World Dictionary* (1984), "extrapolate" means "to arrive at (conclusions or results) by hypothesizing from known facts or observations." Thus, when confronted with certain observations in nature that resemble those found under controlled laboratory conditions, scientists hypothesize about the possible functional relations involving the observed phenomena. This is what is meant by scientific interpretation. As Palmer (1991) points out:

> Interpretation has served, and continues to serve, an honorable role in science, so honorable that we often fail to distinguish between an interpretation and an experimental analysis. Newton's explanation of ocean tides is an interpretation based on his experimental analysis of phenomena such as the motion of pendulums and colliding balls of wool, glass and cork. No one, least of all, Newton, has attempted to establish experimental control over the tides. Yet Newton's principles (to a reasonable approximation) are so firmly established and the extrapolation to this phenomenon so plausible, that we accept his interpretation as if it were the direct outcome of an experimental analysis. (p. 261)

The key to a plausible interpretation, then, is that it proceeds from a foundation of well-established principles derived from a rigorous program of basic research. Even when scientists haven't directly experimented with the events in question, we give more credibility to their hypotheses or interpretations than we do to the guesses of nonscientists. Because behavior analysis does possess a foundation of empirically derived principles, it is in a unique position to be able to interpret behavioral events which have not yet been directly subjected to an experimental analysis.

CRITERIA FOR EVALUATING SCIENTIFIC THEORIES

Since theory in science is derived from the laws that it comprises, we should attempt to establish some criteria that must be met before any statement can qualify as a scientific law. According to McCain and Segal (1988):

> (1) The statement must be about kinds of events and not directly about any singular event. (2) The statement must show a functional relation between two or more kinds of events ("kind of event" refers either to things or to properties of things). (3) There must be a large amount of data confirming the law and little or none disconfirming it. (4) The relation should be applicable to very different events (although there may be limiting conditions). (p. 52)

Again, one can see from this list the interdependent relationship between scientific laws and the functional relations that precede their development. We will refer back to these criteria in chapters 2 and 3. But what about the larger issue of theory? Just as scientific laws may be judged according to certain criteria, so may scientific theories. Although the list that follows is not exhaustive, it does contain five criteria that many authors (e.g., Bachrach, 1972; Green, 1989; Mazur, 1990; Sidman, 1960) agree are among the most important by which to judge scientific theories.

Generality (or Inclusiveness)

A scientific theory has merit if it can deal with a great number of phenomena. These phenomena must be other scientific facts and, thus, must be functional relations, like the facts that comprise the theory. For a theory to be general or inclusive, it should explain other related scientific facts (i.e., functional relations), and not just any observation. For example, Freud's theory of psychoanalysis seems to be able to explain almost any observation. Indeed, this apparent generality may very well have led to the success and popularity of psychoanalysis during the first half of this century. But there is something suspicious about the way psychoanalysis explains everything, especially when one considers that the theory itself is not a scientific theory; in other words, it is not based on scientific facts. So, it is not enough that a theory possesses generality or inclusiveness; it must first qualify as a scientific theory; it must itself be a generalization from and of the scientific facts and laws that it comprises.

Of course, it is rarely possible for a theory to be tested against every new functional relation that is observed, so scientists need to interpret these facts. Interpretations are extensions of the theory to areas that have not yet been subjected to experimentation and analysis. But they must potentially be subject to analysis. When McCain and Segal (1988) said that the purpose of theory was to "describe and explain *observable* events," we can infer that they were probably referring to events that are potentially observable and testable even though not yet tested. In psychology, generality refers to the range of behaviors the theory claims to explain and the range of conditions under which it does so (Poling et al., 1990).

Testability

Testability is one of the most important characteristics of a scientific theory. According to Green (1989), "A theory that is testable can be objectively verified" (p. 19). In order for a theory to be testable, it must possess both empirical and logical support. *Empirical support* consists of the observations that relate to the theory. For example, the observations that relate to Piaget's theory of cognitive development consist of children's solutions to the various problems that Piagetian researchers present to them. The *logical support* of a theory means that the mechanisms proposed by the theory must be plausible, that is, potentially observable and measurable (Poling et al., 1990). Since Piaget's theory of cognitive development proposes cognitive structures that have not been observed and are not potentially observable, its logical support is weak, and the theory is untestable.

In order for a theory to be testable, its claims must also be specific enough to be used in making predictions. Predictions are in the form of "If A then B," where A refers to the manipulation of some independent variable and B refers to the effects on some dependent variable. For example, we can predict that when food deprived rats are placed in an operant conditioning chamber where lever presses have been previously followed by food only in the presence of a light, turning on the light now will increase the momentary frequency of lever pressing. Whether or not the specific predictions hold true is the issue of accuracy or external validity (see below). It is important to point out that a theory can be testable but wrong and, thus, inaccurate (Green, 1989).

External Validity (or Accuracy)

The accuracy of a theory depends on the extent to which predictions made from it are accurate (Sidman, 1960). It is not always possible to test every prediction a theory makes, but it should be possible to test at least some of them. The success of these predictions depends in part on how precise they are, specifically, whether they identify clear independent and dependent variables and relations between them. As Mazur (1990) states, "a scientific theory must make definite predictions, because if there is room for reinterpretation and modification of the predictions after the data are collected, any result can be explained by the theory" (p. 7).

Fruitfulness (or Utility)

The fruitfulness of a theory is determined by "the number of interesting and new phenomena" to which it directs attention (Sidman, 1960). In simpler terms, the theory must be able to stimulate research that might not have otherwise been conducted. Relatedly, some scientists have suggested that a scientific theory must possess utility, that is, it must be potentially able to generate useful applications. The natural sciences enable scientists to understand natural phenomena and also to change them in the "real" world. As Schwartz (1989) has put it, "science has delivered the goods"

(p. 3). The technological applications of the natural sciences also lend credibility to the claim that the scientists understand at least a part of nature. A good theory in psychology should generate practical applications that can be used to change behavior reliably, especially in applied settings such as the home or school. If such practical applications can be found, then psychology can perhaps claim modestly that it understands at least a part of human nature.

Simplicity (or Parsimony)

The concept of parsimony is well known in psychology, but what does it mean? According to *Webster's New World Dictionary* (1984), parsimony comes from the Latin *parcere* meaning to spare. One who is parsimonious is one who is overly careful in spending. In science, a theory is parsimonious if it attempts to account for a body of data with the fewest number of assumptions and statements. Parsimony in science has also been referred to as theoretical economy and according to Green (1989), it can be assessed in two ways. First, if two (or more) theories purportedly explain the same phenomenon, then, all things being equal, the theory with the fewest assumptions is the preferred explanation. Second, if two theories make the same number of assumptions, then the theory that explains more phenomena is the preferred theory. Consider, for example, the tantruming of a 6-year-old child. Freudian theorists might propose that the underlying cause and, therefore, explanation of the behavior is an unresolved conflict between the boy's id and superego: The id's demands for attention dominate the reasoning of the ego and the super-ego's requirement for appropriate behavior. In contrast, behavior analysts might propose that the tantruming has been followed by consequences, such as attention, that have increased the behavior in the contexts in which it has been observed. Which one of these theories is the most parsimonious? The behavior analytic theory requires fewer assumptions about events that are unobserved and unobservable, while at the same time suggesting relationships between tantruming and reinforcing stimuli that are potentially observable and testable. This by itself does not mean that the Freudian theory is wrong, only that it is not very parsimonious in scientific terms.

SCIENTIFIC UNDERSTANDING

Scientific understanding of natural phenomena is usually achieved at several levels of specificity. Although it may be possible to speak of understanding at the level of specific functional relations or even classes of functional relations, it is probably safer to begin after having established scientific laws. A good scientific theory will both deepen and broaden that understanding in at least three ways, according to Hempel (1966):

> First, such a theory offers a systematically unified account of quite diverse phenomena. It traces all of them back to the same underlying processes and presents the various empirical uniformities they exhibit as manifestations of one common set of basic laws. (p. 75)

This is similar to the criterion of inclusiveness. In psychology, a good theory of development should be able to explain many seemingly different behavioral phenomena according to the same basic set of laws or principles. Hempel (1966) continues to state:

> A theory will also deepen our understanding in a different way, namely by showing that the previously formulated empirical laws that it is meant to explain do not hold strictly and unexceptionally, but only approximately and within a certain limited range of application. (p. 76)

This is also related to the criterion of inclusiveness. In psychology, a good theory of behavior should acknowledge the conditions under which it may not explain behavior or under which it is less accurate. For example, a theory of behavior would have to acknowledge the genetic and biological variables that may limit the applicability of the theory. Hempel (1966) concludes:

> Finally, a good theory will also broaden our knowledge and understanding by predicting and explaining phenomena that were not known when the theory was formulated. (p. 77)

This is similar to the criterion of generality. In psychology, a good theory should continue to predict and explain behavioral phenomena as they are encountered.

In summary, it is important to remember that, "The purpose of a theory is to unify and thereby explain a body of data" (Green, 1989, p. 21). As the aforementioned quotes by Hempel (1966) suggest, a good scientific theory goes even farther to increase our understanding by stating the range of conditions within which the laws that make up the theory will hold and also by explaining phenomena that have not yet been explained. In other words, it is not tied only to the observations that were known when the theory was first formulated.

The present book will make the case that behavior analysis, more than any other psychological theory, can satisfy these requirements in the area of child development. In order to support this claim, we must be able to evaluate how successfully behavior-analytic theory meets this purpose. Therefore, we have introduced several criteria of scientific worthiness.

Although there are many theories that may possess some of these criteria to varying degrees, this is not enough to make the theory a good scientific theory. The strongest scientific theory meets most, if not all, of the criteria. This book makes the argument that behavior analysis is the strongest scientific theory of the many different theories in the area of developmental psychology.

SUMMARY

This chapter discussed science and scientific theory. Theory is essentially a summary, either in verbal or mathematical form, of numerous facts which, themselves, consist of repeatable functional relations between objective variables. Thus, theory, as the term is used by scientists, is not a guess or conjecture but the extension of these summary forms to novel instances of the subject matter. The existence of a set of reliable facts enables scientists to control and predict the subject matter, two of the goals of the natural sciences. This chapter also presented several criteria for evaluating the merit of a scientific theory. These include the theory's generality, testability, external validity, utility, and simplicity. Finally, this chapter addressed the issue of scientific understanding—a third goal of science. Scientific understanding is usually achieved at several levels of specificity, beginning with simple functional relations, and extending, inductively, to scientific laws.

2

Developmental Psychology

Chapter 1 presented the concept of theory in science. This chapter describes the general approach to behavior by developmental psychologists. Among the topics discussed in this chapter are structural approaches to the study of behavior, correlational research strategies, and the types of explanations of behavior that may follow from both.

THE CONCEPT OF BEHAVIOR IN
DEVELOPMENTAL PSYCHOLOGY

The field of developmental psychology has been said to consist of various "minitheories," each purporting to account for limited behavioral phenomena, specific domains, or particular periods (Horowitz, 1987). For example, there are different theories for social–emotional development, cognitive development, perceptual development, moral development, language development, and so on. Moreover, within each of these domains there are sometimes several different theories. There is currently no "overarching, comprehensive developmental theory" which can offer a systematically unified account of the diverse phenomena that comprise the field of developmental psychology. In fact, Horowitz (1987) states what seems to be accepted at least implicitly by authors of many developmental textbooks, that is, that the current "minitheory" status of developmental psychology is "a healthy state of affairs." Many developmental psychologists might then agree with Hetherington and Parke (1986) that, "No theory is able to account for all aspects of human development" (p. 5). While this is certainly true, it implies that no single theory may be powerful enough to provide the level of scientific understanding suggested by Hempel (1966), as described in chapter 1. It also implies that many different theories are needed to explain the apparently different behaviors that comprise the topical subareas of developmental psychology. As a consequence, almost no textbook in developmental psychology shows a preference for any particular theory, although most adopt a generally cognitive approach. (See chapter 3 for a brief comparison of the cognitive and behavior analytic approaches to behavior.)

One reason that developmental psychology is so theoretically diverse is that the subject matter is so varied. For example, most developmental textbooks deal with such disparate areas as biological and behavioral development, as well as the genetic and environmental influences on both. This means that theories of genetics, biology, and the environment will have to contribute to a complete understanding of behavioral development. Although we should be able to find in the field of developmental psychology some unified theoretical account of the environmental influences on behavior change, we still find dozens of different theories, few of which are "scientific" according to the criteria set forth in chapter 1.

STRUCTURAL APPROACHES TO BEHAVIOR

A second reason for the theoretical diversity within developmental psychology has to do with the way most developmental psychologists conceptualize behavior. It has been standard practice in psychology in general, and developmental psychology in particular, to classify behavior largely according to its form or structure. This practice is so pervasive in developmental psychology that examples are easy to come by. In fact, most of the areas in developmental psychology illustrate a structural approach to the subject matter. For example, behavior is categorized according to whether it is motor behavior, social behavior, emotional behavior (emotion), cognitive behavior (cognition), perceptual behavior (perception), or language behavior. Behaviors are classified into these categories according to the form of the behavior, that is, what the behavior looks like.

Consider the area of early social relationships, especially the relationship between an infant and parent called "attachment." Developmental psychologists have classified types of attachment based largely on the behaviors of the infant in certain situations. For example, infant behaviors are classified according to whether they represent secure or anxious attachment (Ainsworth, Blehar, Waters, & Wall, 1978). These classifications depend on what the infant does when placed in an unfamiliar situation with unfamiliar adults or when separated from a parent. If the infant leaves the side of the parent and explores the unfamiliar environment, she is securely attached. If she clings and shows signs of distress when the parent leaves, she is said to be anxiously attached. This approach is structural because it looks primarily at the topography (i.e., form) of behavior. Whether the child leaves the parent's side or stays close becomes the important indicator of development. The assumption implied by this practice is that leaving the parent's side and exploring the unfamiliar setting is a different set of behaviors than staying close, and may require a different explanation. Leaving the parent's side indicates secure attachment, and staying close indicates anxious attachment. While this assumption may be true, one cannot tell based on form alone. By concentrating primarily on form, structural approaches frequently ignore or overlook the function of the behavior. This is an important oversight because behaviors that differ in form may have similar functions. Hence, they might be classified differently in terms of their form, but similarly in terms of their function. For example, the behavior of leaving the side of the parent in an unfamiliar situation may be reinforced by what the infant finds, such as new toys or even another adult who reinforces their approach. But the behavior of clinging may also be reinforced by the parent by holding or consoling the infant contingent on such behaviors in certain situations. Without a functional analysis, we might believe that the behaviors that define secure and anxious attachment are fundamentally different and represent some "fundamental qualities of attachment" (Collins & Kuczaj, 1991, p. 111), especially if the behaviors persist over time.

Another problem with classifying behaviors largely according to form is that most behaviors can be potentially classified according to more than one formal category. For example, suppose that upon seeing her mother enter the room, a 6-month-old infant reaches for the mother, but only when the mother is close enough to be touched. The behavior in this context might be explained as (1) memory—the infant recognizes and remembers the mother by responding to her in similar ways as in the past; (2) perception—the infant perceives appropriate size and distances by reaching only when the mother is within touching distance; (3) motor behavior—the behavior of reaching is well coordinated and appears to be voluntary (vs. reflexive); or (4) social behavior—the behavior of reaching toward another person. Although classifying behavior according to form helps developmental psychologists organize and communicate about their subject matter, it hinders the more important functional analysis of behavior. In contrast, behavior analysis accounts for behavior according to a common set of principles regardless of how the behavior is formerly classified.

The present discussion of form versus function doesn't imply that behavior does not have form or cannot be classified according to its form. The problem is to discern which is the most profitable way to conceptualize behavior in terms of the goals of science. In the previous example of attachment, there are at least two different forms of the behavior, one that we can call secure attachment, and one which we can call anxious attachment. However, because they both may have similar functions, that is, they may be determined by the reinforcers that follow in that particular circumstance, they may be explainable according to the same scientific principles. In a comprehensive account of behavior, both form and function are important. If we are interested in how and why behavior occurs, then we need to concentrate on its function(s).

Structural Approaches and Explanations of Behavior

When behavior is distinguished only on the basis of structural characteristics, it becomes easier to assume that different theories or explanations are required to explain the development of each type of behavior. Different forms of behavior are assumed to be qualitatively different. To illustrate, in most developmental textbooks, one can find several competing theories of different categories of behavior. For example, Piaget's cognitive developmental theory, the information-processing approach, and Lev Vygotsky's social cognition theory all account for cognitive development (Berndt, 1992). Likewise, theories by both Freud and Erikson are intended to explain personality and social development, while both Piaget and Kohlberg have proposed different theories of moral development. In addition, there are ethological theories of attachment and contextual theories of individual and cultural relationships.

Even within single theoretical systems, structurally different behaviors are afforded different explanations. In Piaget's theory, for example, different cognitive structures are inferred to explain object permanence, conservation, egocentrism, and so on. In fact, the entire field of child development itself implies a domain that is functionally distinct from adult psychology, as if humans were governed by different psychological principles at different ages. It is not surprising that students may be confused by this theoretical eclecticism.

This structural approach in developmental psychology is based on the assumption that classes of behavior, which are distinguished primarily on the basis of structural properties, are separate functional classes requiring different explanations. All too often, however, the theories and explanations used to account for the development of these behaviors are arrived at through logical error or circular reasoning. First, the behavioral class is given a name. Second, the name is treated as if it referred to a (concrete) material object (i.e., it is reified), so that the name itself becomes the object of study. Finally, the name for the behavioral class becomes the explanation of the observed behavior.

Much of the Piagetian approach to development illustrates this process. For example, by about 24 months of age, infants are able to behave effectively toward absent objects as if the objects were present. Piaget and other developmental psychologists have termed these observed behavior–environment interactions "object permanence" (see chapter 7). When studying the development of these behavioral relations, these researchers say they are studying object permanence or the emergence of the "concept" of object permanence, which implies that what is being studied is something within the child other than the observed behavior-environment relations. When infants are finally able to behave appropriately with respect to objects that are out of sight, some psychologists say it is because the infants now possess the concept of object permanence or the mental capacity to represent objects. Object permanence, which began as the name for certain observed behavioral relations, has become a thing (a structure or process) located inside the child that is responsible for the observed behavior. The use of the concept of object permanence as an explanation of the observed behaviors is an example of a circular and a reified explanation.

By definition, a circular explanation is one in which the only evidence for the explanation is the behavior(s) to be explained. In the example of object permanence, the only evidence for the concept of object permanence as an explanation is the very behavior it is said to explain, namely, the behavior of continuing to search for objects when they are removed from sight. Therefore, this is a circular explanation. Consider an example in the area of early infant attachment. Infants supposedly show "attachment" if they exhibit behaviors such as "clinging, touching, and crying at separation" (Collins & Kuczaj, 1991, p. 109). If these behaviors are then explained as occurring because the child is attached, as they frequently are, then it is a circular explanation; the behaviors are the only evidence for the attachment. In essence, the behaviors are named—"attachment"—and the name is then used to explain the behaviors. It should be obvious that circular explanations are not explanations at all; they skirt the issue of the real determinants of the behavior. Worse yet, they may stop us from looking for more scientific explanations.

Consider the following excerpt on attachment:

> Psychologist Mary D. S. Ainsworth … has argued that attachment behaviors vary in the degree to which they reflect this feeling of security.… In infancy, security means that the baby feels confident of the caregiver's availability and responsiveness. This confidence is essential to healthy psychological growth, because it allows securely attached infants to move away from their caregivers to explore the world around, with the assurance that they can return to the caregiver as a safe haven if threatened. Insecurely attached infants are those who feel uncertain that their caregivers will respond quickly and appropriately to their needs.… Their lack of confidence will inhibit exploration and impede the development of independence and competence that is essential to psychological health.… (Collins & Kuczai, 1991, p. 109)

There are several circular explanations in this excerpt. The first is when the concept of the feeling of confidence (i.e., the feeling of security) is used to explain the infant moving away from the caregiver to explore the world around. The second is when the lack of confidence is used to explain the inhibition of exploration. We know whether an infant feels secure or feels confident only if she leaves the caregiver and explores the setting. But we can't then turn around and use those feelings of security and confidence to explain the behaviors from which they were inferred in the first place. When all is said and done, this excerpt says nothing more than the following: Some infants will leave the side of the caregiver and explore and some infants won't. These are the behaviors that require an explanation. Although the logical errors in this type of theorizing have been noted by psychologists who are not behavior analysts (e.g., Dworetzky, 1990; Flannagan, 1991), little has been done to diminish such practices.

RESEARCH AND THEORY IN DEVELOPMENTAL PSYCHOLOGY

Correlational Research

The theoretical diversity in developmental psychology is also a result of the type of research that characterizes much of the field and, consequently, the data that comprise the subject matter. In addition to the number of different theories, developmental psychology is also noteworthy for the large number of observations researchers have collected. Unfortunately, many of the observations have been generated by nonexperimental, mostly correlational, research methods, and, therefore, do not represent the types of basic facts that characterize a natural science approach, namely, functional relations between controlled variables (see chapter 1). For example, there is a negative correlation between the age at which men die and the level of education of their wives. It would be a mistake, however, to infer from this that a woman's educational level has any direct effect on how long her husband lives. This is an example of a correlation that we would want to interpret cautiously. Remember this caution: Correlation does not mean causation.

Since much of the correlational research found in developmental psychology involves the child's age as one of the variables and some developmental change as the other variable, it is often implied that functional relations have been discovered between the two variables when they have not. In such accounts, the so-called independent variable is the child's age or some invented cognitive structure that develops and is conveniently age-specific. (Recall that independent variables are "those whose values are directly manipulated by the experimenter," because experimenters are interested "in establishing functional relationships between independent and dependent variables" [McCain & Segal, 1988, p. 103]). Although a child's age cannot be an independent variable, many researchers make just such a claim. Consider the following example:

> Suppose we wish to study differences in mathematical problem-solving ability at different ages. Mathematical performance is the dependent variable.... In addition to the dependent measure, the hypothesis specifies age as another variable of interest. Furthermore, because differences between boys and girls in mathematical ability have frequently been hypothesized and reported, it also makes sense to consider gender. Thus, both age and gender are independent variables; they are under the control of the experimenter who chooses the children to participate in the study. (Collins & Kuczai, 1991, p. 19)

A well-known developmental textbook presented this example as an illustration of experimental research. It should be obvious that neither age nor gender is an independent variable, at least as defined by most scientific researchers. In the above example, neither a child's age nor gender can be directly manipulated by an experimenter. In fact, the experiment suggested by these authors is not an experiment but a correlational study. Age and gender are variables that are correlated with mathematical performance. Not all developmental textbooks, of course, make this mistake (e.g., see Berndt, 1992; Bukatko & Daehler, 1992, for two exceptions). Regardless of how developmental textbooks define experimental research, much of the research reported by developmental researchers is correlational, with age as one of the correlated variables. Consider the following two examples of age-correlated research:

1. Attachment in 2- and 3-year-old children of depressed mothers was compared with attachment in children of nondepressed mothers (Radke-Yarrow, Cummings, Kuczynski, & Chapman, 1985). The findings showed that 55% of the children of depressed mothers were insecurely attached as compared with only 29% of children of nondepressed mothers. In broader terms, insecure attachment in children (however it is measured) is positively correlated with depression in mothers.

2. Bryant, Bradley, Maclean, and Crossland (1989) asked 3-year-old children to recite five popular nursery rhymes. Then, their phonological knowledge and reading skills were assessed periodically until the children were 6 years old. The researchers found that reading skills were positively correlated with their knowledge of nursery rhymes at 3 years of age.

The value of correlational research is twofold. First, it allows some prediction of behavior. Thus, in the first example, one might predict cautiously that a child of a clinically depressed mother would exhibit behavior that developmental psychologists would call "insecure attachment." In the second example, one could predict that if a child can recite nursery rhymes well at the age of 3, then she is more likely to be a better reader at the age of 6 than a child who didn't recite as well.

Correlational research is also valuable in that it can suggest something about the independent variables. Hence, we might observe that clinically depressed mothers behave differently toward their children than do nondepressed mothers. For example, they might not encourage independence and might reinforce clinging and whining instead. Also, the mothers might engage in similar behaviors themselves, thus modeling the behaviors for their children. A correlational study, however, can only hint at these functional variables; true experimentation is needed to isolate them from nonfunctional variables. It would certainly be incorrect to say that depression in mothers *causes* insecure attachment in children. This is especially important when we consider that the aforementioned study showed that 29% of nondepressed mothers had children who were insecurely attached. Presumably these nondepressed mothers behaved in similar ways toward their children as the depressed mothers who had insecurely attached children, thus producing similar behaviors in their children. Thus, depression is neither necessary nor sufficient to produce insecurely attached infants.

The study on reading ability suggests that something related to successful nursery rhyme recitation at the age of 3 is related to reading well later on. But it would be a mistake, and it would sound odd, to suggest that reciting nursery rhymes well at age 3 *causes* children to read well at age 6. One would have to look for other variables that might cause the child both to recite well at age 3 and to read well at age 6, such as parental encouragement. Although most developmental researchers realize that correlation does not mean causation, many of the conclusions concerning these studies found in developmental textbooks leave the reader with the wrong impression. For instance, one might conclude that if you want your child to read well at 6 years of age, you should get them to recite nursery rhymes when they are 3. Or even worse, if your child doesn't learn nursery rhymes at 3, there is little hope that she will become a good reader.

Finally, the purpose of much of the correlational, normative research in developmental psychology seems to be to demonstrate whether a behavior is present or not at a particular age, but not how the behavior came to be. Baer (1970) has called this an "age irrelevant concept of development." For example, much of the research by Piagetian psychologists is done to demonstrate whether a child of a certain age is capable of solving a particular problem. Consider the problem of conservation of volume. Piagetian psychologists have demonstrated that, in general, children do not conserve until the age of 6 or 7. While this may or may not be interesting from a normative, sociological standpoint, it suggests very little about *how* the behavior itself emerged, that is, the processes responsible for the change. In many cases, age becomes the cause of the behavior and fixed biological theories are suggested.

In a developmental psychology based largely on establishing relations between the ages of children and changes in their behavior, the outcomes of development become the subject matter. For behavior analysis, the subject matter consists of the analysis of the processes that produce behavioral outcomes (Baer, 1970).

Correlational Research and Stage Theories

In developmental psychology, there is a strong relationship between correlational research and theory construction. Because age is used so often as one of the variables in developmental research, it should not be surprising that it becomes an important part of many developmental theories. Since changes in age and changes in behavior are frequently positively correlated, developmental theories are often stage theories. Many textbooks in the field include discussions of whether development is best considered to be continuous or discontinuous (i.e., occurs in stages). Some have suggested that stages in some theories, for example Piaget's, are used primarily as organizing frameworks to help researchers think more clearly about their subject matter (Horowitz, 1987). But the reader of developmental textbooks is often left with the impression that the stages represent fixed, biological or physiological changes in development that may be relatively independent of any behavior–environment interaction.

For example, Piagetian psychologists describe the development of object permanence during several substages of the sensorimotor period. Each change in children's behavior with respect to hidden or displaced objects is correlated with changes in their ages. During stages 1 and 2 (1 to 4 months), objects that are "out of sight" are literally "out of mind." In other words, infants will not continue to behave toward absent objects as though they were present. By stage 6 (18 to 24 months), however, they will. Both age and a corresponding (unobservable) developing mental structure are often identified as independent variables (causes) that enable children to respond to hidden objects. Because the mental structure presumably develops maturationally, age seems to be a logical reflection of changes in it, and vice versa. Because the cognitive structure itself cannot be observed, age is what is measured and correlated with the changes in the behavior, thus excluding any other possible observable behavior–environment interactions that may actually be functionally related to the child's developing skill. Such structural, normative approaches form the basis for many of the major theories in the area of human development and have encouraged the construction of stage theories of behavior change by Piaget, Freud, Greenspan, Kohlberg, and Maslow, to name a few.

In conclusion, the results of correlational research in developmental psychology, especially where one of the variables is age, should be seen as normative or descriptive, not causal. Correlational research does allow for a form of prediction, but the control of the relevant variables, which is the hallmark of a natural science approach, is absent and, as a result, so are scientific prediction and understanding.

Problems with a Structural Approach to Behavior Change

The concept of stages and structures in developmental psychology is not without merit; it has aided in the organization of data and in communication between researchers (Horowitz, 1987; Lipsitt, 1981). However, the problems generated by structural, normative approaches have thus far outweighed these benefits. Lipsitt (1981) has listed several of these problems. First, structural approaches to behavior posit structures that are not directly observable. Classic examples are Freud's ego, superego, and id; Piaget's cognitive structures, schemas, concepts, and rules; and the input, storage, and retrieval systems of the information-processing model. A second problem noted by Lipsitt is that the emphasis on hypothetical structures and processes has tended to obfuscate other, perhaps more central, underlying behavioral processes. For example, an interest in hypothetical cognitive structures and processes might interfere with the search for more objective environment–behavior interactions as determinants of behavior change. Third, as we have already noted, structural, normative approaches tend to confuse description with explanation. According to Lipsitt, the transitional nature of behavior change, which is an important process in its own right, is overlooked when normative descriptions lead us to believe that we have explained a transition in behavior by saying, for example, that the child is now in "the preoperational stage." A fourth problem is that inferred "constitutional–maturational determinants" of behavior change are emphasized at the expense of more direct environmental or physiological variables. A fifth problem is that structural concepts reduce optimism about the potential of humans to benefit from environmental manipulations, especially those in education. If behavioral development is indeed constrained by the stage-wise development of underlying structures and processes, then it would be difficult to accelerate that development. Sufficient evidence exists to force serious reconsiderations of this interpretation, so much so that the concept of maturational stages as important determinants of behavior is seriously threatened (see Dworetzky 1990, pp. 262–266; Lipsitt, 1981). Finally, structural–normative interpretations easily fall into the logical trap of reification. According to Lipsitt (1981),

> The empirical hazard is that we come to regard those stages as real conditions of the organism rather than as artifacts of our observational procedures and methodologies. Conceptualizations of development in terms of stages are usually followed closely by the adoption of a structural view of the mind. The postulation of structures is usually based upon behavioral observations, to be sure, but the language quickly becomes metaphorical. The special words, initially devised merely to abbreviate complex behavior patterns, now become taskmasters and slaves. (pp. 31–32)

The problem of reification leads to another troublesome verbal practice in developmental psychology. Locating the determinants of behavior inside children makes it easier to describe children as the originators of their actions. Thus, some psychologists suggest that children "sense," "perceive," "remember," "think," "judge," "decide," and so on. Once described this way, behavior can be more easily attributed to these presumably internal activities. Ironically, the most conspicuous examples of this are found in clear-cut cases of operant or respondent conditioning. For example, according to Kalnins and Bruner (1973), conditioning studies with infants provide evidence that infants are able not only "to anticipate an outcome," but also to "choose" and "deploy" "means for achieving it." Moreover, they suggest that infants have the "ability to correct and coordinate behaviour in a fashion that would lead it more directly to the goal" (p. 307). Although these are words of common usage and are easily understood, they divert attention away from the variables of which behavior is a function. This way of talking about infants does not explain or help us understand their behavior.

In their study, Kalnins and Bruner (1973) showed that when sucking a non-nutritive nipple at a certain rate produced a focused picture, sucking rates increased; and when it produced a blurred picture, sucking rates decreased. The facts are clear, and the interpretation is simple. The process of strengthening the sucking rates by presenting a focused picture is called reinforcement. Conversely, the process of weakening sucking rates by presenting a blurred picture is called punishment. Saying that the child is "able to carry out skilled, voluntary-controlled, adaptive behaviour that leads him to goals" does not add anything to the facts and is unscientific. There is no objective evidence of the child's goals or voluntary choice making separate from the behavior being explained. Such descriptions divert our search for the objective variables of which changes in rates of sucking are a function (i.e., the clarity of the picture) to some hypothetical and untestable agent inside the child. Such language is not completely objective either: It states more than the facts allow, and it adds little to the prediction and nothing to the control of the behavior. Moreover, it reduces the likelihood that the true range of environmental determinants of the behavior will be identified.

DEVELOPMENTAL THEORY ASSESSED

We can use the scientific criteria presented in chapter 1 to evaluate the structural–normative approach outlined in this chapter. Let us first consider the criterion of generality or inclusiveness. Recall that a scientific theory has more merit when it can deal with a large number of phenomena. These phenomena must be other scientific facts, and thus must be functional relations, like the facts that comprise the theory. It could be argued that there are few scientific facts in developmental psychology. This does not mean that there are no sound experiments; there are many, and this book discusses several of them. The problem is not the soundness of the experiments but, rather, the absence of basic functional units of analysis (see chapter 3). Without a functional analytic unit, it is unlikely that scientific facts can or will be discovered or that scientific theories will emerge. Instead, any units are likely to be structural units, like Piaget's object permanence or Ainsworth's secure attachment. The result is, at best, a collection of what Horowitz (1987) termed "minitheories," each accounting only for limited behavioral phenomena, specific domains, or particular periods. No single theory can encompass more than its own limited domain. The various theoretical factions in the field of developmental psychology seem content with this state of affairs, so that these specific domains are presented in developmental textbooks as if they were functionally distinct from one another.

The second criterion of a scientific theory is its testability. You will recall from chapter 1 that in order for a theory to be testable, it must possess both empirical and logical support. Empirical support consists of the observations that relate to it, whereas logical support means that the mechanisms proposed by the theory must be plausible, that is, potentially observable and measurable. This means that any theory that proposes unobservable, hypothetical events, especially if those events have no observable counterparts, fails in its logical support. Thus, theories that rely exclusively on hypothetical, cognitive structures and processes cannot be tested. Thus, for example, predicting when object permanence is most likely to be observed in a child is not a sufficient test of Piagetian theory. Such a demonstration only means that the norms derived from the correlations are in fact norms. But simply demonstrating the norms in no way supports any theory of underlying processes responsible for the behavioral changes. We can concede that reasonably accurate predictions can result from normative research, but no amount of prediction, without control of the suspected variables, will adequately provide the test for a theory.

The third criterion is whether the theory possesses external validity or accuracy. Recall from chapter 1 that a theory's accuracy increases if it can make precise predictions. Precise predictions specify clear independent and dependent variables, and the functional relationship between them. Recall Mazur's (1990) caution that "a scientific theory must make definite predictions, because if there is room for reinterpretation and modification of the predictions after the data are collected, any result can be explained by the theory" (p. 7). Again, we come back to the issue of functional units of analysis. If a theory is not based on classes of functional relations between observable events, then precise prediction becomes almost impossible. Remember, we are not talking about the prediction made possible by correlational–normative research, but rather about predicting the value of the dependent variable given the value of the independent variable. The only theory that meets this criterion is behavior analysis.

The fourth criterion is the fruitfulness or utility of a theory. A theory is considered to be fruitful if it directs attention to new and interesting phenomena and, thus, is able to stimulate further research that might not have been conducted otherwise. This is perhaps the only one of the scientific criterion that many developmental theories meet, depending on how one defines "interesting phenomena." For example, Piaget's cognitive developmental theory has directed attention to many interesting phenomena, such as the various types of conservation (e.g., conservation of volume, weight, number). But these are largely interesting because of Piaget's contention that they each represent underlying changes in cognitive structures or processes. If, instead, they represent more complex instances of stimulus control (see chapter 9), then they may still be interesting, but not new.

Recall also that good scientific theories possess utility when they are able to generate useful practical applications. Although claims have been made supporting the usefulness of some mainstream developmental theories, these claims may need to be tempered. Let's consider two examples, one derived from a specific study and the other derived from an overall theoretical approach. The first case involves the practice adopted by many hospitals of encouraging skin to skin contact between a mother and her newborn immediately after birth. The rationale for this came from studies by Klaus, Jerauld, Kreger, McAlpine, Steffa, and Kennel (1972) and Kennel, Jerauld, Wolfe, Chesler, Kreger, McAlpine, Steffa, and Klaus (1974) (see Dworetzky, 1990). As Dworetzky (1990) points out, however, the conclusions from these studies have been challenged on a number of grounds, not the least of which has been possible methodological flaws in the studies themselves. Apparently Kennel and Klaus have retracted their claims somewhat, saying that it is unlikely that any life-sustaining relationship between mother and child depends primarily on one process—bonding—that must occur right after birth (Dworetzky, 1990). They still "believe," however, that the bonding effect is a real one. This is especially interesting because scientific belief should be tied closely to basic research and the reproducibility of the results.

Consider the application of Piaget's theories to education as a second case. Dworetzky (1990) lists several ways in which Piagetian "theory" influenced American education. For example, teachers and educators in the United States were encouraged to reorganize curricula so that they were geared to the children's current stages of cognitive development. Because Piaget thought that teaching children directly would inhibit their own creative strategies for discovering things on their own, many schools phased out direct, structured teaching practices and replaced them with less structured approaches that emphasized the individual learner. Such practices are currently called "whole learning" or "discovery" approaches. Piaget's theory does not qualify as a scientific theory, at least according to the five criteria described in chapter 1. Therefore, we should question the value of modifying social practices, such as the education of young children, according to a theory that does not even meet the basics of scientific credibility.

Admittedly, some of the changes suggested by Piagetian theory might be useful. For example, according to Piaget's theory, early childhood education should emphasize the activity of the child. This suggestion is based on Piaget's premise that cognitive development proceeds as the child interacts with the environment and actively adapts to it (Ginsburg & Opper, 1988). From a behavior analytic perspective, this is a good idea, because the more the child's behavior interacts with the environment, the more chances there are for learning to take place. As a result, the child's behavior becomes more and more varied and, at the same time, specific to its circumstances. So some Piagetian suggestions may work, but not for the reasons his theory states.

The fifth criterion is that of theoretical parsimony or economy. Theories that require the fewest assumptions and explain the most number of phenomena are said to possess the greater theoretical economy. Another problem with most developmental theories is that many of their assumptions concern structures, events, and processes that are hypothetical. This makes it impossible to discover scientific facts, to construe scientific laws, and, ultimately, to develop scientific theories. Of course (referring again to chapter 2), scientific understanding must also suffer, because according to Hempel (1966, p. 75), a good scientific theory will deepen and broaden scientific understanding by offering a systematically unifying account of diverse phenomena. It does this by tracing all of them back to the same basic *processes* and presenting the various empirical uniformities they exhibit as manifestations of one common set of basic laws.

Not all developmental psychologists take only a structural approach to their subject matter. More and more, the functional nature of behavior is being considered along with structural characteristics (e.g., Karniol, 1989; Lockman & Hazen, 1989). Even so, these more functional approaches are the exception and not the rule. And they rarely acknowledge the laws and principles of behavior analysis.

In conclusion, the general theoretical approach found in developmental psychology does not meet the criteria for scientific worthiness and, therefore, does not succeed well at explaining behavioral development. In chapter 3, we will take a look at behavior analysis to see if it succeeds better at achieving scientific understanding of behavioral development.

SUMMARY

This chapter presented a view of contemporary developmental psychology. In that view, modern developmental psychology consists of several different minitheories without one overarching unified theory of behavioral development. Further, it appears that many developmental psychologists don't just accept this status of their field, they welcome it. Developmental psychologists generally take a structural approach to the understanding of behavior, in which the form more than the function of behavior is stressed. Although a structural approach helps developmental psychologists organize and simplify their subject matter, it has several potential pitfalls. One is that functional variables may be overlooked. Another is that structural approaches are more likely to result in circular explanations of behavior in which the evidence for the explanation is often just the behavior to be explained. A final problem is that the most common research tool for many developmental psychologists is the correlational study in which age is used as one of the variables. Although correlational research may provide valuable information, it is no substitute for experimental research involving objective, reliable variables. The former can only hint at functional relations; the latter can reveal them. Additionally, although various approaches to developmental psychology meet some of the scientific criteria presented in chapter 1 some of the time, many consistently fail. The conclusion is that the general structural approach does not succeed well in explaining behavioral development.

3

Behavior Analysis

This chapter describes the essential features of behavior analysis and behavior analytic theory. Its purpose is to show that behavior analysis more closely resembles a natural science approach than the developmental psychology described in chapter 2. The chapter begins by presenting the views on theory and research in psychology by the foremost spokesperson of behavior analysis, B. F. Skinner. Next, it discusses several implications of behavior analytic theory, including those related to basic units of analysis, the conception of behavior and the environment, the issue of where the determinants of behavior are to be found, the role of inference, and the role of genes and physiology. Finally, a brief section concludes the chapter by contrasting behavior analytic and cognitive approaches to explaining behavior.

A LITTLE HISTORY: ARE THEORIES (OF LEARNING) NECESSARY?

The role of theory in behavior analysis has been a subject of debate in psychology, especially since the appearance of a well-known paper by B. F. Skinner (1950) titled "Are Theories of Learning Necessary?" As the title indicates, Skinner asked whether theories of learning were necessary to explain the data from learning experiments. His answer was no.

Based on this, many people concluded that Skinner was opposed to theory in general. Since then, Skinner has erroneously been portrayed as antitheory, and behavior analysis as atheoretical. In his paper, B. F. Skinner did not argue against use of any theory in psychology, but only against use of those theories that appealed to hypothetical, internal events as explanations of behavior. For Skinner, such theories were actually detrimental for a science of behavior because they represented a diversion from the analysis of real behavior as a function of objective variables. As for the title of the paper, Skinner simply meant that theories of learning that appealed to hypothetical, internal events and processes could not be directly tested,

31

and, moreover, were not necessary to explain behavior. In other words, Skinner thought that there were explanations that were easier to test and more parsimonious. He claimed that his research program had already resulted in the discovery of classes of functional relations that were being formulated into scientific laws, and that the theory emerging from these laws was sufficient to explain the same facts without inferring hypothetical events.

Since the present book makes extensive use of behavior analytic theory derived from Skinner's own research and theoretical writings, let us look at Skinner's views on science. We begin with Skinner's use of the term "theory."

SKINNER ON THEORY IN SCIENCE

Skinner discussed scientific method and theory in many places (e.g., 1938, 1947, 1950, 1956). More recently, Zuriff (1985) summarized Skinner's (and the behavior analytic) position on scientific theory. According to Zuriff, Skinnerian theory consists of concepts that express "empirical functional relationships between behavioral and environmental variables...." Zuriff explains:

> Theory, in the acceptable sense, evolves in the attempt to present the collection of empirical facts in a formal and economical way. A formulation using a minimal number of terms to represent a large number of experimental facts is a theory. As the theory develops, it integrates more facts in increasingly more economical formulations. Theoretical concepts thus merely collate observations and do not refer to nonbehavioral processes. A Skinnerian theory is, therefore, a simple, comprehensive, and abstract description of a corpus of data. (p. 89)

Zuriff's description of Skinner's theory essentially mirrors the definitions of theory found in *Webster's Seventh New Collegiate Dictionary* (1965) presented in chapter 1. It may help to repeat them here. According to *Webster's*, a theory is (1) "the analysis of a set of facts in their relation to one another"; (2) "the general or abstract principles of a body of fact," or a "science"; and (3) "a plausible or scientifically acceptable general principle or body of principles offered to explain phenomena." Thus, Skinnerian theory is an organized collection of empirical facts (specifically functional relationships) and includes the formulation of principles (i.e., scientific laws) derived inductively from those facts using a minimum number of terms and concepts.

The relation between fact and theory discussed in chapter 1 has also been addressed by Skinner. In elucidating his position on the relation between fact and theory, Skinner (1947) wrote:

A theory ... has nothing to do with the presence or absence of experimental confirmation. Facts and theories do not stand in opposition to each other. The relation, rather, is this: theories are based upon facts; they are statements about organizations of facts. The atomic theory, the kinetic theory of gases, the theory of evolution and the theory of the gene are examples of reputable and useful scientific theories. They are all statements about facts, and with proper operational care they need be nothing more than that. But they have a generality which transcends particular facts and gives them a wider usefulness. Every science eventually reaches the stage of theory in this sense. (p. 28)

Theories are summaries (either statements or equations) of classes of functional relations (scientific facts) that have themselves been ordered into scientific laws. Moreover, implied in Skinner's quote, and stated directly by Skinner elsewhere (e.g., 1957), is the idea that the theoretical principles of a science do more than explain already observed events; they are used to interpret (i.e., understand) novel empirical observations (e.g., Skinner, 1957). This is the role of extrapolation, or scientific interpretation, discussed in chapter 1. The interpretation of novel behavioral relations using established principles has been a consistent practice in behavior analysis for many years (e.g., Bijou, 1976; Bijou & Baer, 1978; Donahoe & Palmer, 1994, Palmer, 1991; Schlinger, 1992; Skinner, 1957; Whaley & Malott, 1973). It is part of a long tradition in the natural sciences of using theoretical laws and principles induced from scientific facts to understand phenomena that are usually more complex than those studied in the laboratory. Behavior analysis is generally concerned with lawful relations between observable events, namely, behavior and its environmental determinants. Consequently, the theory is maximally descriptive. This is why behavior analysts are so strict about using objective language to describe behavioral relations.

Behavior analysis consists of the laws and principles—derived from the experimental analysis of basic units of behavior—that describe known functional relations between behavior and environment. Behavior analysis includes, but is not limited to, the laws of respondent (Pavlovian) conditioning and the operant laws of reinforcement (and punishment) and stimulus control.

BASIC UNITS IN BEHAVIOR ANALYSIS

Chapter 2 briefly mentioned that a main advantage of behavior analysis is its use of functional units of analysis in understanding behavioral development. A basic unit of analysis is the smallest functional relation that displays order. In behavior analysis, the most fundamental unit is a functional relation between three events: a motivational variable or establishing operation, a class of behavior, and a consequence, for example, a reinforcer ($EO{\rightarrow}R{\rightarrow}S^R$) (Schlinger & Blakely, 1994). This functional relation is called a contingency, where "contingency" refers to the functional relation between the three events. Addition of a discriminative stimulus (S^D) expands the contingency or relation:

$$\begin{matrix} S^D \\ \\ EO \end{matrix} : R \rightarrow S^R$$

In behavior analysis, as in the other natural sciences, the key to the emergence of scientific laws has been the discovery of basic units of analysis. In fact, the success of any science depends on whether that science has discovered "proper units" of analysis. Zeiler (1986) has noted:

> A well-defined unit clarifies the way phenomena are conceptualized and thereby guides research and theory. Isolation of a unit brings order to otherwise discrepant phenomena; invalid units easily lead to confusion as to the meaning and significance of the data. (p. 1)

Notice that these characteristics of well-defined units resemble the characteristics of a strong scientific theory. They must be able to explain already existing phenomena (inclusiveness), guide research and theory (fruitfulness), and offer a unified account of diverse phenomena (generality).

The basic units of modern behavior analysis were first described by Skinner (1935). He defined stimuli and responses (i.e., environment and behavior), not as independent structural units, but as functional classes. Thus, stimuli were not defined by their physical energy, and responses were not defined by their form or topography. Rather, both were defined by their respective effects on one another. Consequently, Skinner discovered fundamental units in the analysis of behavior. Several behavior analysts have described the importance of this discovery for a science of behavior (e.g., Branch, 1977; Catania, 1973; Zeiler, 1986). According to Zeiler (1986):

> The fundamental units (operants, respondents, discriminative operants) are the smallest entities that display the full characteristics of adaptive behavior. The previous structural entities (stimuli and responses in isolation) now become components of the basic units, analogous to nuclei and cytoplasm as components of cells. Research can involve the variables determining how generic classes are constructed and the factors responsible for particular forms of coordinated behavior, but never is it necessary to move to a nonbehavioral level of analysis. (pp. 4–5)

Three issues in this quotation are important in the discussion of behavioral development. The first concerns the issue of adaptive behavior. Behavior analysis is limited to understanding and explaining the effects of the environment on behavior as a result of their interaction. Behavior change as a result of environmental interaction is the essence of adaptive behavior. Behavior analysis assumes that genes and biology play an important role in behavior, and, more importantly, that these variables set broad (vs. narrow) limits within which behavior can be changed by environmental variables (Baldwin & Baldwin, 1988). Thus, behavior analysis is a scientific theory of adaptive behavior.

The second important issue is that of structure versus function. The concept of basic units of analysis has implications for the distinction between structural and functional approaches to behavior. Behavior analysts don't deny that behavioral units can have structure. But they assert that the units must first be functionally defined. Branch (1977) explains:

> The crux of the issue is not whether units can have structure; they do. The important question is, to what is the structure due? A structural account points to structural aspects of the behaver ... whereas a functional account will emphasize the role of manipulable variables in the *formation* of units. (p. 172)

Behavior analysts are interested in the variables that cause adaptive behavior to have structure in the first place. The variables responsible for the formation of units of behavior are to be found largely in the individual's environment, although biology does play a role in the initial and boundary conditions.

The last issue of importance is that of scientific explanation and, more specifically, Skinner's (and the behavior analytic) position on the role of explanation in the study of behavior. With its fundamental units, behavior analysis can bring order, clarity, and unity to developmental psychology. Just as the discovery of the cell as a basic unit of biology integrated the disciplines of anatomy, embryology, botany, and zoology into the unified field that we now call the biological sciences (Zeiler, 1986), the basic units of behavior analysis can help to unify the various subareas of developmental psychology. The present book is an example of one way this might be accomplished.

THE ENVIRONMENT

The Traditional View of the Environment

The behavior analytic concept of environment differs from that found in other psychological approaches. Most standard views of the environment are not only structural in nature, but also molar. In developmental psychology textbooks, the environment is typically defined as the people (e.g., parents, teachers, friends) and institutions (e.g., schools, communities) (Collins & Kuczaj, 1991) or the experiences in a child's life (Scarr,

Weinberg, & Levine, 1986). For example, in the debate about the effects of early, adverse experiences, the environment is described either as enriched or as impoverished (e.g., Collins & Kuczaj, 1991). The context of social development as described by developmental psychologists includes the family, its socioeconomic status, the number of siblings, and the occupations of the parents. Although specific interactions are sometimes alluded to, the environment is usually viewed as a structural entity (e.g., a child's family) with properties that can be quantified (e.g., the number of siblings) and included in correlational calculations with the child's age or developmental progress.

These conceptions of environment may aid in conducting correlational studies, but they fall prey to some of the same problems described earlier concerning structural conceptions of behavior. Specifically, they tend to obscure more fundamental environmental variables. Finally, most psychologists think of the environment only as the things that surround us. This is not surprising since the noun "environment" is derived from the verb "environ," which means "to surround." Behavior analysts, however, view the environment quite differently.

A Behavior Analytic View of the Environment

Behavior analysts view the environment in both structural and functional terms. First, behavior analysts view the environment as consisting of energy changes (i.e., stimuli) of various sorts that not only affect the sensory receptors of organisms but, more importantly, affect their behavior. Thus, stimuli and behavior can form orderly functional relationships. It is these functional relations between behavior and environment that form the basic units from which the principles of behavior analysis have been induced. For behavior analysts, the environment is not defined prior to the study of behavior or by what it looks like, but rather after functional relations have been established, that is, by how it functions. A stimulus is only a functional stimulus if it affects some behavior in a particular manner.

A functional conception of the environment implies that the traditional definition of the environment—something that surrounds us—is incomplete. If, in fact, environment is defined functionally as all of the stimuli that enter into functional relationships with an organism's behavior at any one time, then we must expand our view of the environment to include events both inside as well as outside the body. Therefore, the skin is simply an arbitrary structural boundary. We may now view the environment from a thoroughly functional perspective.

A functional conception of the environment enables us to deal in part with the difficult problem of internal events. Behavior analysts, contrary to most reports, do not discount the role of internal events in their analyses. Rather, they consider them to be physical and potentially observable events that, like external physical events, can affect behavior. Such "private" events include interoceptive somatosensory stimuli (e.g., kinesthetic, vestibular) and behavior (e.g., self-talk) that cannot be observed by others. Rather than making inferences about cognitive and mental events, behavior analysts assume that internal events are real events that possess structure and, more importantly, can affect behavior and, thus, enter into functional relations with behavior.

LOCUS OF CONTROL

Any discussion of environment raises the problem of where the determinants of behavior lie. The issue of locus of control is a central one in behavior analysis, and it is one of the features that most distinguishes behavior analysis from other psychological approaches to behavior. Previously, I described an example of how developmental researchers interpreted a relatively simple demonstration of operant conditioning in infants by placing the determinants of the behavior inside the child (Kalnins & Bruner, 1973). You will recall that these researchers demonstrated that a focused picture was used to reinforce a particular sucking pattern in infants. The researchers neglected environmental factors in their explanation of the infants' behavior. Instead, they described the interactions as voluntary behavior in which the infants were seen as the agents (i.e., originators or initiators) of their own actions.

Behavior analysts register several objections to such agent→action accounts of behavior (e.g., Hineline, 1990). The most obvious objection is that the control of behavior is ultimately not inside the child, but in the environment. The Kalnins and Bruner (1973) study is a perfect example. The rates of sucking changed whenever the experimenters changed the outcome of sucking which was the clarity of the picture. Thus, changes in the environment were responsible for the changes in sucking behavior. Similarly, an experimenter who repeatedly operantly conditioned and then extinguished a rat's lever pressing behavior could not then attribute the changes in behavior to the rat's own decision making and voluntary control. At the very least such descriptions are redundant and add nothing new to the understanding of behavior. At worst, they lead researchers away from the controlling variables and in search of untestable, hypothetical explanations of behavior. Another, more subtle objection is that, from a purely functional standpoint, the environment operates not on the organism per se, but on the organism's behavior. Thus, the laws of behavior analysis are really "laws of responses rather than laws of organisms" (Baer, 1976). The organism is more accurately described as the "host" for the responses, or as the locus where various determinants of behavior (e.g., genetic and environmental) come together (Baer, 1976; Skinner, 1972).

Behavior analysis attributes human behavior to a constellation of variables, including the individual's genes and physiological makeup, but stresses the role of the environment, both past and present. According to a behavior analytic view of development, differences in behavior between individuals are a function of differences in the functional aspects of their environments rather than of differences in genetic or biological variables. Since the causes of behavior can often be unequivocally traced to environmental interactions in a controlled laboratory, behavior analysis can predict or explain behavior outside of the laboratory as well. This is the issue of interpretation in science discussed in chapter 1.

THE ROLE OF INFERENCE IN BEHAVIOR ANALYSIS

Skinner was opposed to explanations of behavior that appealed to inferred, hypothetical events when more objective explanations were available. Examples of such events include cognitive processes and structures, mental events, concepts, thoughts, strategies, and so on. The issue is not whether the events or processes to which these labels refer have any independent existence—that is at present not a testable hypothesis—but whether inferring them is necessary to explain behavior. Cognitive psychologists would say that it is necessary to infer such events to explain behavior (Baars, 1986), and behavior analysts would say that it is not. Behavior analysts also make inferences, but their inferences are about potentially observable environmental events. For example, when a behavior analyst suggests that some form of reinforcement might be responsible for maintaining the tantruming behavior of a 6-year-old, he or she is making an inference based on observing the behavior in its context. The main difference between this inference and the Freudian's inference about conflicts between id, ego, and superego is that the former can be directly tested and verified while the latter cannot. Inferring potentially testable, environmental events as causes of behavior represents the use of behavior analytic theory to interpret behavior in a natural setting (see chapter 1). The advantage of the behavior analytic approach is that it infers events (environmental stimuli) that can be potentially observed, manipulated, and, thus, directly tested.

A BEHAVIOR ANALYTIC TAXONOMY

As stated in the Preface, this book assumes that prospective readers will have had some instruction in the basic principles of behavior analysis. A brief presentation of the basic principles of behavior, however, is warranted. Just as there are functional classification systems in the natural sciences, it is possible to classify functionally the environmental variables that affect behavior. The purpose of this section, then, is to present an outline of such a taxonomy, since these terms and concepts will appear throughout the remainder of the book. The outline of a functional taxonomy of stimulus functions presented here is based on Michael's (1993a) classification and taken more directly from that of Schlinger and Blakely (1994).

Stimulus Functions

Behavior analysts distinguish between immediate versus more enduring effects of environmental events on behavior (e.g., Catania, 1992; Michael, 1983, 1986; Reynolds, 1975; Skinner, 1938, 1953; Thompson & Lubinsky, 1986). In his *Primer of Operant Conditioning* (1975), Reynolds described the distinction between these two generic classes as follows:

> There are two kinds of environmental determinants of behavior: the contemporary and the historical. The behavior of an organism at any one moment is determined by the currently acting, contemporary environment but also by the organism's previous experience with these, or similar environmental conditions. (p. 3)

Michael (1983, 1986) has classified these environmental operations according to whether they immediately, but momentarily, strengthen behavior, or whether they produce a more lasting effect, "which can best be observed when the conditions that preceded the event are again present" (1983, p. 21). The term "evoke" is used to denote the former effect, and the term "function-altering" is used to denote the latter effect (Michael, 1993a; Schlinger & Blakely, 1994).

Evocative Functions

The term "evoke" is used to describe the fact that some environmental operations (e.g., the presentation of stimuli) produce momentary changes in behavior. As this term refers only to a temporal controlling relationship, it may be used for both operant and respondent controlling relations. With respect to respondent relations, the term "evoke" is equivalent to "elicit"; with respect to operant relations, it is equivalent to "set the occasion," or simply, "occasion." Events that evoke behavior include unconditional and conditional stimuli (USs and CSs), discriminative stimuli (S^Ds) and establishing operations (EOs), and sign stimuli (also called releasers) (Michael, 1983). For example, in a typical discrimination procedure with rats, lever pressing is followed by reinforcement only in the presence of a light. When the light is illuminated, all things being equal, a lever press immediately occurs. Therefore, light onset "evokes" the lever press. Likewise, if a parent tells a child, "please turn off the TV," and the child immediately does so, we say that the command "evoked" the child's behavior. In both examples, some stimulus momentarily increased the probability of the behavior. In the strictly temporal sense of the word "cause," we can say that the stimuli "caused" the behavior to occur.

Many stimuli have acquired their evocative functions in the evolutionary histories of the respective species. Such stimuli include sign stimuli, unconditional stimuli, and unconditional establishing operations. Such effects are straightforward and are treated more extensively elsewhere (see Fantino & Logan, 1979; Slater, 1985, for a concise introduction to ethology). In this book, however, we are more concerned with the ways in which the environmental histories of individuals establish and modify or alter the behavioral functions of stimuli. The specific operations are therefore referred to as function altering (Schlinger & Blakely, 1994).

Function-Altering Operations

Environmental operations that alter the evocative functions of stimuli include all procedures in which stimuli are correlated with one another and with responses, including respondent (or classical) and operant conditioning. For example, the respondent procedure of pairing (correlating) a bell with food in the mouth results in the bell acquiring evocative functions with respect to salivation. In this example, the food evokes (or elicits) salivation as an unconditional stimulus (US). But after the function altering operation of correlating the two stimuli, the bell evokes salivation as a conditional stimulus (CS). Similarly, the sound of a mother's voice, which usually precedes nursing an infant, will establish evocative control over the infant's behaviors of turning the head and looking in the direction of the mother. In other words, the sound of the mother's voice produces immediate, momentary changes in the infant's behavior. In this example, the sound of the mother's voice becomes a discriminative stimulus (S^D). Of course, providing food to a food-deprived individual results in food deprivation acquiring evocative control over whatever behavior produces food. That is, food deprivation produces momentary changes in the behavior.

The operation of food deprivation is called a motivational variable or establishing operation (Michael, 1982; 1993b).

Function-altering operations not only strengthen or weaken evocative stimulus functions, but also establish other function-altering operations. For example, pairing (correlating) the sound of the mother's voice with food establishes the sound of the mother's voice as a conditioned reinforcer (S^r). This can be tested by immediately following some new behavior in the infant with only the sound of the mother's voice and observing whether this alone increases the evocative control of the EO or S^D over that behavior. There are many other types of function altering operations, including modeling and imprinting (Schlinger & Blakely, 1994). Verbal stimuli can alter the functions of other stimuli in ways that mimic the effects of respondent or operant conditioning (Allesi, 1992; Schlinger, 1993; Schlinger & Blakely, 1987).

A BEHAVIOR ANALYTIC VIEW OF DEVELOPMENT

The next three sections deal with the concept of development, the behavior analytic view of the respective roles of genes and biology in child behavioral development, and the issue of proximate and ultimate causation. Because this is a book on behavioral development in childhood, it is important to talk about the concept of development from a behavior analytic perspective. Because genes and biology play a significant role in behavioral development, a few words about how behavior analysts view these influences are also in order. Finally, because cognitive psychologists stress proximate causes of behavior and behavior analysts stress ultimate causes of behavior, the last section describes briefly the difference between these two levels of causation.

The Concept of Development

When asking about the meaning of a word, we are really asking how that word is typically used. Of course, it is the nature of human language that individual word use is often controlled by circumstances in the individual's history. The term "development," as used in many developmental textbooks, refers simply to change related in an orderly fashion to time. Such a definition has led, not surprisingly, to the practice of encouraging structural and normative theories of development. This is unfortunate because such conceptions only describe what behavior occurs and not how it occurs. When pressed with the question of how behavioral development occurs, psychologists look to the most obvious variable that is correlated with changes in behavior—changes in age. But age (or time) is not a manipulable variable (see chapter 2); and, therefore, age itself cannot explain how behavior change occurs. Consequently, many developmental psychologists are forced to infer some underlying biological or cognitive structure that changes. Age is simply the most objective reflection of this underlying developmental structure. Thus, in the attempt to find some meaning in the changes in behavior, psychologists borrow from developmental biology and invent stages through which the behavior is said to progress.

With all of this confusion regarding the term "development," is there any way to salvage the crux of the definition, that is, the notion of change over time, and still maintain a scientific approach? One possibility is that we could slightly alter the use of the term to read change *in behavior* over time. This alteration would have the fortunate byproduct of shifting the emphasis from invented time-related variables to "the processes that produce, facilitate, or retard change" (Horowitz, 1987, p. 159), that is, to environmental events as independent variables. This does not mean that normative data are useless; in most instances they represent clues about environmental changes rather than about underlying genetic or biological changes, as many developmental psychologists believe. For example, when a child's behavior displays object permanence during the first 2 years of life, we should look at how the interactions between the child's behavior and the environment have changed over the 2-year period. This is why some behavior analysts (e.g., Bijou & Baer, 1978) have defined psychological development as "progressive changes in interactions between the behavior of individuals and the events in their environment" (p. 2). This is how the term "development" will be used in the present book.

Finally, a word about the inclusion of the term "progressive" in Bijou and Baer's definition is necessary. As Berndt (1992) points out, not all changes in behavior may be considered to be developmental; such a definition would be far too inclusive. Berndt suggests that we adopt Lerner's condition (1986, cited in Berndt, 1992) that "developmental changes are systematic rather than haphazard and successive rather than independent of earlier conditions" (p. 5). The use of "progressive" by Bijou and Baer (1978) is meant to take these features into consideration.

Genes, Brain, and Behavioral Plasticity

One of the many misconceptions and misunderstandings of behavior analysis concerns the role of inheritance and biology on behavior. Behavior analysts do value the very powerful role evolution and genes play in the development of behavior. It is precisely because of our (human) genetic endowment and the nature of our brain that our behavior is so malleable (i.e., adaptive). Behavior analysis, then, is simply the science of this behavioral plasticity, but at the level of behavior and environment, not at the level of the underlying neurological or genetic events. In other words, behavior analysts acknowledge that genes determine the structure of the brain that endows human behavior with its seemingly infinite adaptiveness. In fact, behavior analysts agree with evolutionary biologists who assert that human evolution is characterized by the natural selection of behavioral plasticity (Dobzhansky, Ayala, Stebbins, & Valentine, 1977; Futuyma, 1979). Futuyma (1979) has written:

> On balance, the evidence for the modifiability of human behavior is so great that genetic constraints on our behavior hardly seem to exist. The dominant factor in recent human evolution has been the evolution of behavioral flexibility, the ability to learn and transmit culture. (p. 491)

Obviously this behavioral plasticity is realized in some manner in the structure of the brain. After all, the genetic code is a recipe for the production of protein, and like the rest of the human body, the brain is protein. One of the main distinguishing features of the human brain is its capacity to change (Geschwind, 1979).

The issue for the present discussion is how and at what levels behavior should be studied. The behavior analytic view is that behavior can be fruitfully studied in its environmental context without reference to either genetic or neurobiological information. This is not to say that genetic or neurobiological variables are unimportant, only that they are not necessary to understand how the environment affects behavior at the level of behavior–environment interactions. Obviously, the more we learn about the relative contributions of genetics and neurophysiology, the more we will understand why the environment affects behavior the way it does. But we need not await those developments before we can begin to scientifically understand how behavior adapts to the environment or, more accurately, how the environment selects behavior that we call adaptive.

Proximate and Ultimate Causation

One of the persistent problems with a behavior analytic approach to psychology concerns the status of the causation of behavior. It is not uncommon to hear researchers speak of the brain *causing* behavior. For example, a recent newspaper article mentioned a strong correlation between the severity of the symptoms of schizophrenia and the size of a part of the temporal cortex. Although the data were correlational, the report stated that the size of the particular part of the temporal cortex may *cause* schizophrenia. Similarly, cognitive psychologists speak of cognitive structures and processes *causing* behavior. For example, according to Piagetian theory, when encountering an object like an apple, a child's perceptual knowledge *causes* him or her to abstract certain physical properties of the apple like its roundness. Notwithstanding the serious problems in this kind of theorizing (see chapter 2), in both examples some current event is said to be responsible for the observed behavior. In such cases, the cause is referred to as a proximate cause, that is, a cause that is temporally (or spatially) close to the effect.

While behavior analysts are interested in proximate causes—these are the events that evoke behavior—their real interest is in ultimate causation. In other words, behavior analysts want to understand how proximate events come to affect behavior. If it is true that a part of the temporal cortex affects behavior called schizophrenic (proximate cause), behavior analysts would ask what happened to affect the temporal cortex in that manner (ultimate cause). Ultimate causes are located both in the evolutionary history of the species and in the history of the individual. Thus, in the example of schizophrenia, we may speculate that the part of the temporal cortex that "causes" schizophrenia was altered by either genetic or by environmental variables. Cognitive psychologists posit inferred, internal, and often hypothetical structures and processes as the (proximate) causes of behavior, even though they may agree with behavior analysts that experience with the environment establishes the cognitive events in the first place. Behavior analysts emphasize ultimate mechanisms, like conditioning history.

APPLYING A BEHAVIOR ANALYTIC INTERPRETATION

What follows in the remainder of the book is an illustration of how behavior analysis might be applied to several research areas in child development that are not typically presented as being theoretically related. A behavior analytic interpretation relates them by examining them as examples of adaptive behavior, that is, behavior as a function of environmental variables and subject to the same natural laws. Research in developmental psychology is valuable and therefore should not be disregarded by behavior analysts. Moreover, since behavior analysts have contributed proportionally less of this research, they should take the opportunity to evaluate it according to behavior analytic theory.

One of the problems that a behavior analyst encounters when attempting to interpret research conducted by researchers with other theoretical orientations is that different paradigmatic assumptions often lead to different ways of doing research: Different questions are asked, and certain research strategies determine how those questions are answered. In psychology, the two general theoretical orientations toward behavior are the cognitive and the behavior analytic. The cognitive orientation is currently dominant in psychology; accordingly, much of the research in the area of development has been generated from a cognitive orientation.

Cognitive and Behavior Analytic Approaches to Behavior

Many standard psychological terms in psychology and in ordinary language imply a cognitive approach to behavior. Consider the term "memory." The importance of the concept of memory for cognitive approaches to psychology cannot be overstated. To the extent that the study of memory cannot be separated from the general study of what is called information processing (Cohen & Gelber, 1975), it is possible to view it as the very essence of modern cognitive psychology. As a result, a vast and complicated theoretical network has emerged around the concept of memory, and this raises difficulties for a behavior analytic interpretation of the development of memory in children. It is unrealistic, for example, to expect behavior analysts to make sense out of concepts such as memory traces, storage locations, and retrieval systems.

Theoretical questions in the "memory" literature also present difficulties for behavior analysts. For example, cognitive psychologists raise the questions: "Is there only one storage system in which traces are set down?" Is there "a limited capacity short-term memory in which items are held for only brief periods of time, and a high-capacity long-term memory in which items are complexly coded thereby greatly reducing information loss due to forgetting or retrieval failure" (Cohen & Gelber, 1975, pp. 348–349)? These questions are unanswerable because the proposed theoretical entities are not accessible to empirical methods. The behavior analytic view is to understand and explain behavior according to the established laws and principles of behavior analysis and to disregard the particular inferred theoretical constructs such as remembering, thinking, problem solving, etc.

As previously stated, behavior analysts' opposition to inferences is not an absolute one. When confronting a psychology based in large part on inferred, hypothetical events, the task of behavior analysis is to examine the behavior from which the hypothetical events are inferred. This raises another difficulty for behavior analytic interpretations of concepts like memory. Attempting to interpret units of analysis defined by cognitive psychologists means accepting the general cognitive strategy of identifying units of analysis prior to their measurement "merely on the basis of their putative structure or topography" (Branch, 1977, p. 171). The concept of memory and all of its components (e.g., short-term and long-term memory) qualifies as such a unit because memory as a cognitive structure or process is presumed to exist before psychologists begin to study it. In contrast, the behavior analytic approach is to identify some behavior of interest, and then attempt to either analyze it experimentally or interpret it according to already established laws.

Recall that for cognitive psychology, behavior seems to be important largely insofar as it reflects inferred, internal events. So, cognitively oriented psychologists are less likely to define behavior on the basis of its functional relation to environmental variables than on the basis of what it suggests to them about inferred, hypothetical structures and processes. The behavior analyst who attempts to interpret data derived from this fundamental assumption does so at some risk because the data may not have been derived from a natural science research methodology like that employed by behavior analysts. Despite these difficulties, this book will look at how behavior analytic theory might approach some of the facts that comprise various topics in child development.

Summary

This chapter described the main features of behavior analysis, beginning with the position of behavior analysts on scientific theory. It also countered the frequent claim by nonbehavior analysts that behavior analysts are antitheory. Theory in behavior analysis is consistent with the inductively derived theories of the other natural sciences, the features of which were described in chapter 1. In those theories, the laws and principles of the science are generalizations of the classes of functional relations discovered through a rigorous program of experimental research. The laws and principles, and the functional relations upon which they are based, are derived from the discovery of basic units of analysis: the smallest functional relations between classes of independent and dependent variables that display order.

This chapter also discussed both traditional and behavior analytic views of the environment and of the locus of control; that is, whether the variables determining behavior reside inside the child, which is the traditional view, or in the environment, which is the behavior analytic view. Experimental behavior analysts have discovered several functions of environmental operations on behavior. These functions have been classified according to whether they produce immediate or more enduring effects on behavior.

Finally, this chapter introduced a behavior analytic view of development. That view emphasizes the importance of looking at the processes responsible for the outcomes of development, rather than the outcomes themselves. Behavior analysts view these processes as involving "progressive changes in interactions between the behavior of individuals and the events in their environment" (Bijou & Baer, 1978, p. 2). Finally, this chapter discussed some of the problems behavior analysts encounter when approaching the field of child development, which is dominated largely by cognitive psychologists who frequently infer hypothetical variables as explanations for behavior. The task for the behavior analyst is to look at the behavior from which the hypothetical variables are inferred and to try to understand it according to the laws and principles of behavior analysis.

4

The Development of Memory

The study of memory, especially in infants, is difficult because so many different behaviors are used as evidence of memory. For example, cognitive psychologists claim that "imitation, object permanence, attachment, conditioning, and preference for novel stimuli all imply that the infant is remembering something" (Cohen & Gelber, 1975, p. 353). For most developmental psychologists, the term "memory" is usually used to refer to certain cognitive operations, and the explication of memory must therefore involve understanding the development of these cognitive processes. In contrast, behavior analysts would suggest that instead of inferring hypothetical processes, it would be more scientific to study the behavioral relations observed when developmental psychologists speak of memory. Explanation of memory, then, would involve basic behavioral processes.

This chapter concentrates on two broad areas of research in infant memory: (1) visual recognition memory procedures and (2) visual operant conditioning procedures. Behaviors related to memory, such as pattern recognition, attachment, and object permanence, will be considered in later chapters under different topics. This chapter makes the point that, when developmental researchers speak of "memory" in infants, they mean that the basic laws of habituation and operant conditioning have been shown to apply to infant behavior. In other words, these laws are sufficient at present for understanding the observed behavioral relations called "memory." Much of the research presented in this chapter comprises the core research that is cited in standard developmental writings. This chapter will demonstrate how behavior analysis can account for the results without inferring hypothetical structures, mechanisms, or processes.

THE CONCEPT OF MEMORY IN DEVELOPMENTAL PSYCHOLOGY

One developmental textbook defines memory as "a person's mental record of an event" (Scarr, Weinberg, & Levine, 1986, p. 232). This definition has all of the attendant problems of structural approaches to behavior described in chapter 2. Briefly, behavior is observed in certain situations and given a name, in this case, "memory." The name is then reified and treated as though it had a physical existence (i.e., as a memory or a "mental record of an event"). The memory or mental record is never directly observed. Finally, the term "memory" is used to explain the behaviors it represents, thereby creating a circular explanation. For example, the relatively poor memories of preschoolers have been attributed to their "limited information-processing capacity," a "lack of meaningful organization" of the memories, and an "inadequate knowledge base" (Scarr et al., 1986)—descriptions all inferred from the behaviors to be explained in the first place. Describing child behavior in this way creates surrogates for the actual behavior that are moved inside the child without any independent, empirical confirmation of their existence. Scarr et al. (1986) discuss the concept of poor memory organization in the following excerpt:

> One might compare the storage area of the human mind to a vast library, filled with endless shelves of information. To recall a particular experience or retrieve certain information, the child must search the shelves to find what she needs. If her memory collection is organized in a meaningful way, if it is cataloged, the search is much easier. (pp. 233–234)

Concerning the limited information-processing capacities, they state:

> When faced with a memory task, an older child automatically begins grouping items in his mind, rehearsing the lists of words, and applying other strategies to the task. He has a program or scheme for memorization. The younger child does not have such a scheme. She has to think about how she is going to learn the pictures or words. This uses up mental "space," leaving less room for actually storing information. (p. 234)

The first quotation is clearly metaphorical, but the second one implies the existence of mental structures (schemes) and processes. Metaphors probably do make communication easier, but there is no evidence that the brain is like a library or computer. In these descriptions, events do not happen in the world of behavior and environment, but in another world of hypothetical constructs. While all of this appears relatively benign, it contributes little to understanding the behavior from which it is inferred. Moreover, concentrating on memories and other inferred mental structures directs researchers away from investigating more fundamental and observable processes, like the environmental contingencies responsible for the observed behaviors.

Behavior analysis takes a different approach. Behavior analysts have no difficulty using the term "memory" to describe phenomena that share certain characteristics (Branch, 1977; Palmer, 1991). They do have a problem, however, when behavior is said to reflect underlying processes that are called memory, and when those hypothetical processes are said to be responsible for the behavior (a circular explanation).

RESEARCH ON INFANT MEMORY

Visual Recognition Memory

Psychologists often distinguish between recognition memory and recall memory. In recognition memory, children simply indicate whether they have encountered the stimulus before. In recall memory, they actually produce a verbal response that names the stimulus (Bukatko & Daehler, 1992). Because infants are not yet capable of verbal behavior, researchers can only employ tests of recognition memory. Most of these tests use visual stimuli, so the type of memory studied is called visual recognition memory. Visual recognition memory is inferred "when infants respond differentially to familiar and novel stimuli" (Werner & Siqueland, 1978, p. 79). Investigators have used (single-stimulus) habituation (e.g., Bornstein, 1976) and novelty preference (or paired comparison) procedures (e.g., Fagan, 1970; Fantz, 1964), as well as novelty discrimination procedures (e.g., Werner & Siqueland, 1978), to test for recognition memory.

Experiments Using (Single-Stimulus) Habituation Procedures

In a typical single-stimulus habituation procedure, a single patterned visual stimulus (e.g., a pattern consisting of simple forms, simple colors, or simple color–form combinations) is presented repeatedly until visual fixation time toward it decreases. Then, in test trials, this familiar stimulus and other novel stimuli are successively presented. The dependent measure is the difference in the infant's fixation time between the two types of stimuli. If the fixation time to the novel stimulus is greater, then it can be inferred that the infant remembered the familiar stimulus. For example, consider an experiment by Bornstein (1976) on whether 4-month-old infants would display recognition memory for hue. One group of infants was shown a 570 nanometers (nm) (greenish yellow) hue on 15 trials with each trial lasting 15 seconds with 7.5-second intertrial intervals. This was the habituation phase. As expected, the amount of fixation time to the 570 nm stimulus declined across trials. Immediately after the habituation trials, 9 test trials were conducted in which two other hues—560 nm (yellowish green), and 580 nm (yellow)—were presented with the 570 nm hue. As predicted, fixation time to the 570 nm hue was the shortest. Fixation time to the 580 nm hue was also brief. Although fixation time to the 560 nm hue was shorter than the initial fixation time to the 570 nm hue during the habituation phase, it was the longest in test trials.

What is the best way to explain these results, especially when fixation time was significantly shorter to one novel stimulus (580 nm) than to the other novel stimulus (560 nm)? In this experiment, as in single-stimulus habituation experiments in general, memory is inferred if fixation times to the novel stimuli are longer than to the habituated stimulus. But is it really necessary to infer memory to explain the results? By definition, "habituation" is the name given to the process of repeatedly presenting an unconditional stimulus that results in a decrease in unconditional responding evoked by that stimulus. Based on the principles of habituation, we would predict that after habituation, responding to novel stimuli would be greater than to the habituated stimulus. Therefore, is it not sufficient to say simply that habituation to hue has been demonstrated in 4-month-old infants? After all, this extends the information about habituation to a different population (4-month-old infants) and to a different stimulus class (hue). This information also tells us something about infants' early perceptual abilities; that is, their visual systems are sensitive to small differences in hue. The behavior analytic view is that the results of such experiments can be understood in terms of stimulus control as predicted by the extant experimental literature on habituation, rather than by appealing to inferred hypothetical events (i.e., recognition memory). Theoretical parameters such as rate of habituation, interstimulus interval, generalization, spontaneous recovery, and dishabituation may be used to understand the experimental results of habituation studies. Thus, for behavior analysts, it is sufficient and parsimonious to account for infants' behaviors, that are commonly called memory, on the basis of what is already known about habituation, the facts of which occupy part of behavior analytic theory.

As a result, it is unnecessary to infer memory, as cognitively oriented psychologists do. In their defense, they claim that these results may help researchers "gain some insight into infants' conceptual systems" (Bornstein, 1976, p. 190). But what are these conceptual systems? Such an account illustrates a typical cognitive interpretation, because it takes the observable behavior–environment relations and infers internal processes. Of course, habituation may in fact be "understood" at another, though scientific level, that of underlying cellular processes (e.g., Kandel, 1975). But this does not negate understanding at the level of behavior and environment. Talking about habituation at either the behavioral or cellular level does not require an appeal to hypothetical, cognitive entities or processes. Habituation has been studied in many species other than humans, including those with relatively simple nervous systems, such as the marine invertebrate, Aplysia, a sea snail (see Kandel, 1975), without inferring hypothetical cognitive events to account for the facts. Cognitive psychologists also tend to describe experimental results using ordinary language in which the infant is the initiator of her own actions. For example, Bornstein (1976), writes, "The fact that the infants confuse 580 nm with 570 nm following habituation to 570 nm indicates their qualitative grouping of wavelengths in the range 570–580 nm" (p. 189). The term "confuse," however, complicates the simple observation that infants responded similarly to both 570 nm and 580 nm. In fact, the principle of stimulus generalization would have predicted this result. Perhaps it is correct to say that infants respond to wavelength according to categorical similarity rather than specific wavelength. In the study just described, infants responded similarly to 570 nm and 580 nm because they are both yellowish. But what about the increased response to the novel 560 nm (yellowish green) stimulus? That stimulus is as close to the original 570 nm hue as is the 580 nm stimulus, yet fixation time was much greater. Shouldn't we expect comparable stimulus generalization to both novel stimuli? Shouldn't the infant respond similarly to 560 nm and 570 nm because they are both greenish as they did to 570 nm and 580 nm because they are both yellowish? It is clear that just as the generalization from 570 nm to 580 nm occurred, discrimination between 560 nm and 570 nm occurred. The explanation for this apparent discrimination is not as clear. It is possible that, as Bornstein suggests, infants "encounter the world with certain" visual "biases," that is, "their ... memory for surface qualities, like hue, appear to be organized into categories prior to formal training or tuition." It is also possible, and perhaps more parsimonious, that the infant's visual behavior had already undergone subtle forms of discrimination training prior to the experiment. Evidence from studies on the effects of early visual experience on the brain and behavior lend plausibility to this suggestion (e.g., Hirsch & Spinelli, 1971; Wiesel, 1982).

The habituation procedure might reveal something about how infants' brains and physiological systems work. But does it reflect the brain's hard wiring or programming by experience? The infants in the preceding study were already 4 months old. This means that they had already had a significant number of experiences with hue, including habituation and probably operant conditioning. In fact, it is possible that many of these experiments may not be studies of habituation per se, but of operant stimulus control. That is, the movements of the eyes described by the phrase "visual fixation" may be functionally related to the consequence of seeing the stimulus display. In other words, seeing the familiar (or novel) stimuli may reinforce further looking. This might be especially true in infants because we know that many types of visual stimuli seem to function either as (unconditioned) positive reinforcers for behavior that produces them (e.g., Kalnins & Bruner, 1973; Siqueland & DeLucia, 1969), or as unconditional eliciting stimuli (Fantz, 1961). In any case, behavior analysts would be interested in teasing apart the controlling variables by systematically examining the functional relationships between them.

Experiments Using Paired-Comparison (Novelty Preference) Procedures

The paired comparison or novelty preference procedure, which may be viewed as a variation on the habituation procedure, involves simultaneously presenting two identical patterns to infants, one on the left side and the other on the right side. After this is done repeatedly and fixation time to both stimuli decreases, test trials occur in which novel stimuli are presented simultaneously with the familiar stimuli. Although there are some variations on this procedure (e.g., Fagan, 1970), the dependent measure is the proportion of visual fixation to the novel versus the familiar stimulus. Any differences between the two imply memory of the familiar stimulus (Cohen & Gelber, 1975).

One of the first experiments to use this procedure was conducted by Fantz (1964). Infants ranging in age from 6 to 25 weeks of age were positioned in a small hammock crib inside a test chamber. Two stimulus cards were placed over holes in the top of the apparatus directly over the infants' heads. Of the 11 cards used, 6 were color photographs and 5 were black and white. For each infant, one photograph was a constant pattern, presented for 1 minute, 10 times in succession, during which it was paired with one of the remaining 10 patterns. The dependent measure, the amount of time the infant's eyes fixated on a particular pattern, was measured by observing the corneal reflection of each eye through a small hole in the top of the chamber. Even though there was a great deal of variability among infants, the results seemed to show no difference in fixation times to either the constant or novel patterns for the youngest infants (1–2 months of age), whereas for all other infants, fixation time to the constant pattern decreased as the number of successive exposures increased. How can we interpret these results?

The author concluded that "incidental visual experiences can be retained by infants over 2 months of age, at least for a short period of time" (p. 670). But what is the nature of these "experiences," and why are they referred to as "incidental"? Actually, the simplest explanation, which Fantz seems to support, is that after an initially high level of fixation to the constant stimulus, habituation occurs and the duration of fixation de-creases. The novel stimuli are not presented long enough to get past the initial high level of fixation, hence, the differences in fixation times. There-fore, it is unnecessary to use obscure terms, like the retention of "visual experiences," when habituation adequately explains the results.

Results of both types of procedures (i.e., single-stimulus habituation and novelty preference procedures) show generally that visual fixation is proportionally longer to novel stimuli (Miranda & Fantz, 1974). There are at least two questions we can ask: (1) what is being measured, and (2) how should the results be interpreted? The answers provided by traditional developmental psychologists and behavior analysts reveal the differences in their respective approaches. For traditional developmental psycholo-gists, what is purportedly being measured is recognition memory, which is inferred from differential fixation times. That is, if there are differences in fixation times, recognition memory exists; and if there are no differences, then there is no recognition memory. The cognitive explanation of the behavior of the infants under these tests of "short-term memory" seems to be the same as the memory itself and, thus, is circular. For example, some have concluded that "the infant is able to take in and retain information from a visual stimulus and thereby to differentiate between that stimulus and an unfamiliar one" (Miranda and Fantz, 1974, p. 651). But is this saying anything more than that there are different fixation times to different stimuli? In fact, the only evidence for taking in and retaining information and differentiating between stimuli is the very behavior to be explained—differential fixation times.

According to a behavior analytic view, one way of understanding the results of the Fantz (1964) study is in terms of the relation between the unconditional eliciting effects of certain visual stimuli (called novel), and the decreased unconditional eliciting effects of other visual stimuli (called familiar). As Fantz (1964) states, "Response to novelty might thus be described as an unlearned visual interest in a complex stimulus which has not been habituated by experience" (p. 669). If the habituation explanation is valid, then demonstrating it in very young infants extends the principles of habituation to this population and indicates something about the kinds of visual stimuli to which infants are sensitive.

An alternative behavior analytic explanation is in terms of operant principles. As we have already pointed out, several studies have shown that sucking patterns in infants can be reinforced by manipulating various aspects of visual stimuli (e.g., Kalnins & Bruner, 1973; Siqueland & De-Lucia, 1969). It is possible that rather than viewing the responses to novel visual events as instances of unconditional responses, they may be seen as operants. Of course, the very first response may be an orienting response and, thus, elicited; however, the frequency of subsequent responses may increase because of the visual consequences of the behavior.

These responses may be special operants in the sense that they are specific to the visual systems of infants; that is, there may be some biological variables that contribute to their strength. Thus, the decrease in fixation time may either reflect satiation (an establishing operation) or operant extinction (a function-altering operation). Satiation effects of visual reinforcers have been shown when nonnutritive sucking was maintained by visual reinforcers (Siqueland & DeLucia, 1969). Operant extinction may also play a role. For example, it is possible that behavior maintained by visual reinforcers extinguishes faster than other types of behavior. In general, consequences that are effective reinforcers may be those that represent the most stimulus change (Michael, 1975). Thus, after a visual stimulus is presented and the infant's eyes have scanned the array, the amount of stimulus change decreases. In other words, there is nothing new to see. The "redundancy" in the reinforcing stimulus, then, may be another way of describing the effects of an establishing operation or operant extinction. This general reinforcement hypothesis can be tested simply by arranging the visual events to be presented contingently on some other response such as nonnutritive sucking. It might be possible to separate the unconditional eliciting and reinforcing effects of such events, but they may also be impossibly interconnected, functioning as a kind of symbiotic process for behavior change in the infant. In other words, the visual stimulus initially elicits looking as an unconditional elicitor and then the consequence of that looking—seeing the visual stimulus—ensures continued looking.

Experiments Using Novelty Discrimination Procedures

Visual recognition memory has also been studied using novelty discrimination procedures (e.g., Milewski & Siqueland, 1975; Werner & Siqueland, 1978). The novelty discrimination procedure combines aspects of the paired-comparison (novelty preference) procedures and operant conditioning procedures (see below). In general, novelty discrimination studies have used visual stimuli as reinforcers for high-amplitude sucking (HAS) in infants. The sucking is measured by using a nonnutritive nipple that is connected both to a polygraph which records individual sucks and to the power supply of the lamp of a slide projector, thus controlling the illumination of slides containing visual stimuli. A single suck raises the illumination of the lamp only slightly while a burst of sucks increases the illumination maximally. This type of reinforcement schedule has been termed a "conjugate reinforcement schedule" (see Rovee-Collier & Gekoski, 1979, for a review) because the intensity of the consequence is directly proportional to the intensity of the response.

In an experiment by Werner and Siqueland (1978), the visual stimuli consisted of slides showing red and white or green and white checkerboards. There were three phases in their experiment. The first was a baseline phase in which sucks were recorded in the absence of visual consequences. The second phase lasted 3 minutes, during which the HAS contingency was in effect; that is, sucks produced conjugate reinforcement. The performance criterion for this phase was a 20% decrement in sucking for two consecutive minutes. This "familiarization" criterion was established so that the effects of the shift to a novel stimulus as a consequence in phase 3 could be assessed. In other words, a novel stimulus as a consequence of HAS should produce an increase in high-amplitude sucks. The increase would be more easily observed if the frequency of high-amplitude sucks in the previous conjugate reinforcement phase were lower. The results showed that HAS in newborns increased when the novel stimuli were contingent on the HAS relative to the pre-shift criterion (i.e., familiarization) levels.

The Werner and Siqueland (1978) study is similar to studies using novelty preference procedures. Specifically, some stimuli serve as the familiar stimuli, while others serve as the novel stimuli. In this study, however, the familiar stimuli are "familiar" in that they have had reinforcing functions, and those reinforcing functions diminished either through satiation or extinction. Just as with the novelty preference studies, results from this novelty discrimination study have been discussed in terms of infant memory. Thus, Werner and Siqueland (1978) concluded the following: "The findings of this study show that visual recognition memory, in some rudimentary form, is evidenced in the conditioned sucking of ... infants within the first days of life" (p. 92). From a behavior analytic perspective, however, we see that operant conditioning with visual stimuli as reinforcers has been extended, this time to newborn infants—nothing more and nothing less.

Experiments Using Operant Conditioning Procedures

Experiments on infant memory using operant conditioning procedures consist mostly of work by Rovee-Collier and her colleagues (e.g., Boller, Rovee-Collier, Borovsky, O'Connor, & Shyi, 1990; Fagen & Rovee-Collier, 1983; Hill, Borovsky, & Rovee-Collier, 1988; Rovee & Fagen, 1976; Rovee-Collier, Griesler, & Early, 1985; Rovee-Collier & Sullivan, 1980; Rovee-Collier, Sullivan, Enright, Lucas, & Fagen, 1980; Sullivan, Rovee-Collier, & Tynes, 1979). This body of work represents one of the noticeable instances where behaviorally trained researchers have made a significant research contribution to the mainstream child development literature. Even this body of work, however, recognizes the general cognitive orientation in psychology because its experimental questions were apparently derived from cognitive theory. The working definition of memory by these researchers—"a multidimensional collection of attributes that represent an event" (Rovee-Collier & Sullivan, 1980, p. 799)—reveals the cognitive orientation. Moreover, even though these researchers used operant conditioning procedures, their experimental designs typically consisted of between subject comparisons with large groups of infants such that complex statistical analyses were needed to make sense of the results.

Most of the experiments by Rovee-Collier and her colleagues employed a procedure in which various aspects of infant "memory" were studied using operant foot kicks. In this procedure, the infant's left foot was attached via a cloth ribbon to a mobile hanging above the infant's crib, so that when the infant's foot moved, the mobile would move (see Figure 4.1). The more vigorously the infant's foot moved, the more vigorously the mobile would move. Recall that this type of reinforcement schedule is referred to as a conjugate reinforcement schedule.

In one experiment, Rovee and Fagen (1976) studied "retention" of operant foot kicks in 3-month-old infants. More precisely, their study

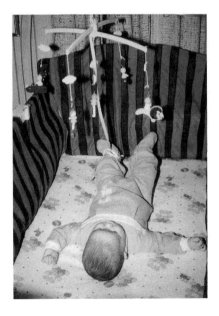

FIGURE 4.1. Conjugate reinforcement procedure with foot kicks. (Photo courtesy of Carolyn Rovee-Collier)

"sought to determine the course of daily acquisition and retention of operant foot kicks for a visual ... reinforcer" (p. 2). The experiment consisted of one 15-minute session on four consecutive days. The first three minutes of the first session constituted a baseline for foot kicks, and the first 3 minutes of the last three sessions were "retention test" periods during which foot kicks were ineffective in producing movement of the mobile (i.e., operant extinction). The 3-minute baseline and retention test periods were followed by a 9-minute acquisition period during which left foot kicks produced the moving mobile. Each session ended with a 3-minute extinction period. On the fourth day, infants in the experimental group were presented with a novel mobile in order to explore, in the authors' words, "the specificity of the information stored in long-term memory" (p. 2). The experimenters recorded visual attention to the mobiles as well as foot kicks.

The findings showed that the frequency of foot kicks during the 3-minute retention test at the beginning of the daily sessions on days 2 and 3 was higher than during both the baseline and extinction periods of the previous day. The duration of visual attention to the mobile also increased during the conditioning trials. Although the duration of visual attention during the retention and extinction trials was lower, it increased in a linear fashion across all the daily retention periods. When the novel mobile was installed at the beginning of day 4, foot kicks by infants in the experimental group declined, while visual attention increased; however, foot kicks quickly increased in most infants once they began to kick and see the new mobile move.

These results prompted the investigators to conclude: "Clearly, 3-month-old infants are capable both of integrating simple perceptual-motor responses and of directing them selectively at later intervals" (p. 10). But it was not the infants who integrated "simple perceptual-motor responses," it was the environment that reinforced the behavior and brought it under the evocative (stimulus) control of the sight of the mobile. From a behavior analytic perspective, the results of the Rovee and Fagen (1976) study showed that operant behavior in 3-month-old infants could be conditioned using a visual reinforcer. This should not have been surprising considering the results of earlier studies in which reinforcement by visual stimuli was demonstrated in infants (Milewski & Siqueland, 1975; Siqueland & DeLucia, 1969).

What do the findings of the Rovee and Fagen (1976) experiment have to do with memory? Recall from chapter 3 that reinforcement is conceptualized as a function-altering operation that, by definition, alters the evocative function of other events (i.e., motivational operations and discriminative stimuli) to evoke behavior. In the Rovee and Fagen (1976) study, the visual reinforcer altered the sight of the mobile (as well as other contextual stimuli) such that it evoked foot kicks. Because this effect endured over time, it is called memory. The endurance of behavioral relations over time is also the essence of operant behavior. What about the dramatic decline in foot kicks and the increase in visual attention by the infants in the experimental group on day 4 when the new mobile was encountered? One could say that in this condition the infants apparently "forgot" the foot kick response. As Rovee and Fagen (1976) suggested, however, this discrepancy is probably an indication of operant discrimination. At the very least, the discrepancy between the decline in foot kicks and the increase in visual attention represents an instance of stimulus-change decrement. That is, when any characteristic of the training stimulus complex is changed, a decrement is predicted in some measure of behavior; for example, lower response rate, smaller response magnitude, longer latencies, etc. This phenomenon has also been demonstrated by Fagen, Rovee, and Kaplan (1976) when they showed that as the number of novel components in the mobile increased, the magnitude of operant foot kicks decreased.

The importance of the Rovee and Fagen (1976) study depends upon one's theoretical orientation. The Rovee and Fagen (1976) study is important to cognitively oriented psychologists because memory may be inferred from the enduring nature of the behavior and because it has been demonstrated in very young infants. The behavior analyst, by contrast, would find the results interesting simply because they seem to extend the basic principles of reinforcement and stimulus control to 3-month-old infants, thus strengthening the generality of behavior analytic theory (see chapter 1). Perhaps the most interesting aspect of this study from a behavior analytic point of view is the demonstration that the sight of a moving mobile can function as a reinforcer for behavior not related to seeing the mobile (i.e., foot kicks). To be fair, even though much of the research conducted by Rovee-Collier and her colleagues has been directed at answering cognitive questions concerning infant memory, some of these studies have contributed directly to the expansion of the behavior analytic database by extending to infants the phenomena of response differentiation (Rovee-Collier, Morrongiello, Aron, & Kupersmidt, 1978) and behavioral contrast (Rovee-Collier & Capatides, 1979), and by providing assessments of reinforcer efficacy in infants (McKirdy & Rovee, 1978).

Now that we have presented the basic paradigm incorporated by Rovee-Collier and her colleagues, we now consider several other studies by these researchers which used the reinforcement of operant foot kicks to investigate infant memory. The titles of these studies reflect experimental questions generated by a cognitive orientation to infant memory rather than a behavior analytic one: "A Conditioning Analysis of Infant *Long-Term Memory*," (Sullivan, Rovee-Collier & Tynes, 1979), "*Reactivation* of Infant Memory" (Rovee-Collier, Sullivan, Enright, et al., 1980), "*Organization* of Infant Memory" (Rovee-Collier & Sullivan, 1980), "*Memory Retrieval*: A Time-Locked Process in Infancy" (Fagen & Rovee-Collier, 1983), "Contextual Determinants of *Retrieval* in Three-Month-Old Infants" (Rovee-Collier, Griesler, & Earley, 1985), and "Continuities in Infant *Memory* Development" (Hill, Borovsky, & Rovee-Collier, 1986) (emphasis added). In fact, even though all of these experiments used simple operant conditioning procedures, the specific procedures were derived not from behavior analytic research but from animal memory studies (Rovee-Collier & Sullivan, 1980). The operant foot kick procedure seems to have been a convenient way to answer some traditional questions in the cognitive literature about the nature of infant memory. Given this state of affairs, the rationale for the inclusion of these studies in this chapter is to provide a behavior analytic interpretation of the results. It will not be possible to describe in detail all of these experiments, so we will focus only on the major experimental findings, followed by explanations of the results, first in the researchers' terms and then in behavior-analytic terms. The major experimental findings of these studies fall into three general categories: the demonstration of long-term memory in infants, the reactivation of forgotten memories, and the contextual control over memory.

The Demonstration of Long-Term Memory in Infants

The study of long-term memory includes demonstrating some of the conditions under which "forgetting" occurs in infants. In several experiments by Rovee-Collier and her colleagues, infants were tested for recall after various intervals of time (e.g., 48, 72, 96, 120, 144, 192, and 336 hours in Rovee-Collier et al., 1979). According to the authors, "no evidence of forgetting was observed for as long as 192 hours following original training" (p. 152), prompting the conclusion that infants are able to retain an acquired association for as long as 8 days following conditioning. In behavior analytic terms, the stimulus control over operant foot kicks has been shown to persist as long as 8 days after training in infants.

In several articles, Rovee-Collier and her colleagues have observed what they termed "forgetting." They report to have alleviated the forgetting by reactivating the forgotten memory. The concept of forgetting, however, is a difficult one. In most instances, forgetting presumably refers to a decrement in responding solely as a function of the passage of time, that is, where there is no opportunity to make the response. For behavior analysts, the issue of forgetting is an issue of stimulus control. It reflects the weakening ability of discriminative stimuli to evoke responses. What is responsible for the weakening of stimulus control? Is it simply the passage of time which reflects some underlying decay of the memory? In general, behavior analysts believe that there is "no known behavioral process by which stimulus control declines in an orderly way *solely as a result of the lapse of time*" (Palmer, 1991, p. 266, emphasis added). In fact, there is some question as to whether forgetting occurs at all. For example, Skinner reported that pigeons who had been trained to produce a high, steady rate of responding and then were returned to the same setting 4 years later responded at similar levels (Skinner, 1950; see also Skinner, 1938, pp. 92–93). For behavior analysts, accounts of response decrement in terms of known processes and principles must be eliminated before any other accounts would be considered. Toward that end, Palmer (1991) has suggested three alternatives to the "decay hypothesis" expressed in terms of stimulus control. They are (1) the failure to reinstate all of the stimulus conditions that were relevant to the original response strength; (2) competing responses to the same stimuli; and (3) competing responses conditioned to other stimuli.

Let us consider the results of the experiments by Rovee-Collier and her associates in light of these alternatives. In most of the experiments using operant foot kicks, there were only two training days, with one session per day. Each session lasted 15 minutes. The first 3 minutes (baseline in the first session and retention test in subsequent sessions) and the last 3 minutes of each session consisted of extinction trials; the middle 9 minutes consisted of conditioning trials. During the extinction trials, the context was altered; the mobile was placed on the other side of the infant's crib and the satin ribbon was not attached to the infant's leg. This is an example of the failure to reinstate all of the stimulus conditions that were present during the original training. From an observer's perspective, the stimuli associated with the retention test constitute quite a different stimulus complex than those associated with reinforcement. Whether it was important to the infants' behavior is unclear, but it could explain some of the forgetting reported by the experimenters.

In behavior analytic terms, the different conditions associated with training and retention tests resemble the procedure of discrimination training. In the presence of one stimulus, certain complex responses are reinforced; and in the presence of a different stimulus, those responses are not reinforced, or different responses are reinforced. That the frequency of foot kicks was higher during the 3 minute retention tests than during the previous 3 minute extinction period might reflect the continuing development of discrimination. After more training, the frequency of foot kicks would probably begin to decline during all extinction periods. If the differences between the training and test (extinction) conditions were minimized, perhaps the foot kick behavior would have persisted longer than was observed in the studies reported here.

The presence of other procedural problems makes the results of the various Rovee-Collier experiments difficult to interpret. First, the experiments were all conducted in the infants' home cribs, and it is not clear what kinds of interactions occurred during the time when the experimenters were not in the home. Second, foot kicks were recorded by human observers, and it seems possible that observers would have more difficulty counting foot kicks when the ribbon was not attached. Also, infants received only three sessions, the first two separated by 24 hours and the third occurring at differing, but later times. And it is clear from some of the reports that considerable between infant differences in conditioning occurred from the first to the second day. Looking at group results may have prevented the experimenters from isolating variables responsible for those individual differences.

Despite these potential problems, what can we say about the general results of these experiments in light of the concept of forgetting? In most cases, responding during the first 3 minute retention session (of the 2nd day) was higher than the preceding 3 minute baseline day, although lower than the 3 minutes of conditioning on the preceding day. As already stated, in addition to demonstrating evidence of operant conditioning, the within session discrepancy in responding between extinction and conditioning demonstrates, at the very least, a stimulus–change decrement and, possibly, the beginnings of discriminative responding. It is also possible that the apparent loss of control demonstrated during the retention tests actually represents competing responses to the same stimuli, a second alternative interpretation to a forgetting hypothesis. As Rovee and Fagen (1976) reported, visual attention to the mobile, as well as foot kicks, increased linearly across all retention tests. While foot kicks declined in the experimental infants when the novel mobile was presented in session 4, visual attention increased, which may have competed with the foot kicks. Whereas the lower responding during the retention tests after longer delays (e.g., 144, 192, 336 hours) seemed to be a function solely of the delays, eliminating the problems just discussed should make it more difficult to infer the passage of time as the critical independent variable, especially when one considers that individual infants did respond just as vigorously after the longest interval (336 hours) (see Sullivan et al., 1979, experiment 2, subjects 3 and 6). Thus, rather than appealing to a general memory process called "forgetting," behavior analysts would attempt to discover the environmental variables responsible for these individual differences. Palmer (1991) notes:

> [T]he failure of a discriminative stimulus to occasion a response may be due, not to a loss of control, but to competing responses and missing contextual support. However, demonstrating that decay is not at least partly responsible for a decrement in performance may be impossible, since it is not clear how to put the matter to experimental test. (p. 267)

The Reactivation of Forgotten Memories

Rovee-Collier and her colleagues have shown that if a moving mobile was briefly re-presented to the infant 24 hours before a long-term retention test, responding which had become weak (presumably due to forgetting) would rebound and remain stronger than if the moving mobile were not re-presented. They termed this procedure a "reactivation treatment," presumably because the presentation of the moving mobile "reactivates" the forgotten memory. According to the researchers, "An infant's reencounters with contextual aspects of prior training or an earlier experience can prime or recycle the remaining memory attributes and enhance access to them, alleviating forgetting ..." (Rovee-Collier et al., 1980, p. 1161). Notice that this account appeals to inferred, hypothetical constructs, such as memory attributes, and processes, such as priming or recycling.

The behavior analytic interpretation again would appeal to principles of stimulus control. It is likely that the "reactivation treatment" simply reinstated stimulus control that, for whatever reason, had weakened. Rovee-Collier et al. (1980), however, seem to discount this interpretation. Even though the infants were seated in a reclining seat which presumably "minimized foot kicks and altered the topography of those which did occur" (p. 1160), it is still possible that the function of the foot kicks that occurred was still related to the moving mobile. Although the mobile was not directly tied to the infants' feet, its continued movement, even though independent of responding, could still have maintained already conditioned foot kicks superstitiously (Neuringer, 1970). In other words, once foot kicks had been conditioned and the mobile had been disconnected from the infant's foot, any movement by the mobile might have reinforced foot kicks. Thus, when the infants were placed in the original testing context the next day, the frequency of foot kicks was higher than in infants who had not received the reactivation treatment. The question is whether a cognitive or a behavior analytic interpretation better explains the findings. A behavior analytic interpretation is backed by established scientific facts and principles that do not require appeals to hypothetical and untestable events as explanations.

The Contextual Control Over Memory

In several experiments, Rovee-Collier and her colleagues have shown that when novel mobiles (Rovee & Fagen, 1976) or novel components of mobiles (Fagen et al., 1976) are presented to infants, the frequency of operant foot kicks declines. They have also shown that the frequency of foot kicks was lower in a 2-week retention test in the presence of a novel crib bumper (Rovee-Collier, Griesler, & Earley, 1985). The authors' conclusion regarding the results is that normal memory retrieval in infants is a process that is dependent on the context, even if that context was never exclusively paired with reinforcement. But this simply represents a demonstration of stimulus control not only by the stimuli used in training but also by the contextual stimuli. This explanation, therefore, does not require an account based on memory and retrieval phenomena. In fact, behavior analysts know that when compound stimuli are correlated with reinforcement for responding to them, the actual stimulus components that acquire control may differ from subject to subject (Reynolds, 1961), and those differences may be traced, in part, to the subject's reinforcement history (Johnson & Cumming, 1968).

COGNITIVE AND BEHAVIOR ANALYTIC VIEWS OF MEMORY

To repeat, behavior analysts account for memory phenomena largely in terms of stimulus control. In the following quotation, however, note the cognitive manner in which the authors describe the stimulus control of behavior:

> Retrieval is presumed to occur when attributes noticed during a retention test are identical or highly similar to those that comprise the representation. Once noticed, they arouse the corresponding memory attributes that, in turn, can arouse or prime other stored attributes that are part of the same memory. (Rovee-Collier & Sullivan 1980, p. 799)

This is nothing more than a redescription of the observed facts of the experiment. That is, the more similar the stimuli presented during a retention test are to those that comprised the context in which operant conditioning originally occurred, the stronger the resulting behavior (stimulus generalization). Cognitively oriented psychologists, however, can take even straightforward demonstrations of operant conditioning in infants and interpret them as evidence for inferred events. For example, Cohen and Gelber (1975) have interpreted operant conditioning in infants by saying that, "Whatever is stored ... must include some information about the appropriate response and therefore may be an instance of enactive memory" (p. 351). Watson (1967) has likened the memory required for operant conditioning in infants to a "computerlike process" in which "the memory records of stimulus input and response output are scanned under the guidance of a 'learning instruction' reading: 'Find and repeat the response which preceded the reception of the reward stimulus'" (p. 55). Needless to say, the view of this book is that these hypothetical processes are unnecessary obstacles to understanding the behavior from which they are inferred.

In conclusion, in the particular environments found in the experiments of Rovee-Collier and her colleagues, foot kicks were adaptive; that is, foot kicks came under the stimulus control of the particular settings by producing a reinforcing consequence, the moving mobile. Of course, neither the experiments nor the present interpretation explains why the sight of the moving mobile functions as a reinforcer. If we are interested in the parameters of reinforcers for human infants, that is another experimental question. Any analysis of operant foot kicks in terms of the concept of memory is unnecessary because we can account for the observed changes in behavior without it. For behavior analysis, this operant behavior is important in its own right and not as an indicator of hypothetical, underlying structures or processes. A behavior analytic interpretation takes nothing away from the infant; on the contrary, as the studies by Rovee-Collier and her associates have shown, a behavior analytic approach demonstrates a way of more thoroughly investigating the behavioral capabilities of young children.

SUMMARY

This chapter averred that the concept of memory as "a mental record of an event" represents an instance of reification. The term "memory" is simply a name for behaviors observed in particular contexts; the memory itself is never independently observed. Furthermore, when the concept of memory is used as an explanation for the behavior from which it is inferred, that represents a circular explanation. The chapter then described and provided examples of several procedures for the investigation of visual recognition memory as well as procedures that employed operant methodology. In both cases, the chapter argued that it is unnecessary to infer hypothetical memory processes to explain the results of this research because behavior analytic explanations, for example, those in terms of stimulus control, are more parsimonious and scientific.

5

Motor Development

When developmental psychologists speak of the development of motor behavior, they are referring to changes in behaviors such as sitting, crawling, standing, walking, reaching, and grasping. These behaviors are obviously important because it is through them that humans mechanically act upon and interact with their environment. In this chapter, two broad (structural) categories of motor behavior will be considered: body control, including postural control and locomotion, and manual control (prehension), including reaching and grasping.

At first glance, it might seem that the development of motor behavior is due almost solely to maturational factors (see below); however, there is a substantial amount of evidence pointing to the strong influence of environmental factors. Maturation plays a significant role in the development of motor behavior, but the powerful role of operant conditioning has not been fully appreciated by many developmental psychologists. Because behavior analysis looks at the environmental determinants of behavior, it can help us understand this aspect of motor development. In fact, the development of motor behavior illustrates nicely the position of behavior analysis on the respective roles of genes (maturation) and environment, which might be stated as follows: Excluding anatomy and physical structure, genetic and biological variables set broad, as opposed to narrow limits within which behavior can be changed by environmental variables (Baldwin & Baldwin, 1988).

Developmental psychologists often link the development of motor behavior in infants to the development of "voluntary" control. This implies, among other things, that the control of behavior is conscious, and that it comes from within the infant. The behavior analytic interpretation of motor behavior presented in this chapter will reiterate and clarify the behavior analytic position on "voluntary" behavior presented in chapter 3, namely, that like all operant behavior, "voluntary" behavior is selected by the environment.

As already stated, motor development refers to changes in behaviors that both act upon and interact mechanically with the (external) environment. This chapter will discuss the topic of motor development as it is usually presented in the standard developmental literature.

BASIC CONCEPTS IN MOTOR DEVELOPMENT

With the exception of certain infant reflexes and rhythmical stereotypies (see below), motor development can be classified as either postural/locomotive behavior or prehensile behavior. Postural/locomotive, as the name indicates, consists of behaviors which control the body, arms, and legs. Prehension, or manual control, concerns the changing abilities of the hands to manipulate the environment.

Perhaps more than any other behavior in infants, changes in motor behavior seem to occur in a fairly fixed sequence and at fairly predictable times. The sequence of motor behavioral development has been described as cephalocaudal and proximodistal. Cephalocaudal (i.e., head to foot) development means that the control and coordination of the body occurs in the direction from the head to the feet. In other words, control over the upper body (e.g., head and neck) occurs before control over the lower body (e.g., legs and feet). Likewise, proximodistal (i.e., near to far) development means that body parts closest to the center of the body, such as the arms, become coordinated before parts farther out, such as the hands and fingers. As developmental psychologists point out, although the ages at which the major motor milestones occur vary somewhat, the sequence is fairly uniform. This would seem to implicate maturation as an important determinant of motor development. But maturation does not determine the development of the behavior per se. Rather, it determines the sequence of anatomical and structural (i.e., musculoskeletal) development and sets the limits within which the behavior may develop.

MATURATION AND EXPERIENCE IN MOTOR DEVELOPMENT

Developmental textbooks often discuss the relative roles of maturation and experience in the development of various behaviors, and motor development is no exception. *Maturation* is usually defined as "a genetically determined biological plan of development" that is "relatively independent of experience" (Dworetzky, 1990, p. 106). The phrase "relatively independent of experience" should probably be recast as "all environmental influences being equal," because no biological plan of development can occur independent of experience. The problem with maturational accounts of development is that, in many cases, the environment is seen in molar, structural terms (see chapter 3), and the moment-to-moment interactions between behavior and functional, environmental variables are overlooked as a result. If developmental psychologists are not aware of the environmental events, as described in this book, then it is not surprising that the regularities and similarities between individuals with respect to a given form of behavioral development will more likely be attributed to inferred maturational variables. And just as behavioral similarities between individuals are said to be due to genetic similarities, behavioral differences are said to be due to genetic differences. This locution is a convenient way of explaining behavior without having to address the role of the environment.

In discussions of the relative roles of maturation and experience on the development of motor behavior, it is frequently concluded that, although maturation determines an age range within which motor development must occur, the environment, or experience, can and does play a significant role in determining whether motor skills will actually develop. Unfortunately, in most standard treatments, the concepts of "experience" and "environment" are never precisely defined. For example, experience is said to refer to "factors within the environment that may alter or modify the appearance of various developmental characteristics through the process of learning" (Gallahue, 1989, p. 15). This is accurate so far as it goes. However, the description of learning says only that "experience is prerequisite." It is rarely mentioned that the laws of behavior theory are "the factors within the environment that may alter or modify" behavioral development. Some have written that "the environment can play a role [in motor development], by encouraging the infant to display a skill at a particular time" (Vasta, Haith, & Miller, 1992, p. 175). But what does it mean to say that the environment encourages the infant? This is the critical question to answer. However, no standard treatment of motor development even suggests the importance of the laws of behavior analysis. Instead, many developmental textbooks say that practice is important (e.g., Bukatko & Daehler, 1992; Dworetzky, 1990; Vasta et al., 1992). Let us consider some examples.

In one study (Zelazo, Zelazo, & Kolb, 1972), researchers made certain that infants practiced the walking reflex for 12 minutes (four 3-minute sessions) each day. As a result, the walking reflex in these infants lasted longer than it does on average, and the infants began walking earlier than those who had no such experience, or those whose legs were passively moved back and forth. Most developmental textbooks also report studies showing that children walk on average earlier in societies where parents believe it is important to teach children to walk. It is not clear from these reports exactly what is going on when infants are made to "practice" motor skills. It could be that the "practice," especially as described by Zelazo, simply strengthens muscles and thus increases muscle mass relative to other body (e.g., fat) mass (Thelen, 1983). It is also possible that in many instances the "practice" is operant conditioning involving reinforcement of walking.

Dworetzky (1993) cites research showing that children in the United States today typically walk alone a few months earlier than they did 60 years ago. Since it is highly unlikely that the gene pool has changed drastically in that span of time, experience is likely to be the major factor. What kind of experience is necessary? Dworetzky (1993) offers several suggestions. First, 60 years ago, children grew up in the Great Depression and may not have had adequate nutrition. Another factor may be related to sociocultural factors. Parents today are more eager to see their children walk earlier and thus "encourage" earlier walking, whereas parents 60 years ago had larger families and might not have been as excited about encouraging their fourth or fifth child to walk earlier. Dworetzky even suggests that the introduction of wall-to-wall carpeting might play a role. Sixty years ago when babies took their first steps and fell, it was usually onto a hard floor (probably functioning as a form of punishment), whereas today they fall upon a much softer surface (which, if punishing, probably represents a smaller magnitude of punishment). The point of this discussion is that these experiential factors increase the average age within which normal motor development is seen in human infants, in particular, by expanding the lower end of the age range. This illustrates that maturation sets somewhat broad limits within which behavior is sensitive to environmental selection.

Let us now consider a behavior analytic view of some of the research relating to the development of postural–locomotive and prehensile motor development. To begin, it is important to discuss briefly infant postural reflexes and rhythmical stereotypies, because, for many developmental researchers, infant reflexes and rhythmical stereotypies are functionally important to the development of later motor behavior.

RHYTHMICAL STEREOTYPIES AND REFLEXES

Rhythmical Stereotypies

One constituent of the behavior of the newborn is rhythmical behaviors called "rhythmical stereotypies" (Thelen, 1979). Thelen (1979) has observed, cataloged, and classified rhythmical stereotypies into four structural groups: (1) movements of the legs and feet; (2) movements of the torso; (3) movements of the arms, hands, and fingers; and (4) movements of the head and face. The most frequently occurring stereotypies she observed were leg kicks, foot rubs (where the surface of the heel of the flexed leg was rubbed along the surface of the ankle and foot of the extended leg), arm waves, banging the hand against a surface with and without holding an object, and finger flexes (Thelen, 1979). Figure 5.1 shows these most commonly occurring stereotypies. Several facts indicate that these rhythmical stereotypies are largely maturational in nature. First, they are found in all healthy human infants, although not all infants exhibit all of the stereotypical movements observed by Thelen. Second, Thelen (1979) observed several "developmental trends." One is that the frequency of these movements peaks at between 24 and 42 months before declining, and another is that the number of different stereotypies increases over the first year.

Thelen has hypothesized that because the development of these rhythmical stereotypies is correlated with neuromuscular maturation, there must be a strong intrinsic component to them. There is evidence to suggest, however, that the environment may also play a role (Thelen, 1979). For example, Thelen has observed that rhythmical stereotypies "may be elicited by certain environmental stimuli (for example, the approach of the mother, being placed in the feeding chair or nursing position, or grabbing an object)" (p. 712). This indicates that the rhythmical stereotypy functions either as part of a respondent relation or as part of an operant discriminative (or motivative) relation. For example, the sight of the mother, the feeding chair, or the nursing position may elicit certain behaviors if those stimuli were reliably associated with stimuli involved in feeding or social contact. Or the behaviors may be evoked by these stimuli because in the past, for whatever reason they initially occurred, the behaviors were correlated with reinforcing consequences (e.g., nourishment or attention from the mother).

Other evidence for the role of environmental factors comes from the observation that there are significant individual differences in the age of onset and the particular types of stereotypies observed. Although such differences could be due to differences in rate of maturation between individuals, they may also be due to subtle differences in operant contingencies between individuals. For example, regardless of how the behaviors originate, the consequences they produce may be responsible for the subsequent increase in their frequency. Using the conjugate reinforcement of foot kicks procedure (described in chapter 4), Thelen and her colleagues (Thelen & Fisher, 1983, cited in Thelen, Kelso, & Fogel, 1987) showed that

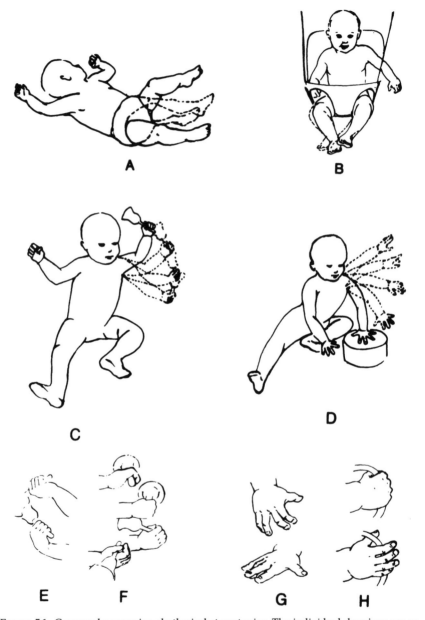

FIGURE 5.1. Commonly occurring rhythmical stereotypies. The individual drawings are as follows: (A) leg kicks; (B) foot rubs; (C) arm waves with object; (D) banging the hand against a surface without holding an object; (E) and (F) hand flexes; (G) and (H) finger flexes. (SOURCE: Adapted from Thelen [1979] and reproduced with permission from Academic Press, Ltd. Courtesy of Esther Thelen.)

leg movements they described as "spontaneous" could be "converted" into operant behavior. In their example, the reinforcing consequence was obvious because it was manipulated by the experimenters; but in the normal rhythmical stereotypy, the reinforcing consequence may not be as obvious. It is possible that the reinforcer for body movements is the sensory feedback produced by the movements themselves. For example, foot rubs produce both proprioceptive and tactile feedback, leg kicks produce proprioceptive and often visual feedback, and banging the hand against a surface results in proprioceptive, tactile, maybe visual, and certainly auditory feedback.

But how can this interpretation explain the similarity in rhythmical stereotypies found between infants? A behavior analytic interpretation would simply suggest that the capacity for such sensory feedback to reinforce the movements that produce them may be inherited. It wouldn't be the first case where the capacity of a particular stimulus to function as a reinforcer, and not the specific behavior, was inherited. Peterson (1960) exposed newly hatched ducklings to a moving yellow light in an experimental chamber. The ducklings then began to follow the yellow light whenever it moved. This following behavior is what Lorenz called "imprinting." However, Peterson went on to show that the moving yellow light could be used as a reinforcer to shape the behavior of pecking a plexiglass disk. Based on this observation, Skinner (1974) suggested that perhaps the behavior of moving away from the yellow light (the opposite of the normal imprinting behavior) could be reinforced by arranging the yellow light to move closer to the duckling when the duckling moved away. The experiment by Peterson (1960), as well as others on imprinting stimuli (e.g., Bateson & Reese, 1968, 1969; Hoffman, Searle, Toffey, & Kozma, 1966; Hoffman, Stratton, & Newby, 1969), have shown clearly that the following behavior in newly hatched precocial birds is not inherited per se. Rather, the evocative and reinforcing functions of the imprinting stimulus are established by the chicks' early exposure to it.

The similarity of rhythmical behaviors observed in human infants may also result from similarities in physical and anatomical structure. In addition, only a few behaviors are sufficient to produce the reinforcing sensory feedback. For example, only banging the hand against a surface produces that type of auditory feedback and only moving the foot of one leg against another object produces a particular kind of tactile feedback. An operant analysis would lead researchers to look for functional classes, that is, classes of responses that produce a common reinforcing consequence, rather than purely structural ones based only on the form of the particular behavior.

A behavior analytic view of rhythmical stereotypies is testable, albeit indirectly. Some of the feedback proposed, for example visual or auditory feedback, could be delivered for arbitrary behaviors. Something of the sort was done by Kalnins and Bruner (1973) when they made the clarity of a focused picture contingent on patterned sucking (see also Milewski & Siqueland, 1975; Werner & Siqueland, 1978), and by Rovee-Collier and her colleagues (e.g., Rovee & Fagen, 1976; Rovee-Collier, Sullivan, Enright, et al., 1980; Rovee-Collier & Sullivan, 1990) when they made the movement of a mobile contingent on foot kicks. Also, McKirdy and Rovee (1978) made auditory feedback contingent on foot kicks, Watson (1967) made auditory and visual feedback contingent on directional looking, Watson and Ramey (1972) made visual stimulation contingent on head presses against a pillow, and Finkelstein and Ramey (1977) made auditory-visual stimulation contingent on arm pulling responses. All of these demonstrations indicate that a variety of sensory events contingent on some type of motor activity can increase the frequency of such behavior. We will return to this hypothesis when we examine the ontogeny of postural, locomotor, and manual development.

Reflexes

There are several reasons why most texts include a section on infant reflexes prior to discussing motor development. In the chronology of motor development, reflexes, like rhythmical stereotypies, precede more coordinated and controlled motor behavior. Most researchers view many infant reflexes as necessary precursors to this development, although there is debate about the specific relation between infant reflexes and the appearance of later coordinated motor behavior.

Developmental researchers agree that "reflex movements are evidenced in all fetuses, neonates, and infants to a greater or lesser degree, depending on their age and neurological makeup" (Gallahue, 1989, p. 143). Reflexes, also called unconditional (or unconditioned) reflexes (by Pavlov and, subsequently, by behavior analysts), are stimulus–response (S→R) relations in which the presentation of the stimulus (S) elicits the response (R) without any prior learning; that is, the stimulus–response relation is not conditional on any other experiences. For example, if you stroke the side of a neonate's face near the mouth (S), this will cause the infant's head to turn in that direction (R). This reflex, called the rooting (or search) reflex, can be demonstrated in all healthy human neonates. These facts support the contention that this reflex relation is inherited. Reflexes are sometimes described as automatic or involuntary, usually to distinguish them from "voluntary" behavior, but, as we will see later, this is not a useful distinction. For the present purpose of attempting to understand the relation of infant reflexes to later motor skills, this chapter will only consider those reflexes that seem to be related to postural–locomotive and prehensile motor development.

Postural Reflexes

Table 5.1 lists the postural reflexes with their corresponding ages of onset and disappearance. The postural reflexes include labyrinthine righting, pull-up, parachute and propping, neck and body righting, crawling, primary stepping, and swimming reflexes (Gallahue, 1989). In the *labyrinthine righting reflex*, if the infant is tilted forward, backward, or to the side (S), the head moves in the direction opposite to that in which the trunk is moved (R). This reflex is important in maintaining an upright head and body posture. In the *pull-up reflex*, if the infant is held by one or both hands in an upright position and tipped forwards or backwards (S), the arms will flex to maintain an upright position (R). The parachute and propping reflexes consist of "protective reactions of the limbs in the direction of the displacing force" (R), which "occur in response to a sudden displacing force or when balance can no longer be maintained" (S) (Gallahue, 1989, p. 155). For example, the forward parachute reflex is demonstrated by holding the infant vertically in the air and tilting her toward the ground (S) which elicits arm extension (R) (as if anticipating a fall). The downward parachute reflex is demonstrated by holding the infant in an upright position and quickly lowering the infant (S) which elicits extension and tension of the limbs (R). The propping reflex may be observed by moving the infant off balance from a sitting position (S) which also elicits extensions of the arms. In the neck righting reflex, if the infant's head is turned

TABLE 5.1. Postural Reflexes and Their Approximate Ages
of Onset and Disappearance

Reflex	Age of onset	Age of disappearance
Labyrinthine righting	2nd month	1st year
Pull-up	3rd month	1st year
Parachute and propping	4th month	1st year
Neck and body righting	2nd month	6th month
Crawling	birth	3rd month
Stepping	birth	4th month
Swimming	birth	4th month

to one side while the infant is in the prone position (S), this elicits turning of the body in the same direction (R). In the body righting reflex, if the infant's body is turned to one side while the infant is in a side-lying position (S), this elicits turning of the head in the same direction (R). In the crawling reflex, if the infant is placed in a prone position and pressure is applied to the sole of one foot (S), this will elicit crawling movements (R) using both upper and lower limbs. In the primary stepping reflex (which we have already mentioned), if the infant is held erect and leaned forward (S), this will elicit walking movements of the legs (R). Finally, in the swimming reflex, if the infant is placed in a prone position in or over water (S), this will elicit "rhythmical ... swimming movements of the arms and legs" (R) (Gallahue, 1989).

As we will see, these postural reflexes are structurally similar to later behavioral relations that are characterized as postural or locomotor control.

STRUCTURAL CATEGORIES OF MOTOR DEVELOPMENT

Motor development has been classified by researchers according to the ever increasing coordination of behaviors related to maintaining an upright posture, moving in the environment, and reaching and grasping. The term "control" is used by researchers to refer to this increasing coordination of behavior in the environment. However, for behavior analysts, the term "control" can be used to refer simply to the cumulative effects of operant conditioning (in combination with maturational factors) on the stimulus control of motor behavior. This section is divided into two subsections: body control and manual control. Body control includes changes in postural and locomotor behavior and manual control includes changes in reaching and grasping.

Body Control

Postural Control

Postural control can be described as being able "to make a continuous sequence of changes while maintaining motion stability" (Keogh & Sugden, 1985, p. 37). Postural control is considered separately from locomotor control, because general body posture must be controlled before the control of other movements is possible. As Gallahue (1989) states, "The infant is involved in a constant struggle against the forces of gravity in the attempts to obtain and maintain an upright posture" (p. 168). Keogh and

Sugden (1985) describe the early development of postural control in terms of three progressions: head control, sitting, and standing. Notice that the overall progression illustrates the principle of cephalocaudal development. Figure 5.2 presents the major postural milestones during the first year of life that define these three progressions.

The first general progression (from about 1 to 3 months) involves the increased control of the head, from being able momentarily to lift the head from the prone position to being able to hold the head erect and steady while being held and moved by another person (see Figure 5.3). The second progression (from about 3 to 7 months) involves being able to achieve and maintain an upright posture in a sitting position (Keogh & Sugden, 1985), from being able to sit with slight support while keeping the head steady to getting to the sitting position from a supine or prone position. The third progression (from about 5 to 11 months) involves changes in getting to and maintaining a standing position, from maintaining a standing position while holding a support to pulling to a standing

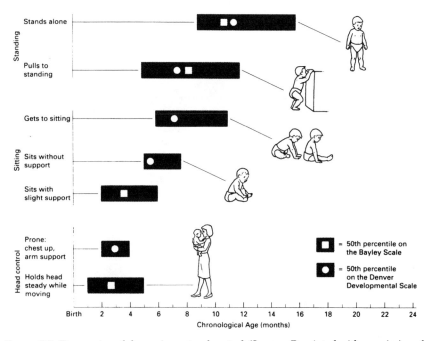

FIGURE 5.2. Progression of change in postural control. (SOURCE: Reprinted with permission of Macmillan College Publishing Company from *Movement Skill Development* by Jack Keogh and David Sugden. Copyright 1985 by Macmillan Publishing Company, Inc.)

position and then standing alone. Once locomotor movements begin to dominate the infant's behavioral repertoire sometime after the first year, changes in postural control become much harder to identify because they are inextricably tied to all movements. Keogh and Sugden (1985) explain:

> The control of all movements depends on the control of a postural position while the movement is being made. Babies at the end of their second year can walk quickly, run haltingly, do many interesting variations of sitting and walking, and do rudimentary forms of throwing and kicking. All of these achievements indicate improved postural control. (p. 34)

In order to better understand the changes in postural stability, Keogh and Sugden (1985) have characterized this development in terms of three general interdependent movement problems that must be solved before postural control can occur. These include (1) the problem of maintaining a steady position in relation to gravity; (2) the problem of changing and achieving a new position; and (3) the problem of maintaining equilibrium while moving. These problems are solved initially by the presence of certain postural reflexes, so called because they resemble the later controlled postural movements. For example, the problem of maintaining a steady position in relation to gravity is partially solved in early infancy by

FIGURE 5.3. An infant lifts her head from the prone position. (Photo by H. Schlinger)

the labyrinthine righting and the pull-up reflexes; the problem of changing and achieving a new position is partially solved by the neck and body righting reflexes; and the problem of maintaining equilibrium while moving is partially solved by the primary stepping and the swimming reflexes.

These three problems are solved ultimately by the appearance of what developmental psychologists call "voluntary" postural control. Although voluntary control depends on mature nervous and musculoskeletal systems, its presence depends largely on the effects which the relevant behavior produces on the environment. The view of the author is that "voluntary" behavior is in fact operant behavior (see below). One of the important questions in the development of motor behavior concerns the origin of such behavior. Does it evolve out of the related postural and locomotor reflexes or rhythmical stereotypies; that is, do they share some functional characteristics or are they functionally and developmentally separate?

A Behavior Analysis of Postural Control

A behavior analytic view of postural control, while not taking a specific stand on the debate about the role of infant postural reflexes in the development of later postural movements, asserts that the nonreflexive behaviors that result in postural control or stability are operant and, thus, determined (i.e., selected) by their consequences. The consequences that select the postural behaviors probably consist of proprioceptive and visual feedback. For example, consider the following excerpt by Keogh and Sugden (1985) concerning the development of behaviors that result in changing a position and achieving a new position:

> Changing a position may be achieved in many different ways which require coordinated movements by the arms, legs, and head. Babies will move their limbs and heads in a bewildering array of movements that seem intended to roll the trunk over, but they are initially not effective. When once successful in rolling the trunk over, limb and head movements soon can be used in several coordinated combinations to roll over whenever desired. (p. 36)

Successful rolling over, including the altered proprioceptive, tactile, and visual changes, may be viewed as the reinforcing consequence that selected the behaviors. The operant class in this case consists of any behaviors that comprise the class of coordinated behaviors that result in rolling over.

The same analysis may be made with respect to changing from any one position to another, including changing from a nonsitting to a sitting position and from a sitting to a standing position. In both cases, not only are there distinct proprioceptive and tactile consequences, but there are also unique visual consequences. We have already mentioned the strong experimental evidence that a variety of visual stimulus changes are potent reinforcers for arbitrary behaviors in infants (e.g., Kalnins & Bruner, 1973; Rovee & Fagen, 1976; Watson and Ramey, 1972). Consider the changes in visual stimuli inherent in the following changes in movement. When an infant moves from a prone to a supine position the functional visual stimuli change from what the infant can see while lying face down to all of the visual events that come into play when the infant is lying face up, especially once head movements have come under operant control. Turning the head from side to side makes possible a visual world of approximately 180°. Moving from a lying to a sitting or a standing position increases that visual world to the horizon and, ultimately with the correct head (or body) movements, to 360°. Such a hypothesis has received some support from a study by White (1967) discussed in the section on "Reaching and Grasping" in this chapter.

Based on this discussion, it is clear that changing a position and achieving a new one require not only postural control but also movement skill.

Locomotor Control

We have said that postural control is necessary before locomotor control can occur, but we have also noted that, beyond a certain point in this development, it is difficult to separate the two. The point at which infants first become mobile is usually sometime during their sixth month; however, postural and locomotor control begin to be interdependent earlier than that. According to Gallahue (1989), "The infant's movement through space is dependent on emerging abilities to cope with the force of gravity. Locomotion does not develop independently of stability; it relies heavily on it" (p. 172).

We can trace the beginnings of locomotor control as far back as the first month, when the infant changes from a supine to a prone position. Figure 5.4 presents the major locomotor milestones during the first 2 years of life. Keogh and Sugden (1985) classify the early development of locomotor development into two general progressions: (1) prewalking, which ends with crawling or creeping, and (2) walking, which ends with walking without support or help.

Prewalking. As with postural control, the first signs of locomotion are seen in certain postural reflexes, most notably the crawling, primary stepping, and swimming reflexes. As we have noted, some researchers believe that these reflexes are either necessary precursors to actual locomotion or, at the very least, are functionally related to later locomotor control. The

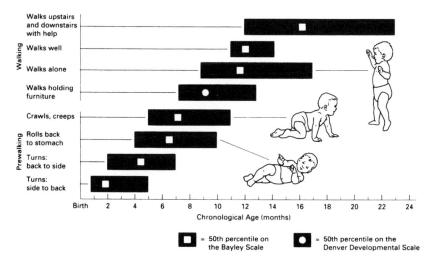

FIGURE 5.4. Progressions of change in locomotion. (SOURCE: Reprinted with permission of Macmillan College Publishing Company from *Movement Skill Development* by Jack Keogh and David Sugden. Copyright 1985 by Macmillan Publishing Company, Inc.)

first major sign of locomotor control (i.e., mobility) is when, at 6 months, the infant rolls over from a supine to a prone position and back. Prior to that, when the infant is in the supine position, there is a great deal of movement in the limbs (rhythmical stereotypies), but true mobility is not possible until the infant can get into a prone position. When infants are placed on their side during the first and second months, they can move to their back, and by the fourth month, they can move from their back to their side "as a precursor to locomotion" (Keogh & Sugden, 1985).

Crawling and Creeping. The prewalking stage ends with crawling and creeping. In crawling, which usually occurs by the sixth month, "the arms are used to pull the body forward while the legs push" (Keogh & Sugden, 1985, p. 39). Of course, not all infants crawl, and not all crawl in the same way. For example, sometimes only the arms are used, and sometimes only the legs are used. What all of these different forms have in common is that infants are in the prone position with their stomach and chest either touching the ground or slightly elevated. In creeping, which usually evolves from crawling, "the legs and arms are used in opposition to one another from a hands-and-knees (i.e., an all-fours) position" (Gallahue, 1989, p. 39).

Walking. Walking represents true mobility for the infant; however, it does not appear spontaneously. As Figure 5.4 shows, the progression ending with unassisted walking begins when the infant is able to pull herself into a standing position. From there, the infant can cruise, or take steps, while holding onto some object for support. Soon thereafter, independent walking occurs (see Figure 5.5). Galahue (1989) writes:

> An infant's first attempts at independent walking ... are characterized by a wide base of support, the feet turned outward, and the knees slightly flexed. These first walking movements are not synchronous and fluid; they are irregular and hesitant and are not accompanied by reciprocal arm movements. In fact they only vaguely resemble the mature walking pattern of early childhood. (p. 174)

This statement implies that independent walking is modified and refined from its earliest appearance to its final, mature form. This progression requires the solution of difficult movement problems, many of which are themselves created by the walking movements. According to Keogh and Sugden (1985),

> The body in an upright position is less stable because the center of gravity is higher and the base of support is smaller than when on the ground on all-fours or in a prone position. Also, the center of gravity must be moved outside the base of support to produce forward motion. Motion stability must be established by moving fast enough to overcome or minimize the resistance to forward motion. Footsteps are placed more in line to reduce resistance to forward motion, which also reduces the base of support. Leg movements must be continuous rather than discrete, with a coordination of movement sequences and positions of arms, trunk, and head. The walker also must adjust to physical conditions, such as walking downhill on a wet pavement, and be prepared to stop and change directions in relation to environmental conditions. Walking becomes an automatic yet flexible movement skill by age 2 or 3, and each person establishes a style that often is recognizable to others. (p. 41)

A Behavior Analysis of Locomotor Control

A behavior analytic view of the development of locomotor skills is that when maturational factors (e.g., increases in muscle mass, skeletal rigidity, and changes in body proportion) have been taken into account, locomotion is operant behavior. As Bijou (1979) writes, "Motor development originates in the interaction between the maturing biological structures and the stimulus antecedents and consequences of the behavior they make possible" (p. 178). This approach does not mean that genes are unimportant. The very capacity for operant conditioning is a function of our genetic inheritance. The differences between species in the capacity for

FIGURE 5.5. A toddler exhibits unassisted walking. (Photo by N. Schlinger)

operant conditioning are genetic. For example, there is a good chance that in human infants visual stimulus changes, movement relative to the external environment, and the successful manipulation of objects all function as unconditioned reinforcers. These are implied in certain discussions on the development of locomotor behavior. For example, Thelen (1979, p. 152) refers to the "growing intentional or goal-directed motivation to move" during the first year of life. She further states, "Infants appear ... to have the motivation to move forward in the service of a goal long before they have the motor capability to use their limbs for locomotion" (1979, p. 153).

The motivational variables that determine the strength of these reinforcers and evoke the relevant locomotor behavior may be difficult to determine, although in some cases they seem rather clear. Bijou (1979) offers an example in which an infant is lying on a toy with hard, sharp corners. The stimulation provided by the toy functions as an establishing operation, establishing the removal of the stimulation as a (negative) reinforcer and evoking whatever behavior has previously been successful in reducing or removing similar aversive stimulation. With respect to walking and the many difficult movement problems mentioned by Keogh and Sugden (1985) above, there is a constant interplay between the movements that produce imbalance and sometimes falling, and those which result in successful movement and balance. Behavior analytic theory would point to these subtle punishing and reinforcing, that is, automatic, consequences in accounting for the differentiation of behaviors that change immature, awkward walking into mature, fluid walking.

Behavior analysts would also point to other consequences of mobility, including those that bring the infant into visual and tactile contact with distant objects, including caregivers (Green, Gustafson, & West, 1980; Gustafson, 1984), and those that involve the caregivers responding to the infant's locomotion with contingent vocalizations (e.g., West & Rheingold, 1978). For example, Gustafson studied the effects of independent locomotion by infants using infant walkers on the occurrence of other behaviors such as looking, object manipulation, and both directed and nondirected social behaviors. The results showed that there was a significant increase in all behaviors except object manipulation for infants who used the walkers as compared with infants who could not locomote independently. Once in the walkers, infants looked more at the features of the room as opposed to only those things that were directly in front of them, and despite the fact that differences in object manipulation were not statistically significant, the infants spent more time manipulating distant objects. According to Gustafson (1984), "The ability to locomote thus was shown to engender specific behavioral capabilities and performances, which might, in turn, alter the probabilities of specific types of feedback from infants' social and nonsocial surroundings" (p. 402).

These studies on the effects of locomotion seem to support the suggestion that locomotive behavior produces a variety of consequences that might function to strengthen that behavior, and that independent locomotion results in the opportunity for other behaviors (e.g., looking, object manipulation, and directed social behavior) to occur and to produce consequences. These studies also suggest that social antecedent and consequent events play a large role in the development of motor behavior. Infants see other people walking, and as a result, moving about and getting things. They also receive a lot of attention contingent on making even slight movements beginning in the earliest days of infancy. Thus, moving not only results in changing visual stimuli and in bringing the infant closer to objects, it also increases interactions with caregivers. All of these consequences reinforce the behaviors involved in walking that produce that contact (Green, Gustafson, & West, 1980; West & Rheingold, 1978). This is the goal-directedness mentioned by Thelen (1979) above. An operant analysis would suggest that if you take the goal (reinforcer) away, the behavior will not "develop."

Developmental psychologists constantly attempt to explain the vast similarities and regularities in development between infants. The development of motor behavior is no exception, especially because its development is so similar from infant to infant. Of course, one reason for this similarity is that humans share genes. The similarity in human behavior, however, might be explained by more indirect genetic variables. For example, because humans share a common physical structure, there are only so many ways to achieve movement with balance. The individual differences seen in walking style may reflect slight differences in structure, but they may also reflect differences in conditioning histories. Because these variables are subtle and historical, they are difficult to identify.

Manual Control

The second structural category of motor development is manual control. When we speak of "manual control" we are referring to a classification system for the arm and hand movements used to manipulate objects (Keogh & Sugden, 1985, p. 43). Manual control is separated from general body control because of the importance of arm, hand, and finger movements for the human. One index of this importance is the larger size of the motor strip in the motor cortex of the brain that is devoted to arm and hand movement as compared with that devoted to body and trunk movement. Although much could be written on the movements of the arm and hand, we will concentrate our attention primarily on the developmental progressions leading to reaching and grasping which are perhaps the major motor milestones of infancy related to manual control.

First, however, it is important to understand the respective functions of the arm and hand. Keogh and Sugden (1985) have described several functions of each. The functions of the arm are (1) to support the hand, where the arm is kept relatively immobile so as to support the hand in manipulating objects; (2) to position the hand for reaching and grasping; and (3) to generate and modulate the force of the hand when it is manipulating an object. The functions of the hand are (1) to grasp, which includes picking up and holding objects, and (2) to manipulate, where the thumb and fingers are used to move an object (Keogh & Sugden, 1985, p. 44). Of course, most movements of the hand and arm involve coordinated movements of both, in which separate movements of each may become differentiated depending on the task involved.

As they did with postural and locomotor control, Keogh and Sugden (1985) have described the early development of manual control according to three major movement progressions. We will only consider the first two because they relate specifically to reaching and grasping. Figure 5.6 presents these two major milestones that occur during the first year of life. The first of these developmental progressions includes movements of the hand which result in grasping, holding, handling, and releasing an object; the second includes changes in the movements of the arm that result in greater spatial accuracy in hand placement.

The first progression consists of three major grasping achievements that occur during the first year of life beginning with picking up a cube at 3 to 4 months. According to Keogh and Sugden (1985, p. 45), this is the first successful reach and grasp of an object, even though the reach is clumsy and the grasp is without thumb opposition. The next "landmark achievement" is at 5 to 6 months when the infant can pick up the same cube, but this time with thumb opposition. The last major achievement occurs at 8 to 10 months when the infant is able to make a *neat pincer grasp* which involves grasping a smaller object (e.g., a raisin) with the thumb and one finger.

The second major developmental progression concerns visually guided reaching which begins at 2 to 3 months with *hand regard*, that is, infants moving their hands in front of their eyes. At 3 to 4 months, infants can reach and touch an object although not surprisingly, this is done somewhat clumsily at first. By 6 months, infants can position their hands accurately, so further development simply involves these skills occurring in more and more different situations.

A Behavior Analysis of Reaching and Grasping

Reaching and grasping, like most aspects of behavioral development, have been described according to normative stages or sequences. For example, 2-month-old infants will accurately swipe at an object in front of them, but there are no attempts at grasping. By 5 months of age, they reach for and successfully grasp objects in what White (1971) has called "top level reaching." According to White (1971), the final reach and grasp relation involves the rapid lifting of one hand from out of the visual field to the object. As the hand approaches the object, it opens "in anticipation of contact." Moreover, before about 6 months, infants will attempt to grasp a virtual object, for example, an object reflected in a mirror (Keogh & Sugden, 1985, p. 48). (Nowadays, of course, computers create virtual objects in a total virtual environment in what is known as virtual reality.) Readers might recognize this as an instance of operant stimulus generalization in which the reflected image evokes behavior just as the real object has. At 3 months, infants will contact an object by reaching about 40% of the time; but by 4 months, they have few misses (Bower, 1979). The general picture of reaching and grasping is that, although there are crude attempts at both early in life, by the time the infant is 6 months old, accurate and successful reaching and grasping are the norm.

Thus, we know what infants do with respect to reaching and grasping

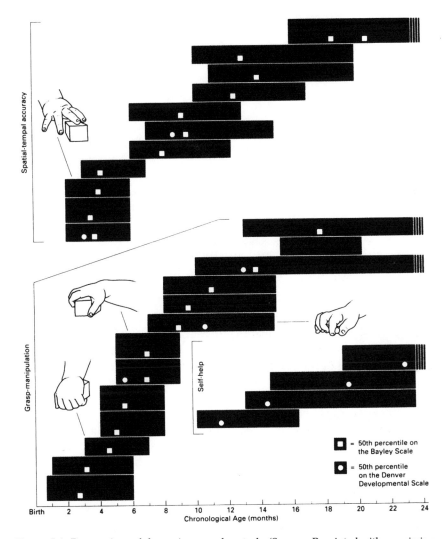

FIGURE 5.6. Progressions of change in manual controls. (SOURCE: Reprinted with permission of Macmillan College Publishing Company from *Movement Skill Development* by Jack Keogh and David Sugden. Copyright 1985 by Macmillan Publishing Company, Inc.)

and when they are likely to do it. However, the more important scientific question concerns how reaching and grasping evolve from the early crude movements to the very refined, differentiated, and coordinated movements observed only a few months later. In other words, we need to understand the processes that determine the development of reaching and grasping in terms of "the moment-to-moment experiences of the child" (White, 1971, p. 89).

Not surprisingly, evidence suggests that experience plays a significant role in the development of visually guided reaching. For example, consider a well-known study by White (1967) in which the environment of a group of 19 infants was "enriched" by (1) increasing the amount of time the infants were handled each day by 20 minutes; (2) increasing the amount of motility, which included placing the infants in the prone position for 15 minutes three times a day and removing the crib liners so that the activities in the ward were visible to the infants; and (3) altering the visual surroundings, including suspending a stabile consisting of highly contrasting colors and forms, and substituting the normal linens and crib liners with ones that were brightly colored. The researchers measured visual attention, prehensory responses, and such visual–motor behaviors as hand regard, hands touching the midline, mutual fingering, and turning of the torso. The most significant result of the White (1967) study was that the median age for the first appearance of top level reaching in the experimental group was 45 days earlier than in the control group. In addition, visual attention also increased dramatically over that in the control group once prehensory contacts with the stabile and the bumpers were possible. A particularly interesting result of the White (1967) study concerned the development of hand regard. "Hand regard" is the term used to describe the fact that infants will move their own hands in front of their eyes. Hand regard normally appears at about 84 days, but the infants in the control group of the White (1967) study displayed hand regard before 50 days of age.

According to White (1971), the results of his study demonstrate the plasticity of several visual–motor developments. Behavior analysts should not be surprised by such findings. For behavior analysts, an "enriched" environment means an environment that is richer in potential reinforcement contingencies with respect to certain behaviors. In the case of White's (1967) study, the environment was "enriched" by creating more functional stimuli, both antecedent and consequent, the infants' behavior of visually guided reaching. Consider the results concerning hand regard. Obviously, the sight of the infant's own hand moving in front of the eyes is a functional stimulus for that very behavior. It is probably the case that the sight of the hand moving reinforces not only the behavior of looking at the hand (visual attention), but also the movements of the hands themselves. Thus, in the nonenriched environment of the control infants, a lack of other forms of reinforcement may explain the fact that hand regard became so prominent so early. For infants in the experimental group, hand regard occurred much less frequently, probably because there were other reinforcers for visual attention and hand movements. Beginning at about 72 days of age, the infants in the experimental group began making swiping movements at the rattles on the stabile, after which the frequency of such behavior increased. The sound of the rattle contingent on the swiping movements was probably the functional consequence (i.e., positive reinforcer) for the behavior.

White (1971) criticizes Piaget's theory because it doesn't deal with the mechanisms of development in terms of the moment-to-moment experiences of the child. Behavior analysis, however, does accomplish this. That is, it identifies the variables responsible for the moment-to-moment interactions that alter visual attention, hand regard, and, ultimately, top level reaching. White's statement that "increased looking at and palpating of nearby objects (induced via enrichment procedures) would result in acceleration of the coordination process" (p. 107), implies that the altered contingencies of reinforcement that resulted from the "enrichment" of the environment are responsible for this acceleration. From the perspective of the present book, the findings summarized by White (1971) support the contention that maturational variables set broad limits within which contingencies of reinforcement may select different forms of motor behavior.

Ecological Reinforcers

Bijou provides a nice example, originally offered by Bijou and Baer (1961), of a behavior analytic interpretation of the development of the manual pincer grasp. He points out that the very young child does not usually show separate finger responses including a pincer grasp, which involves the use of the thumb in opposition to another finger to pick up small objects. On the contrary, the very young child flexes all of the fingers resulting in either an open or closed hand. According to Bijou (1979):

> [T]o differentiate separate finger responses requires an environment in which different reinforcement contingencies operate for movements of one finger than operate for movements of more than one. ... A pea on a table top is an example of such an environment. Attempts to pick up the pea by scooping it into the palm with all five fingers succeed only occasionally and after considerable time and effort, but attempts to pick up the pea with a scissor movement of the thumb and forefinger are likely to succeed more frequently and more easily. (p. 181)

Although Bijou posits that the reinforcer is the pea in the mouth, it is more likely that the reinforcer is the grasping and picking up of the pea. This example illustrates a type of reinforcement called ecological reinfor-

cement (Bijou, 1979). Ecological reinforcers are a type of automatic reinforcer in which the stimulus changes produced by the behavior increase
the frequency of that behavior under similar circumstances. Behavior
analysts use the term "automatic reinforcement," in the ordinary sense of
not requiring mediation by another person (Vaughan & Michael, 1982, p.
218). More specifically, automatic reinforcement is "a natural result of
behavior when it operates upon the behaver's own body or the surrounding world" (Vaughan & Michael, 1982, p. 219). This is an important type of
reinforcement since it does not have to be a tangible item, like candy,
praise, or tokens, delivered by another person. Of course, one of the
strengths of behavior-analytic theory is that reinforcers are not defined a
priori but, rather, by the effect they have on the behavior that precedes
them. The concept of ecological reinforcers is extremely important for a
behavior analytic theory of behavior change because it extends the range
of possible reinforcers and shows how interacting with the nonsocial
environment is sufficient to condition (i.e., to shape, differentiate, and
bring under stimulus control) a wide variety of behaviors. In this chapter,
the point has been made that ecological reinforcers are perhaps the primary source of reinforcement for the development of motor behavior in
human infants.

VOLUNTARY (VERSUS INVOLUNTARY) CONTROL

Previously, we mentioned the importance of the concept of so-called
"voluntary" behavior for many developmental psychologists. In many
developmental texts, the development of motor behavior is closely tied to
the issue of voluntary behavior or control. In fact, many textbooks present
the section on voluntary motor behavior immediately following the section on infant reflexes (i.e., involuntary behavior). This organization is not
accidental. It is true that much motor development is based on preexisting
reflexive behavior. But what happens when the behavioral repertoire of
the human changes from being almost entirely dominated by reflexes and
rhythmical stereotypies to being mostly operant behavior? Are infants
now able to control their own behavior at will? Is their behavior now
voluntary?

The following excerpts from various writings in the area of infant
motor development show that the issue is frequently cast in these terms.
For example, Kopp (1979, p. 9) has referred to motor development as "the
acquisition of voluntary movement." Regarding the rhythmic stereotypical movements of infants, Keogh and Sugden (1985) stated that "they may
be ... initial efforts to produce purposeful movements without sufficient

control to approximate the intention" (p. 24). In their developmental textbook, Bukatko and Daehler (1992) write that, "During the first year of life, infants also begin to display a wide variety of directed, voluntary actions as they gradually gain neuromotor control of head, arms, and legs" (p. 213). Finally, Berndt (1992) asks, "what principles govern the development of voluntary motor behavior" (p. 181)?

It might be instructive first to define "voluntary." According to *Webster's New World Dictionary* (1984), voluntary comes from the Latin word "voluntarius," which is related to the Latin "voluntas," meaning free will, which itself is related to "velle," to will. It is thus not surprising that most of the listings in the dictionary refer to free choice or free will. However, voluntary can also be defined as "intentional, not accidental." These two definitions of voluntary introduce an important distinction that can help us make sense of the issue. From a behavior analytic (i.e., deterministic) view, there is no such thing as voluntary if that means free from causal factors. Therefore, to define voluntary in terms of free choice or free will opposes the deterministic assumption held by scientists. Moreover, it encourages descriptions of infant behavior where infants seem to be autonomous agents directing and using their behavior for various purposes. Such descriptions move the behavior from environmental interactions to internal processes. Interestingly, in cases where the (ultimate) causes of behavior are "inside" the child (i.e., in the genes), as in reflexes, the child is not given credit for the behavior, but when the causes of the behavior are "in the environment," the child is suddenly given credit for being an autonomous agent.

There remains the problem that infant reflexive and rhythmical stereotypical behavior does seem to be distinctly different from later motor behavior. When most developmental researchers describe the former as being involuntary and the latter as being voluntary, they are implying that the infant has no choice over reflexive behavior but has a choice over later motor behavior. Again, these may not be useful distinctions to make. The difference between infant reflexive and rhythmical stereotypical behavior and later motor behavior is not that one is determined (i.e., caused) and the other is a matter of free will but, rather, that the two are controlled by different variables. Specifically, infant reflexes and rhythmical stereotypies are evoked by stimuli because of the evolutionary history of the human species, and later motor behavior is evoked by many more and varied antecedent events because of a lifetime history of operant conditioning. Both are caused; neither is a result of free will. It is true that the variables that evoke infant reflexes are usually more distinct and punctate than those that evoke reaching and grasping or walking, but that does not make one free from external control.

Perhaps a better definition of voluntary is the second definition mentioned above, that is, "intentional; not accidental." In this case, intentional (or deliberate) refers to the control of the behavior by contingencies of reinforcement. In fact, B. F. Skinner (1974) claims that "operant behavior is the very field of purpose and intention" in the sense that "by its very nature it (operant behavior) is directed toward the future ..." (p. 55). What Skinner means by the future is that consequences of behavior in particular situations affect future occurrences of behavior under similar circumstances. The language of purpose and intention arises when the behavior in question is operant and not reflexive.

COGNITIVE AND BEHAVIOR ANALYTIC VIEWS OF MOTOR DEVELOPMENT

For cognitive developmental psychologists, motor behavior is important because it is the means by which infants gain knowledge about the environment (Ginsburg & Opper, 1988). Piaget (1964) was closer to a behavior analytic view when he said "to know an object, is to act on it" (p. 8). For cognitive psychologists, knowledge about the environment is often used as a proximate explanation (see chapter 3) of behavior. In other words, knowledge as a cognitive structure causes infants to act in various ways consistent with that knowledge. The knowledge is reified and subsequently inferred based only on the infant's behavior. When it is used to explain the very behavior from which it was inferred, it represents a circular explanation (see chapter 2).

The cognitive approach to motor development in infancy can be illustrated with a study by Benson and Uzgiris (1985) in which the ability of infants to search correctly for and find a hidden object was assessed following either passive locomotion or self-locomotion. In this study, infants were first "familiarized" with the testing procedures by having them retrieve a toy that was partially and then totally hidden beneath a cloth cover. After two correct searches, each infant was "trained" to move around an apparatus and retrieve a visible toy. Test trials consisted of placing the toy in one of two hiding wells in the apparatus and then assessing the accuracy of searching for the hidden toy either after the infant moved herself around the testing apparatus (self-initiated locomotion) or was moved (i.e., carried) by a parent. The results showed that accuracy of retrieving the toy was greater when the infants self-locomoted rather than when they were carried by a parent. Moreover, the search accuracy for those infants who self-locomoted first did not transfer to conditions when they were then carried. The researchers interpreted these results as support for Piaget's contention that "action-based knowledge during infancy is involved in the achievement of spatial understanding and that the experience of self-initiated locomotion contributes to spatial development" (Benson & Uzgiris, 1985, p. 923).

What is the behavior analytic view of the Benson and Uzgiris (1985) study? In other words, how can the operant unit of analysis be used to interpret these results? Let's begin with the "familiarization" phase. Based on the authors' description, familiarization was really discrimination training in which retrieving the toy was reinforced (by getting the toy) initially when the toy was partially hidden and then when it was completely hidden. The "training" component added to that discriminative repertoire by requiring that the infants move around the hiding box before being permitted to retrieve the visible toy. The fact that the parents "enticed" or "encouraged" the infant to move around the box added to the S^D component of the task during training.

What about the results of the test trials? Behavior analysts would want to know why self-locomoting infants were more successful in retrieving the toy. The answer seems simple. The training trials involved the reinforcement of self-locomotion and accurate toy retrieval even though the toys in this condition were visible. Retrieval behavior when the toy was not visible had already been reinforced during the familiarization phase. The test trials simply tested the combining or merging, perhaps spontaneously, of these two repertoires (Epstein, 1981). The fact that generalization did not occur to conditions when infants were carried even after they had correctly retrieved the toy following self-locomotion simply represents an example of discriminative behavior. In fact, behavior analysts would submit that it is possible to reverse the findings of this study by pretraining infants to correctly retrieve the toy after being carried instead of pretraining self-locomotion. It is true that the normal course of behavioral development is for humans to move around on their own and to manipulate objects at the same time, but not as cognitive psychologists suggest, because they have acquired "spatial understanding" or "knowledge" (e.g., Benson, 1990), but because this is how they normally find and get things they want. For behavior analysts, explanations in terms of hypothetical entities like knowledge or (spatial) understanding are unnecessary, not directly testable, and not parsimonious.

For behavior analysts, motor behavior is important for reasons different than those of cognitive psychologists. All of the different forms of motor behavior are selected by the operant contingencies described earlier as problems in the external environment. In its earliest stages, the behavior is crude and undifferentiated, but some forms are more successful than other forms under certain conditions and, therefore, come to predominate under those circumstances. Cognitive psychologists like to describe much of this behavior as voluntary, or self-initiated; however, behavior analysts would suggest that this is only an illusion resulting from the fact that the conditions that evoke the behavior are subtle and multifaceted. For behavior analysts, motor development is adaptive behavior that is important because it enables humans to survive in the external environment.

SUMMARY

Motor development includes progressive changes in interactions between environmental variables and behaviors such as sitting, crawling, standing, walking, reaching, and grasping. This chapter discussed two categories of motor behavior: body control, which includes postural control and locomotion, and manual control (prehension), which includes reaching and grasping. The chapter then discussed the relative roles of maturation and experience on the development of these behaviors. Although changes in motor behaviors obviously occur within limits set by maturational factors, the extent of those limits is probably determined by environmental variables. Maturational accounts of motor development, however, often overlook subtle operant contingencies that might better account for many of the observed similarities and differences in motor development between individuals. These operant contingencies often involve automatic reinforcement, that is, reinforcement inherent in the behavior itself and, therefore, not mediated by another person. Developmental psychologists frequently describe the transition from rhythmical stereotypies and reflexes to more coordinated behavior as a transition from involuntary to voluntary behavior. This chapter, however, asserted that it is more parsimonious to describe this as a transition from reflexive to operant behavior, where both are involuntary. Finally, the chapter contrasted briefly the cognitive view of motor behavior as a way to obtain knowledge about the environment with a behavior analytic view of motor behavior as adaptive, that is, operant, behavior.

6

Perceptual Development

When psychologists write about the development of motor control and movement in infants, they frequently include descriptions of the development of sensory and perceptual systems as well (e.g., Gallahue, 1989; Keogh & Sugden, 1985). According to Keogh and Sugden (1985), the analysis of movement "must take into account the natures of the movement problem and the mover in the environmental context" (p. 265). Gallahue (1989) sees the process of infants "learning how to interact with the environment ... as a perceptual as well as a motor process" (p. 183). This chapter describes some of the research in the development of infant perceptual behavior, especially that behavior that is important to movement control. Instead of viewing perception as a thing or as a process, as most cognitive psychologists do, behavior analysts view it as behavior under particular types of stimulus control (e.g., Knapp, 1987; Nevin, 1973; Schoenfeld & Cumming, 1963). The development of perceptual behavior is simply the change from simpler to more complex instances of these types of stimulus control. The primary emphasis of the present chapter is on the development of visual perceptual behavior, that is, the control of behavior by visual stimuli and their interrelations. The present emphasis is justified because of the importance of visual stimuli for such behaviors as locomotion and visually guided reaching, which were discussed in chapter 5. The major topics considered in the present chapter are depth perception (including spatial orientation) and object perception (e.g., object constancies). The development of auditory perceptual behavior will be discussed in chapter 8 on language development.

SENSATION AND PERCEPTION

Psychology textbooks often contrast perception with sensation. The term "sensation" usually refers to the basic effects of stimuli on sensory receptors. Perception, however, has been described cognitively as:

the process by which animals *gain knowledge* about their environment and about themselves in relation to the environment. It is the beginning of knowing, and so is an essential part of cognition. More specifically, to perceive is to *obtain information* about the world through stimulation. (Gibson & Spelke, 1983, p. 2; emphasis added)

Dworetzky (1990) uses the term "perception" to refer to how the organism interprets the sensory experience. According to Gallahue (1989), sensations become perceptions only when "sensory stimuli can be integrated with stored information" (p. 184). The following quote is indicative of the general cognitive approach to the development of perception in infants:

Newborns attach little *meaning* to sensory stimuli. The ability to *integrate* stored data is limited. For example, light rays impinging on the eye register on the retinas and are transmitted to the appropriate nerve centers in the sensory areas of the cortex. The newborn's reaction is simple (sensation); if the light is dim, the pupils dilate; if the light is bright, the pupils constrict and some of the stimulation is shut off (consensual pupillary reflex). Soon the neonate blinks as the stimulus approaches. These simple reflex actions persist throughout life, but in a very short time the infant begins to *attach meaning* to the visual stimuli received. Soon a certain face becomes "mother." An object is *identified* as having either three or four sides. The infant now *attends* to certain stimuli and begins to *apply basic meaning* to them. (Gallahue, 1989, p. 184; emphasis added)

Notice in the above quote that stimuli don't control behavior; rather they have "meaning." It is the infant who "attends" to the stimulus, "identifies" it, and ultimately "attaches" meaning to it. In the behavior analytic view of perceptual behavior, particular stimuli control behavior(s) we refer to as *attending*, certain contingencies of reinforcement are responsible for the behavior(s) we refer to as *identifying*, and stimuli have *meaning* only when they control appropriate behavior. Moreover, if anything "attaches" meaning to a stimulus it is the environmental contingencies involving that stimulus and the behavior of an organism. In other words, all of these labels refer to relations between behavior and environment.

VISUAL PERCEPTUAL BEHAVIOR

According to Keogh and Sugden (1985):

Vision is our principal and most comprehensive means of specifying our environment and provides a display to represent the part of the environment in our visual field. Reading the visual display becomes the general problem in visual perceptual development. Individuals need to find and know specific objects as parts and wholes and to be able to combine them into larger configurations and patterns. They must also be able to see into the environment and perceive distance and depth and detect and follow movement. (p. 282)

This quote serves as an introduction to the following section on visual perceptual behavior. It sets apart the two major areas of visual perceptual development that will be considered, namely, depth perception and object perception (including object constancies). These two related areas of perceptual development are important to the development of movement control (Keogh & Sugden, 1985). As we will see, some perceptual control is apparent before infants have had the opportunity to move much in three-dimensional space.

Before we continue, however, let us first clarify the previous quote by Keogh and Sugden in the context of a behavior analytic perspective. Rather than describing "the general problem" in perceptual development as "reading the visual display," the behavior-analytic view is to account for how the visual display (i.e., stimuli) acquires functional control over the behavior we call perception. Keogh and Sugden (1985) are probably correct in saying that "individuals need to find and know specific objects and their spatial and temporal relationships" (p. 282). In essence, this means that in order to survive in a given environment the individual's behavior must conform to the contingencies relating to objects with which they must interact. This includes contingencies wherein responding to object parts versus wholes, as well as to specific patterns and configurations, especially in relation to other types of stimulation, is important. We must remember that, as with the previously discussed topics of memory and motor behavior, these "perceptions" are not mental or cognitive operations or processes as many authors imply, but rather behaviors that interact with and are changed by operant contingencies. Finally, it is not the infant who must "find and know" objects and their relations to one another, but rather it is the contingencies of reinforcement that select behavior relevant to the objects.

Depth Perception

Depth perception is important not only for moving within and responding correctly to the spatial layout of the environment but also for recognizing objects (Banks & Salapatek, 1983). The fundamental question concerning depth perception is how humans come to respond to three-dimensional aspects of the environment despite the fact that the retinal surface on which optical images are projected is two-dimensional (Banks & Salapatek, 1983).

The ability to react appropriately to distant objects (or depth) depends upon at least three general classes of cues: binocular cues, kinetic cues, and static (monocular) or pictorial cues (Aslin, 1987; Banks & Salapatek, 1983). *Binocular* cues, such as retinal disparity (also called binocular parallax), result from the two eyes being separated slightly and, thus, receiving slightly different retinal images of objects located at near distances. *Kinetic* cues (which are monocular cues) are produced by the differences in speed with which the images of objects at different distances move across the retina. These changes can be produced either by the movement of the objects in space (called *optical expansion*) or by the movement of the observer's head or body (called *motion parallax*). The *static (monocular)* cues (often called pictorial cues because they are used by artists to create the impression of depth) that are important for depth perception include linear perspective, interposition, texture gradients, relative and familiar size, and aerial perspective.

After years of investigation, developmental researchers have determined that depth perception based on these three classes of depth cues first appears in infants between 3 and 7 months of age (Aslin, 1987).

The next three sections describe these three classes of depth cues and some of the experiments that have demonstrated their control over perceptual behavior in infants. When relevant, cognitive descriptions of experimental results will be contrasted with a behavior analytic view.

Binocular Stimulus Control

Depth perception controlled by binocular cues can result from either convergence angle or disparity. The angle of convergence is the point at which the two eyes fixate. Thus, nearer distances produce larger angles. Disparity refers to changes in convergence that are required to fixate an object at a different distance (Aslin, 1987). The perception of relative depth based on disparity is called *stereopsis*. There is general agreement that control by the binocular cue of retinal disparity is first evident in infants between 2 and 3 months of age and is fully present by 5 months of age (Banks & Salapatek, 1983; Granrud, 1986).

Granrud (1986) showed that binocular disparity was a more effective cue for spatial (i.e., distance and size) perceptual behaviors in 4- to 5-month-old infants than were monocular cues. Several studies have in fact demonstrated that the stimulus control of depth-appropriate responding by binocular cues occurs at about 5 months (Bechtoldt & Hutz, 1979; Gordon & Yonas, 1976; Yonas, Oberg, & Norcia, 1978). For example, using a stereoscopic display that simulated the approach of an object on a collision course with the infant's face, Yonas et al. (1978) showed that 5-month-olds, but not 3½ month-olds, exhibited more reaching, head withdrawal, and blinking. Pettersen, Yonas, and Fisch (1980) showed that infants as young as 6 weeks would blink "defensively" in response to an object moving toward their faces and, moreover, that the blink was a function not of air pressure changes but of the visual characteristics of the display.

Banks and Salapatek (1983) have pointed out, however, that studies indicating that depth-appropriate responding does not occur in infants before 4 months of age are not conclusive because it is possible that the responses measured—reaching and defensive reactions—do not appear until about 4 months of age. Thus, it is possible that some control by depth cues is operative before that time but cannot be assessed with reaching or defensive behaviors.

Kinetic Stimulus Control

Kinetic cues result from motion that can be either "observer-induced" (called motion parallax) or "environmentally induced" (called optical expansion). The former involves the observer moving his or her eyes, head, or body; and the latter involves the movement of the viewed object (Yonas & Owsley, 1987). Research suggests that infant behavior is sensitive to control by kinetic stimuli and that kinetic cues may be the only type of depth cue for behavior in very young infants (Yonas & Owsley, 1987).

Perhaps the most famous (and earliest) studies on infant depth perception (in particular, height perception) was conducted by Eleanor Gibson and Richard Walk. Gibson and Walk (1960) devised an apparatus they called a "visual cliff" (see Figure 6.1). It consisted of a large sheet of glass under which a sheet of patterned material was placed. On one side of the cliff, the patterned material was placed flush against the glass; and on the other side, the sheet of patterned material was placed on the floor. The difference between the two sides of the glass gave the appearance of a drop-off, or cliff. Gibson and Walk found that infants of several species of animals, including rats, chickens, cats, sheep, dogs, pigs, and goats, avoided the apparent drop-off when placed on the "shallow" side of the visual cliff. When human infants aged 6 months to 14 months were placed in the center of the apparatus and then called to either the "shallow" or "deep" side by their mothers, most, but not all, of the infants did not crawl to the deep side. In fact, many infants began to cry when their mothers called to them from the deep side of the visual cliff. Gibson and Walk cautiously interpreted these results as demonstrating that human infants can perceive depth by the time they can crawl. However, the results with nonhuman infants (e.g., 24-hour-old chicks) suggested that the perception of height might be inherited (Gibson & Walk, 1960). Gibson and Walk (1960) offered "the rather broad conclusion" that "a seeing animal will be able to discriminate depth when its locomotion is adequate, even when

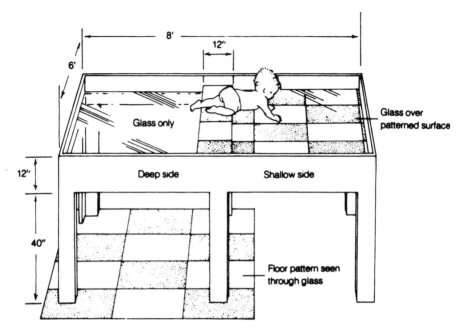

FIGURE 6.1.   The visual cliff. (SOURCE: Reprinted with permission from p. 138 of *Introduction to Child Development* [5th ed.] by John P. Dworetzky; Copyright 1993 by West Publishing Company. All rights reserved.)

locomotion begins at birth" (p. 69). The implication is that the avoidance behavior of the human infants on the visual cliff, like the behavior in other nonhuman species, might have an inherited component.

Gibson and Walk's (1960) demonstrations of avoidance behavior by human infants on the visual cliff prompted other researchers to question whether it was really possible to conclude that the depth perception was innate. Perhaps the biggest problem with the visual cliff studies is that, unlike most of the nonhuman animals used by Gibson and Walk, human infants are not mobile at birth or even shortly thereafter. Thus, by the time infants begin to crawl well, there have been numerous opportunities for learning to take place. It thus becomes difficult to make any conclusions about the innateness of depth perception in humans. Some researchers attempted to correct for this by selecting responses for study other than self-produced movement. For example, Campos and his colleagues showed heart-rate deceleration in infants as young as 2 months old and heart-rate acceleration in 9-month-old infants when they were placed on the deep side of the visual cliff apparatus (Campos & Langer, 1971;

Campos, Langer, & Krowitz, 1970; Schwartz, Campos, & Baisel, 1973). They concluded that the avoidance behavior in human infants did not reflect innate depth perception as in precocial animals. Instead, researchers saw it as a possible function of fear conditioning that could only begin after experience with self-produced movement (e.g., crawling).

Other researchers have challenged this interpretation and argued for an explanation based on maturation. For example, the results of a study by Richards and Rader (1981) showed that the age of crawling onset, and not crawling experience, was the best predictor of avoidance behavior on the visual cliff. Specifically, infants who learned to crawl before 6.5 months crossed the visual cliff, and infants who learned to crawl after 6.5 months avoided the deep side of the visual cliff (Richards & Rader, 1981). The researchers explained these results in terms of a hypothetical, maturationally controlled "perceptual motor program" which supposedly directs crawling in response to visual input. If crawling onset occurs before this hypothetical program is activated, crawling will be controlled more by tactile than visual input (Rader, Bausano, & Richards, 1980; Richards & Rader, 1981). Thus, according to these researchers, there appears to be a critical period for the linking of visual information and crawling (Richards & Rader, 1981). These studies, however, employed correlational methods and, because the proposed independent variables are not potentially observable, the evidence for a maturational program is indirect. One can recognize several problems with this explanation based on our discussion of correlational research methods in chapter 2.

Gibson and Walk (1960) determined that the primary cue controlling the behavior of nonhuman infants on the visual cliff was motion parallax, although older animals were also affected by pattern and texture density. Recall that in motion parallax, which is one of the two primary visual cues for distance (Bower, 1966), images on the retina are displaced when the head turns or is moved (see Figure 6.2). The amount of retinal displacement is a function of the distance and direction of the actual viewed scene from the point of focus (Keogh & Sugden, 1985). In the visual cliff apparatus, pattern elements on the shallow side move more rapidly across the field of vision than pattern elements on the deep side when the animal moves its position on the board or just moves its head. The findings with nonhuman infants on the visual cliff imply that the changes in heart rate in young infants observed by Campos and his coworkers may have been controlled by kinetic cues. Recall that the infants in these studies were too young to crawl, so they were carried across the sides of the visual cliff by the experimenters, thus producing apparent motion of the pattern elements from the shallow to the deep sides.

Although we will deal with size constancy in greater detail in a

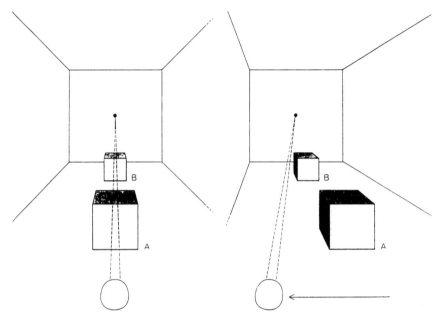

FIGURE 6.2. Motion parallax. If the head moves left and the eyes are kept fixed on a distant point, the nearest object (A) appears to move to the right farther than the more distant object (B) does. (SOURCE: Bower [1966]. Reprinted with permission from *Scientific American*.)

separate section below, it is interesting to point out here that Bower's (1966) report of size constancy in infants as young as 6 weeks of age also implicated the kinetic cue of motion parallax as the primary controlling variable. In order to ascertain which of the depth cues were most salient for these young infants, Bower first operantly conditioned head turning in infants in the presence of a stationary 30 centimeter (cm) cube placed at a distance of 1 meter. After conditioning, generalization was tested by varying the size and distance of the cube. In the generalization tests, the 30 cm cube was placed 3 meters away, a 90 cm cube was placed 1 meter away, and the same 90 cm cube was placed 3 meters away. Figure 6.3 shows the training and test stimuli in their true size and their retinal size. In this arrangement, more responding to the 30 cm cube 3 meters away would be evidence for size constancy even though the retinal image would be smaller than the same cube at 1 meter. More responding to the 90 cm cube at 3 meters would indicate that retinal image size was the main controlling factor because the 90 cm cube at 3 meters produces the same retinal image size as the 30 cm cube at 1 meter. Of the three groups of infants, one viewed real cubes but wore a patch over one eye, thus allowing only motion parallax or pictorial cues (both monocular cues). A second group viewed projected slides instead of real cubes, thus allowing pictorial cues (see below), but lacking binocular or motion parallax cues. A third group wore specially constructed stereoscopic goggles and viewed projected stereograms which prevented motion parallax but permitted binocular parallax and pictorial cues. The results showed that infants in the first (monocular) group responded most to the same cube further away suggesting their behavior was controlled not by the retinal image size, but rather by the actual size (i.e., size constancy). The infants who viewed the slides (groups 2 and 3) did not perform as well. The infants in group 2 who only had access to pictorial cues and the infants in group 3 who had some access to binocular cues did not respond significantly differently to the three generalization stimuli. These results suggested that motion parallax was the most effective cue for depth and size in 6-week-old infants.

In addition to motion parallax and optical expansion, another kinetic cue for depth perception is accretion-deletion of texture. This is produced when movement, either by an observer or by objects in the viewing environment, causes disruptions of the pattern of visible texture projected to the observer's eyes. Yonas and Owsley (1987) describe accretion-deletion of texture as follows:

> Since terrestrial environments are filled with opaque objects and surfaces, the visual world is divided into visible and occluded surfaces at each possible observation point. When the observer moves through the environment, or when an object moves relative to an observer, some surfaces are occluded and others are revealed. (p. 108)

As with control by other kinetic depth cues, researchers have determined that the behavior of infants as young as 5 months old is sensitive to accretion–deletion cues. In one study, Granrud, Yonas, Smith, Arterberry, Glicksman, and Sorknes (1984) used computer-generated random-dot displays in which accretion and deletion of texture provided the only cues for contour or for depth at an edge (see Figure 6.4). When the display moved, the foreground surface moved in front of and occluded a moving background surface (accretion and deletion); and when the display was motionless, it appeared to be a flat array of dots. The researchers found that both 5- and 7-month-old infants reached more often toward the foreground than the background.

The general conclusion from the studies discussed in this section is that infant behavior is sensitive to control by kinetic stimuli and that these cues may indeed be the only type of depth cue for behavior infants as young as 6 weeks old.

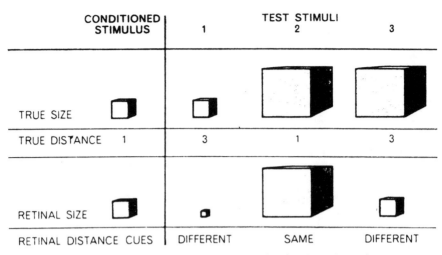

FIGURE 6.3. Training and test stimuli used by Bower (1966) to investigate size constancy. (Source: Reprinted with permission from *Scientific American*.)

Static (Monocular) Stimulus Control

Yonas and Owsley (1987) describe nicely the importance of monocular cues for depth perception:

> If the reader were to look up from this page, the three-dimensional layout of the room would be immediately apparent. If the reader then closed one eye, binocular depth information would be eliminated, yet there would be very little loss of spatial definition, especially if the observer's head were in motion, making kinetic depth information available. If we take this scenario one step further, and remove kinetic information from the array, perhaps by asking the observer to minimize eye, head, and body movement and by preventing object movement, the observer would still perceive a world in three dimensions. The room would not appear as an arrangement of two-dimensional patches of color. (p. 86)

This description implies that some stimuli can control depth-appropriate responding even with only one eye and an optic array that is static. As stated previously these static monocular depth cues are also called "pictorial cues," because they are used by artists to create the impression of depth in two-dimensional displays. The Italian Renaissance artist Leonardo da Vinci was the first person to describe many of the depth cues that painters use.

We have already noted that the control of depth-appropriate behavior by binocular cues occurs by about 5 months of age and control by kinetic

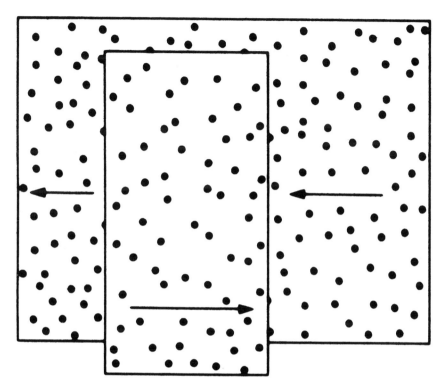

FIGURE 6.4. Computer-generated random-dot displays of accretion and deletion of texture cues. Arrows indicate direction of motion. Interior vertical lines indicate locations of subjective depth cues. (SOURCE: Granrud, Yonas, Smith, Arterberry, Glicksman, and Sorknes [1984]. Copyright 1966 Society for Research in Child Development.)

cues occurs even earlier than that. Interestingly, control by static (monocular) cues appears later than control by binocular cues. Bower (1966) found that the behavior of 6- and 8-week-old infants was sensitive, in descending order, to the cues of motion parallax, binocular parallax, and static (pictorial) cues. As we said, the static (pictorial) cues exerted little or no control over the size-constancy behavior of the 6- to 8-week-old infants in Bower's (1966) study. As discussed before, these findings support the behavior analytic view that the development of depth perception occurs as a result of the progressive interactions between perceptual cues and behavior. Although there are several different types of static (pictorial) depth cues, we will only discuss two of them—linear perspective and familiar size.

Linear Perspective.   Several studies have investigated the control of perceptual behavior in infants by various monocular cues (e.g., Granrud & Yonas, 1984; Granrud, Yonas, & Opland, 1985; Granrud, Yonas, & Pettersen, 1984; Granrud, Yonas et al., 1984; Yonas, Cleaves, and Pettersen, 1978). For example, Yonas, Cleaves, and Pettersen (1978) used a trapezoidal window presented parallel to the fronto-parallel plane (see Figure 6.5) to investigate control by the pictorial cue of linear perspective. When one eye was covered, 6- and 7-month-old infants reached (incorrectly) more to the larger (i.e., pictorially "nearer") side of the trapezoid as if it were closer. When binocular viewing was allowed, infants reached more to different parts of the fronto-parallel display as if they were all equally close. In contrast, 5-month-olds reached about equally often to both sides of the trapezoidal window display, suggesting that pictorial cues were not effective. However, another group of 5-month-olds reached more often to the nearer side of a real rectangular window rotated approximately 45° about a vertical axis suggesting control by kinetic cues (i.e., motion parallax). These results might have been predicted by Bower's (1966) findings on the order in which depth cues control infant behavior. Other studies have supported Yonas et al. (1978) in that the reaching of 5-month-old infants may be controlled by binocular cues but is not well controlled by pictorial depth cues (e.g., Kaufman, Maland, & Yonas, 1981). Once again, this lends support for a behavior analytic view of the development of perceptual behavior as a result of the progressive interactions between infants' behaviors and their environments.

Familiar Size.   Another possible controlling variable for effective distance responding is familiar size. Although familiarity or experience with objects is not necessary for appropriate depth responding, it is clear that the retinal image size can become an effective cue for depth responding if the object is familiar. Consider a study by Yonas, Pettersen, and Granrud (1982). These researchers studied the effectiveness of familiar size as a cue for distance responding using reaching in 5- and 7-month-old infants. The familiar objects were two different sized pictures of the infants' mothers' faces; the unfamiliar objects were two checkerboards of different sizes. All stimuli were presented at the same distance and were viewed monocularly. Results showed that the 7-month-olds reached more often to the larger face but equally often to the two checkerboards whereas the 5-month-olds reached equally to all stimuli. These results suggest that the 7-month-olds, but not the 5-month-olds, exhibited size-appropriate responding to familiar objects. One can conclude that size-appropriate responding is typically present by 7 months of age and that experience plays an important role in spatial perception (Yonas & Owsley, 1987; Yonas et al., 1982).

FIGURE 6.5. The Fronto-parallel Ames trapezoidal window. (SOURCE: "Development of Sensitivity to Pictorial Depth," by A. Yonas, W. T. Cleaves, and L. Pettersen. In *Science*, Vol. 200, 1978, p. 77. Copyright 1978 by the American Association for the Advancement of Science.)

From a behavior analytic perspective, what does it mean to call objects "familiar" or "unfamiliar"? Obviously, objects become familiar depending on experience with them. From a behavior analytic perspective, objects become "familiar" due to a history of reinforcement that has produced appropriate responses to them. In other words, after interacting with objects, they come to exert stimulus control over operant behavior that is appropriate to them. For example, the way an object is handled or held is determined by the consequences of successful holding or handling. Some of this behavior can be described as perceptual if the retinal image size plus the visual angle subtended by the object are a source of stimulus control over appropriate responding (e.g., reaching). (The stimulus control over size-appropriate responding is discussed further in the section on size constancy below.)

In addition to linear perspective and familiar size, Yonas and his colleagues have also determined that the static pictorial cues of *interposition*, in which one object overlaps with or occludes another object (Granrud & Yonas, 1984), and *shading*, which involves variations in luminance in the retinal image (Granrud, Yonas, & Opland, 1985), become effective cues for depth-appropriate reaching between 5 and 7 months of age. Of course, simply demonstrating when during development certain visual stimuli effectively control perceptual behavior does not necessarily shed light on the processes responsible for the change. Although some researchers have argued for a strong maturational component to the development of visual perceptual behavior (e.g., Bower, 1966; Rader et al., 1980), a behavior analytic view is that to the extent that such behavior is affected by experience, the principles of behavior analysis can be used to understand the possible environmental processes.

A Behavior Analytic View of Depth-Appropriate Responding

The first five chapters have asserted that much of human behavior is established, modified, and maintained as a result of interactions with the environment. Behavior appropriate to different circumstances is selected by operant conditioning, just as genetic mutations that are appropriate for different environmental requirements are selected in natural selection. We have referred to such behavior as adaptive. The process by which the behavior of individual organisms is selected by the environmental interaction is called operant conditioning. Although perceptual development has long been considered to result from largely maturational processes, much of the evidence from studies on infants suggests that there is a strong environmental component to its development. This is not to say that there is not an interactive relationship between environment and genetics. However, genes set broad, not narrow, limits on learning. One reason non-behavior analytic researchers probably overlook operant contingencies, especially in perceptual development, is that the researchers are simply not aware of their explanatory power. Another reason is that they might have an erroneous view of just what a behavior analytic view of perceptual behavior is. For example, some developmental psychologists have erroneously assumed that the reinforcers implicit in an operant view of perceptual development must come from other people (Gibson, 1977). On the contrary, perhaps most of the reinforcers in perceptual behavior, as well as in motor behavior, are automatic in the sense that they are not mediated by other people but rather are inherent in the interactions themselves.

As the above discussion indicates, researchers have a good idea about what infants do and when they do it with respect to the stimulus control of depth-appropriate behavior. They also have a better idea about the types of depth cues that control distance responding and at what ages these cues are operable. These normative facts about the emergence of depth-appropriate responding encourage the assumption of maturational processes. Another, equally parsimonious explanation for the development of depth-appropriate behavior is in terms of its adaptive value. For behavior analysts, the question is: What typically happens to infants up to 7 months of age that produces depth-appropriate behavior? Although there may be some inherited behavioral relations involving depth cues (e.g., motion parallax), the fact that so much depth-appropriate behavior in infants is first seen between 5 and 7 months of age supports an environmental explanation just as easily as a maturational one. From a behavior analytic perspective, behavior in infants (e.g., blinking, head movement, reaching, crawling, etc.) comes under the control of various depth cues (stimulus relationships) because successful responding requires that it does so. Moreover, that the stimulus control by depth cues seems to follow a certain order—from binocular, to kinetic, to static (pictorial)—may reflect the order of interactions between the infant and the environment. For example, some depth-appropriate behavior controlled by the kinetic cue of motion parallax is evident in infants as young as 6 weeks of age (Bower, 1966; Campos & Langer, 1971). Because infants at this age are not capable of other depth-appropriate behavior such as reaching, it is not surprising that the behavior they are capable of—head and eye movements—comes under the control of motion parallax cues. A good case can therefore be made for an interpretation of visually guided reaching and locomotive behaviors in terms of discrimination because these behaviors operate on the environment in a more conspicuous manner and are initially uncoordinated and under poor tactile and visual stimulus control. But before we discuss visually guided reaching, let us take a closer look at visual size constancy.

Object Perception

As we move through the environment and view objects, the retinal image associated with those objects changes continually (Banks & Salapatek, 1983). It might seem natural, therefore, that these constant changes in retinal image would pose a problem for accurately recognizing and identifying objects, especially if behavior is initially conditioned to static objects. Keogh and Sugden (1985) describe the importance of object perception, especially object constancy, as follows:

> Newborns see objects as things and do not see the space between them as things. That is, they extract objects for their visual attention rather than space from the visual display. When an object becomes known it becomes recognizable as that object from whatever angle it is viewed. The object will have a

constancy in that it will remain the same shape even though the retinal image has changed. Constancy is established also for size and location. If we approach a stationary object in our visual field, the object will retain the same shape, appear to be the same size, and maintain the same location, even though our retinal image grows bigger and the object changes position on the retina. (p. 283)

How do objects "as things," and not the spaces between objects, come to appropriately control the behavior of children? Although object perception includes a whole class of object constancies, we will concentrate our discussion on perceptual size constancy.

Traditional Approaches to Perceptual Size Constancy

The rule about the constancies of objects can be stated as follows: Even though the size, shape, and position of objects change with respect to the image projected on the retina, the actual size, shape, and position of the objects in the environment remain constant. As Bower (1966) explains, "perception seems faithful to the object rather than to its retinal image" (p. 80). Perhaps it is more precise to say that object-controlled behavior is faithful to the object itself rather than to its retinal image. Dworetzky (1990) defines size constancy as "the learned perception that an object remains the same size, despite the fact that the size of the image it casts on the retina varies with its distance from the viewer" (p. 134). Dworetzky (1990) describes an example of size constancy as follows:

When you look at your parked car as you are walking away from it, your visual sensory system sends a message to your brain. First the image of the car is projected through the lens onto an area at the back of each of your eyes called the retina. As you walk away (still looking at your car), the image projected onto the retina gets smaller and smaller as you get farther from your car.... Although the sensory image of your car is shrinking rapidly you don't perceive that your car is changing size. Instead, you perceive that your car is simply becoming more distant. (p. 134)

It is sometimes said that we "know" that an object is the same size even though it appears smaller. It is even said that although the object casts a smaller image on the retina, we still "see" it as being the same size. In addition, developmental researchers talk about the age at which children "acquire size constancy" (e.g., Day & McKenzie, 1981; Yonas, Granrud, & Pettersen, 1985).

The preceding locutions are confusing ways of talking about the phenomenon and they pose all of the problems of any structural interpretation of behavior. Just as with memory, behaviors are observed in certain situations and given a name, in this case "perception," or more specifically "size constancy." The name is reified as a type of knowledge or cognition about the world although the knowledge or cognition is never directly observed. With this explanation, the child "acquires" and then "possesses" size constancy. This implies that as a result of certain experiences, a structure is created inside the child which then enables him or her to interpret the sizes of objects correctly. Concentrating on this and other inferred structures prevents researchers from investigating more fundamental behavioral processes, like the nature of the experiences themselves (e.g., the reinforcement contingencies that contribute to the observed behaviors). The emphasis of most cognitive accounts is not on the child's behavior, but on inferred surrogates of the behavior called "interpretations" or "recognitions," the only evidence of which is the very behaviors they are said to explain. Perception is really just the behavior of the child in the particular environmental context. This more parsimonious description, however, is overlooked in lieu of inventing internal surrogates which are said to interpret the sensory information.

Experiments on Size Constancy. Although we considered experiments on depth perception in a separate section, it is important to point out that size constancy and depth perception are intimately related. As noted previously, one of the most important static cues for depth-appropriate responding, especially in infants by 7 months of age, is the relative size of objects. Other evidence suggests that sensitivity to distance cues, especially those produced by retinal disparity, is necessary for size-appropriate responding (i.e., size constancy) (Aslin, 1987; Granrud, 1986). Responding appropriately to objects as they move closer to or farther from our visual receptors is part of the very essence of responding to depth, or three dimensional, cues. Of course, as objects move closer to or farther from the visual field, the retinal image grows or shrinks respectively. Researchers have attempted to determine the approximate ages when sensitivity to the cues for depth, and thus size, perception first appear. The determination of size constancy is not as simple as it might appear, however. In fact, researchers have found that size constancy can occur under the control of different kinds of visual cues and that the "development" of this differential stimulus control does not occur all at once (Day, 1987). This gradual development of size constancy provides fuel for the debate on relative significance of maturation versus learning in the development of size constancy (e.g., Bower, 1966; Pettersen et al., 1980).

Although several experiments examining the role of different cues for depth-appropriate responding have implications for size constancy (e.g., Yonas et al., 1978; Yonas et al., 1982), only a few have actually investigated size constancy as a separate phenomenon, to the extent that it is possible (e.g., Bower, 1966; Day & McKenzie, 1981; McKenzie, Tootell, & Day, 1980).

The findings of Bower (1966) on size constancy in infants as young as 6 weeks of age implicated motion parallax as the primary controlling variable. McKenzie et al. (1980) studied size constancy in 18-, 26-, and 33-week-old infants using colored models of human heads as the stimuli because they were more "realistic" than stimuli used in previous studies (e.g., cubes), and thus might inherently (i.e., biologically) control more looking. The researchers used habituation of visual fixation under one of four conditions of object size (one large and one small) and distance (either 30 or 60 cm): (1) the large head presented at 60 cm (the control condition); (2) the large head presented at 30 cm (called the size-constancy condition because only the size was the same as the control stimulus); (3) the small head presented at 60 cm (called the distance condition because only distance was the same as control); and (4) the small head presented at 30 cm (called the visual angle condition because only the visual angle was the same as control). The habituation condition involved the large head presented at 60 cm (the control and test conditions). The results, measured in terms of recovery from habituation, showed that for the 26- and 33-week-old infants, recovery of visual fixation to the large head at 30 cm (the size-constancy condition) and to the large head at 60 cm (the control/test condition) was slight, indicating size-appropriate responding, whereas recovery to the distance and visual angle stimulus conditions was greater. The 18-week-old infants, however, showed recovery to both the size constancy and the distance conditions that were similar to the test condition. The researchers found it difficult to make any conclusions about size constancy, possibly because the objects were stationary and, thus, less salient (Day & McKenzie, 1981).

Day and his colleagues (Day, 1987; Day & McKenzie, 1981) tested the suggestion that size constancy might be evident in infants as young as 18 weeks of age under slightly different conditions, for example, where the stimulus objects moved. Day and McKenzie (1981) conducted an experiment with 18-week-old infants, again using recovery from habituation, but this time the stimulus object, a model head (see Figure 6.6), moved toward and away from the infant along the median axis during the habituation phase. In the test phase, an object of a different size moved throughout the same range of distances and visual angles. Using this design, recovery from habituation during the test phase could be attributed to the size of the object independently of either distance or visual angle (Day, 1987). The results showed that recovery from habituation was greater for a moving object of a different size than for the same object, indicating that the invariant physical size of the object was the controlling stimulus and not its visual angle.

A study by Granrud (1986) may help to clarify the relationship be-

FIGURE 6.6. Experimental arrangement used by Day and McKenzie (1981). (SOURCE: Copyright 1981 by the American Psychological Association. Reprinted by permission.)

tween size-appropriate behavior and depth-appropriate behavior. In a series of experiments designed to elucidate the role of sensitivity to binocular disparity in both depth- and size-appropriate behavior, Granrud (1986) reported the following results: (1) in situations in which monocular cues were similar to those available in the real world, binocular cues were more effective than monocular cues in controlling reaching to two different sized objects that were placed side by side at different distances, thus producing equal sized retinal images; and (2) 4-month-old infants who were sensitive to binocular disparity reached more for the nearer of the two retinally equivalent objects than 4-month-olds who were not disparity sensitive, indicating that the cue of binocular disparity is a critical cue controlling depth- and size-appropriate behavior. Finally, Granrud (1986) replicated the experimental conditions of the Day and McKenzie (1981) study described above with a disparity-sensitive and a disparity-insensitive group of 4-month-old infants. The results showed that the disparity-sensitive group evidenced significantly greater recovery from habituation to the novel object than did infants in the disparity-insensitive group (although the results regarding the disparity-insensitive group were equivocal). According to Granrud (1986), "[T]hese findings indicate that the development of sensitivity to binocular disparity is accompanied by a substantial increase in infants' ability to perceive distances and sizes of objects" (p. 46).

A Behavior Analytic View of Object-Appropriate Behavior

A behavior analytic view of visual perceptual behavior is that it is behavior under complex stimulus control (e.g., Knapp, 1987; Malott & Whaley, 1981; Nevin, 1973; Schoenfeld & Cumming, 1963). However, as indicated in chapter 2, many developmental psychologists are more interested in the relation between changes in child development, visual perceptual behavior in this case, and changes in age. This chapter has cited several studies in which such relationships have been studied. A behavior analytic approach does not dismiss questions about the chronology of certain behavioral changes; instead, it looks for explanations about differences at different ages in the changes in interactions between the behavior and the environment. For example, we might ask *why* control by monocular depth cues appears to develop later than control by binocular depth cues? To answer this, behavior analysts would want to understand the nature of the infant's early visual experiences. They might discover, for example, that from the earliest days after birth, and for the first several months, the infant's visual environment consists largely of objects that move toward the infant or in and out of the infant's visual field (e.g., people's faces, bottles, pacifiers, etc.). In addition to kinetic cues, these moving objects produce the binocular cues of convergence and retinal disparity. In the presence of these events, certain consequences (e.g. being touched, having something placed into the mouth, or simply seeing the object) immediately follow the infant's behaviors (e.g., looking or reaching).

Some of the infant's reactions (e.g., head withdrawal, blinking, and reaching) are probably initially parts of unconditional reflexes and are elicited by objects that move quickly toward the infant's face; however, other behavior (e.g., looking or reaching) becomes operant, and thus comes under the stimulus control of the binocular cues. Reaching in the absence of approaching objects is not followed by reinforcing consequences, but reaching when these things approach is followed by touching or grasping the object. Many of the monocular cues (e.g., linear perspective, interposition and texture gradients) probably become more important once the infant is in a sitting position, which typically occurs between 5 and 8 months of age. The quantity and quality of potentially functional stimuli increases dramatically when the infant's body position changes from the prone to the sitting position and then again from the sitting to the standing position. Behavior analysts ask about the variables that determine changes in the behavior of infants under these functional perceptual cues. Thus, in part by asking different questions, behavior analysis offers an objective and parsimonious way of describing the changes in behavior.

A Behavior Analytic View of Size Constancy

First of all, let's be clear about what happens when the distance between objects and an observer changes. Recall the earlier quote by Keogh and Sugden (1985). They accurately described the nature of object constancy: when the retinal image of an object changes, the object itself retains the same shape, size, and position. Thus, the physical characteristics of objects are constant. They also correctly described the effect on the observer: "[W]hen an object becomes known it becomes recognizable as that object from whatever angle it is viewed" (p. 283). From a behavior analytic viewpoint, objects become "known" and, therefore, "recognizable" as a result of what might be called "contingencies of interaction," which means the contingencies of reinforcement that produce behavior appropriate to objects. Thus, an object becomes recognizable when an observer responds appropriately to it. This can occur in a number of different ways. In size constancy, the image cast on the retina becomes smaller as objects become more distant and larger as objects get closer. If we move away from our car, the image on the retina gets smaller, and however we describe it, we never see it as anything but smaller. Saying that we perceive it as being the same size, means that we still *behave* toward it as being the same size. In other words, the car exerts some of the same stimulus control that it always did. We still label it as a car. We may reach for our keys and walk toward the car when we want to go somewhere and so on.

So, what is size constancy? An objective description of size constancy is that even though we actually see objects as smaller or larger (in terms of retinal image size), we continue to behave toward them in most of the ways we always have. As Keogh and Sugden (1985) noted, size constancy, like all object constancies, is a property of objects in the world; that is, the sizes of objects are constant. It is not necessary to say that the constant sizes of objects are taken in and acquired. Nor is it necessary to infer cognitive structures, behavioral surrogates, or perceptions to explain the size-constant behaviors. For psychologists, it should be sufficient to say that our behavior comes under the stimulus control of objects and either varies or does not as the sensory characteristics of their size, shape, and position change depending upon the operative contingencies. But *how* does this happen? Many accounts of depth perception and the related perception of size constancy allude to experiential factors but offer no interpretations (e.g., Banks & Salapatek, 1983). Because behavior analysis is essentially the science of adaptive behavior, it is in an ideal position to offer an interpretation.

A stimulus control account of size constancy requires the identification of the stimulus characteristics involved when the distances of objects vary. The ability to react appropriately to distant objects (or depth) depends upon several types of cues and experiences. As Day (1987) points out, before infants can respond appropriately to the sizes of objects, they must be able to discriminate size and distance. Infants must have either inherited or learned these perceptual discriminations. Either way, as we have mentioned, there are two general classes of depth cues—binocular cues and monocular cues—that come to control depth- and size-appropriate behavior. The critical question is *how* these cues come to control behavior.

Obviously, any claims of a role for a genetic contribution size constancy must be largely inferential. Claiming a role for learning requires either being able to produce the learning unambiguously, for example, in a laboratory, or providing a plausible interpretation based on already demonstrated scientific principles. The success of this enterprise is aided by citing supportive research. For example, one clue to the role of learning in the development of perceptual behavior comes from Granrud, Haake, and Yonas (1985), who showed that only 6 to 10 minutes of manual handling of (i.e., playing with) previously unfamiliar objects by young infants was apparently sufficient to make the objects "familiar" and to control depth-appropriate reaching. If this kind of learning can occur so quickly and subtly, then it is easy to see why the role of learning in perceptual behavior might be overlooked. In just 6 to 10 minutes, the tactile, proprioceptive, and visual stimuli produced by the manual handling of objects were sufficient to develop the visual stimulus control necessary to effectively control depth-appropriate responding to the objects.

One problem in assessing perceptual stimulus control concerns the behavior to be measured. Perceptual behavior is not a special type of behavior; it includes whichever behavior is under the control of perceptual cues. However, it is possible to argue that, with some behaviors such as visually guided reaching, infants may not be physically capable of the behavior although some other behavior may still be brought under the control of perceptual cues. In some cases, this problem has been overcome by using other measures, such as changes in heart rate or sucking rate (e.g., Campos, Langer & Krowitz, 1970; Kalnins & Bruner, 1973). The implication is that if stimuli don't yet differentially control some behavior, then we don't speak of perception. In other words, psychologists don't use the term "perception" in the absence of some measurable (perceptual) response, just as they don't speak of recognition memory in the absence of differential fixation times. Thus, perception is not something that an individual possesses either mentally or physiologically; it is simply a label for certain behavioral relations.

A Behavior Analytic View of Visually Guided Reaching. One response in infants that comes under the appropriate control of object size and depth cues fairly early is (visually guided) reaching. We previously described research by Yonas et al. (1982) regarding the control of reaching behavior by familiar size. These results are interesting for behavior analysts not only because they indicate that size-appropriate responding is typically present by 7 months of age, but also because they are amenable to a behavior analytic interpretation. Objects become "familiar" due to a history of reinforcement that has produced appropriate responding to them. But behavior analysis must do more than offer post hoc explanations; it must offer plausible processes. Ideally, a behavior analysis of this problem would involve an experimental demonstration in which size-appropriate responding is generated in an organism lacking such behavior. Without such a demonstration, behavior analysts would offer a plausible interpretation according to the laws and principles of behavior analysis. What follows is how behavior analysts might interpret such a behavioral transition in infants in their "natural" environment.

Obviously, reaching can't occur until the underlying musculoskeletal structures have matured, although such development can apparently be accelerated by environmental manipulation (White & Held, 1966; White, Castle, & Held, 1964). Consider an infant lying in its crib. By the time reaching is physically possible, among the first contingencies to which the infant is exposed is the sight of the parent as a stimulus in whose presence reaching out is successful; that is, reaching produces some type of contact or interaction with the parent. Such a stimulus is termed a discriminative stimulus (S^D), and its control over behavior is evidenced when, on subsequent occasions, it evokes the behavior that was previously successful (in producing some consequence) when it was present. In our example, however, successful reaching is only possible when the retinal image of the parent is relatively large (e.g., when the parent is leaning over the crib). When the retinal image is small (i.e., when the parent is farther away), reaching out, which probably occurs during the initial stages of discrimination learning, is not reinforced. In this situation, retinal image size is probably the most important S^D (or S-delta, that is, a stimulus in whose presence behavior is unsuccessful) for the size-appropriate behavior unless either the parent is moving or the infant's head is moving, in which case kinetic cues (e.g., motion parallax or accretion/deletion of texture) become part of the S^D complex.

Consider another scenario. An infant is sitting on the floor of an average sized room. There are two stuffed animals of different sizes. The smaller of the two is next to the infant and the larger one is farther away; however, both stuffed animals produce the same retinal image size, that is, they subtend the same visual angle. There are also other toys in the room, some of which produce the same retinal image size as the farther stuffed animal even though they are closer to the infant, and vice versa. What visual cues are provided by the two stuffed animals and the other toys that determine reaching behavior to the stuffed animals? Traditional approaches might ask how the infant "knows" which stuffed animal is really closer, how the infant "calculates" distances, or whether the infant has "acquired" size constancy. The behavior analyst asks what experiences (i.e., interactions with the environment) produce size-constant behavior? Recall that both stuffed animals produce the same retinal image size, so retinal image size cannot be the primary functional stimulus for size-appropriate reaching. Initially, the infant reaches for both of the stuffed animals. Reaching for the closer one is successful and reaching for the farther one is unsuccessful. The binocular and kinetic cues notwithstanding, most of the other static monocular cues come into play. For example, the closer stuffed animal or other close objects tend to obscure the more distant stuffed animal (interposition). Moreover, any receding lines in the room will appear to converge near the farther stuffed animal (linear perspective). Also, the more distant stuffed animal and other equally distant objects produce a finer grain texture than closer objects. In the presence of this stimulus complex, reaching for the closer stuffed animal is successful (i.e., it is reinforced); and this particular complex becomes an S^D and will, under similar circumstances in the future, evoke reaching for closer objects. Reaching for the farther stuffed animal is not successful; the same stimulus complex becomes an S-delta (i.e., a stimulus that is correlated with failure, or nonreinforcement of responses) and will not evoke reaching for farther objects. Of course, determining the particular properties of the environment that become functionally relevant requires an experimental analysis; the present interpretation can only suggest possible candidates.

Visually guided reaching is not the only example of size-constant behavior. Once verbal behavior is present, that too becomes part of the class of responses controlled by depth cues. For most people, verbal behavior, like nonverbal behavior, is controlled by the sight of objects and is usually acquired under a variety of conditions in which the sensory characteristics of the objects vary. One of the verbal responses that continues to be appropriate despite these changes is called a tact (Skinner, 1957), which is equivalent to the name of an object (see chapter 8). Most verbal communities maintain the constancy of simple tacts regardless of sensory changes in other characteristics of the tacted objects. For example, a chair is called a "chair" regardless of its height, color, shape, etc. The acquisition of this verbal behavior might be expedited through stimulus generalization from the stimulus characteristics present when the tact was first conditioned, or it might require more direct training. For example, the tact "mama" might be acquired when the mother is very close to the infant thus creating a large retinal image. If, however, the mother moves away, her physical features, which remain constant, may still evoke "mama," which would normally be quickly reinforced by the mother reacting to the infant's speaking. If it doesn't, prompting may be necessary. More likely, tacts, like most other behavior, are acquired under varied conditions; thus, stimulus generalization is built in.

Although the discussion of perceptual behavior in this chapter has been limited to the development of behavior controlled by visual stimuli, in particular those related to depth and size, the behavior analysis may be extended to all perceptual behavior, regardless of the type of stimuli that control the behavior. Perceptual behavior, like all other behavior, is seen as behavior operating on the environment and producing consequences that in turn select behavior appropriate to the particular circumstance. There is no need to infer cognitions, perceptions, or any other mental processes to account for the occurrence of the behavior. The use of such terms leads us farther away from the possible environmental determinants of the behavior and into a world where proposed causal mechanisms can neither be confirmed nor refuted.

SUMMARY

This chapter described a behavior analytic view of perceptual development as progressive changes in interactions between behavior and complex types of discriminative stimuli or cues. The chapter discussed two areas of visual perceptual development that are important to movement through space: depth perception and the perception of object constancies, in particular, size constancy. With respect to depth perception, the discriminative stimuli consist of binocular cues which result from the two eyes converging on a particular point, kinetic cues which result either from movement of the observer's head or from movement of external objects, and static (monocular) cues which control depth-appropriate responding even with only one eye. The latter cues include linear perspective and familiar size. Object constancies refer to the fact that as we move through the environment and the retinal images of objects change, we continue to behave the same toward them. For example, size constancy refers to the fact that as we move closer to or farther from objects, their retinal image becomes larger and smaller respectively, yet we still behave toward the objects as being the same size.

This chapter cited several studies conducted by developmental psychologists in which these perceptual cues were isolated in infants. The results were interpreted according to a behavior analytic perspective. In contrast to a more traditional, or cognitive view, which describes perception as a process that is used to explain perceptual behavior, a behavior analytic view is that perception is a label for particular behaviors (e.g., crawling, reaching, etc.) which come under complex stimulus control as a result of those behaviors interacting with operant contingencies of reinforcement.

7

Cognitive Development

The term "cognition" is used often in the developmental psychology literature and it is probably never defined exactly the same way twice. Considering that cognitive events, processes, and structures are wholly invented concepts, it is interesting that the definitions are so similar. Cognition may refer to (1) "knowing" (Vasta, Haith, & Miller, 1992, p. 28); (2) "internal mental processes" (Dworetzky, 1993, p. 241); (3) "thought processes and mental activities, including attention, memory, and problem solving" (Butkatko & Daehler, 1992, p. 317); and (4) the "mental processes ... that human beings use to acquire knowledge of the world" (Scarr, Weinberg, & Levine, 1986, p. 133). Based on these definitions, it is possible to extract two common characteristics of cognition: It consists of (1) internal (mental) processes that (2) enable individuals to acquire knowledge of the world. On the surface, these "definitions" of cognition fail any test of objectivity because the events and processes to which they refer cannot be observed or measured, which means they cannot be directly analyzed. Therefore, in order to make sense of the study of cognitive development, we must look at the specific behaviors that occur in children when cognitive developmental psychologists speak of "cognition."

The present chapter concentrates on the development of such behaviors in infants between birth and approximately 2 years of age. Many readers will recognize this particular age frame as the one Jean Piaget labeled as the "sensorimotor" period of cognitive development. Because Piaget's contributions have become synonymous with cognitive development, the chapter uses his framework as the basis for discussion. As in previous chapters, however, this chapter shows that the behaviors said to reflect cognitive developmental processes can be more parsimoniously explained according to the principles of behavior analysis and, moreover, that it is not necessary to infer cognitive concepts. First, the chapter presents an overview of the sensorimotor period of development in terms of some of the major changes that Piaget emphasized, and juxtaposes a cognitive–developmental and behavior analytic interpretation of those changes. Second, the chapter presents a detailed discussion and analysis of imitation and object permanence from both perspectives.

Before we describe the stages of sensorimotor development, it would be helpful for the reader to have a little background on Piaget's general approach to cognitive development. In the following section, we describe some of his basic ideas that are likely to surface in the later sections and explain them in behavior analytic terms.

PIAGETIAN CONCEPTS

Organization and Adaptation

For Piaget, intellectual or cognitive development, that is, the acquisition of knowledge about the world, results from individuals organizing their psychological structures in order to adapt to the environment. Most readers who have studied Piaget's theory of cognitive development might recall that individuals adapt to the environment through two complimentary processes, assimilation and accommodation. In behavior analytic terms, the behavior of individuals in a particular situation is a function of the success or failure of that behavior in that situation. As long as this behavior continues to be successful, Piaget would say that the individual *assimilates* the current environment (knowledge) into his or her existing psychological structures. If, however, the individual's previously acquired behavior is insufficient to interact successfully with the current environment, then the individual *accommodates* his or her psychological structures so as to adapt to the environmental demands. Ginsburg and Opper (1988) offer the following example of assimilation and accommodation in infancy. In this example, an infant is presented with a rattle with which he has never before had an opportunity to play. First the infant assimilates the rattle into existing cognitive structures:

> In the past the infant has already grasped things; for him grasping is a well-formed structure of behavior. When he sees the rattle for the first time, he tries to deal with the novel object by incorporating it into a habitual pattern of behavior. In a sense, he tries to transform the novel object to something with which he is familiar, namely, a thing to be grasped. We can say, therefore, that he assimilates the object into his framework and thereby assigns the object a "meaning." (p. 19)

When assimilation is not entirely adequate, the infant must accommodate his behavior to the environment:

> The infant tries to grasp the rattle. To do this successfully he must accommodate in more ways than are immediately apparent. First, he must accommodate

his visual activities to perceive the rattle correctly, for example, by locating it in space. Then he must reach out, adjusting his arm movements to the distance between himself and the rattle. In grasping the rattle, he must mold his fingers to its shape; in lifting the rattle he must accommodate his muscular exertion to its weight. (p. 19)

Piaget's conception of the interaction of individuals with the environment is similar to that of behavior analysis. First, both perspectives assume a behaving (that is, active) organism in an environment, although the Piagetian and behavior analytic meaning of "active" are probably not the same. Second, both assume that the child's behavior constantly conforms to the environment. The major difference lies in the processes proposed to account for that behavioral adaptation. In Piaget's approach, it is the organism who does the adapting (either by assimilating or accommodating), whereas the behavior analytic view is that it is the selective action of the consequences of the organism's behavior that gradually shapes the behavior. In Piaget's system, organizing and adapting are intentional, although not necessarily conscious processes and, thus, represent a teleological approach. The behavior analytic view, like the Darwinian theory of evolution, is selectionist.

The behavior analytic view of Piaget's concept of assimilation is simply that the stimuli present when behavior was successful in the past will evoke that behavior in the future; this is the principle of stimulus control. If the behavior is no longer successful in producing the same consequences (extinction), its variability increases, as does the probability that small variations will produce the effective behavioral consequence, and thus come under the control of the present stimulus complex. This is a behavior analytic interpretation of Piaget's concept of accommodation.

The difference between the two approaches is readily seen in the example above. From a behavior analytic perspective, the processes of assimilation and accommodation are relatively simple. As an S^D, the sight of the rattle evokes behavior, for example grasping, which has been successful in similar situations in the past. If the rattle is presented at some distance, then reaching is necessary before grasping can take place, so, the specific form of the grasp may have to be different from previous forms. Because there is inherent variability in behavior, some of the variations in reaching and grasping are successful and some are not. In a very short time, the successful variations prevail; they have been reinforced by the feel and perhaps the sound of the rattle that follows them. In contrast, the Piagetian view is that infants face many problems and must solve them. Infants do not simply reach and grasp. Rather, they "incorporate" and "transform" and "assign meaning" to the novel object. After describing infants as the originator of their actions, it doesn't seem too far a stretch to say that infants "assimilate" and "accommodate" the rattle, as if assimilating and accommodating were actions in and of themselves.

Psychological Structures

According to Piaget, the result of organization and adaptation to the environment is the development of certain psychological structures that differ depending on the child's age. The stages of cognitive development are each characterized by the existence of different psychological structures. Psychological structures are regular patterns of behavior that become more complex as the child grows older and interacts more with the environment. For infants, the organizing structure is called a scheme (Piaget called it a schema); and for children from about 7 to 11 years of age, the organizing structure is called an operation. As we will only be dealing with the development of cognitive behavior in infancy, we will only be concerned with schemes.

Schemes

The term *schemes* is used to refer to ways of acting on the world (Lamb & Bornstein, 1987) or organized patterns of behavior (Ginsburg & Opper, 1988). As Ginsburg and Opper (1988) point out, there are two important aspects to schemes. First, they are actions. In other words, schemes involve behavior. Second, schemes refer to the "basic structure" or the "essence" of behavior. The following quotation by Ginsburg and Opper (1988) on thumb-sucking illustrates these usages:

> If we examine the infant's behavior in detail, we will see that no two acts of thumb-sucking performed by one child are precisely the same. On one occasion the activity starts when the thumb is 10 inches from the mouth, on another when it is 11 inches away. At one time the thumb travels in almost a straight line to the mouth; at another time its trajectory is quite irregular. In short, if we describe behavior in sufficient detail, we find that there are no two identical actions. There is no one act of thumb-sucking, but many; in fact there are as many as the number of times the child brings the thumb to the mouth. (pp. 20–21)

For Piaget the structure of the behavior is important. What does Piaget mean by the structure of behavior? According to Ginsburg and Opper (1988), it is "an abstraction of the features common to a wide variety of acts which differ in detail" (p. 21). What is the common feature that defines thumb-sucking? It is "that the infant has acquired a regular way of getting the thumb into the mouth" (Ginsburg & Opper, 1988, p. 21). This regularity is the Piagetian concept of a scheme. Behavior analysts would recognize this description of schemes, because it is essentially a description of an operant unit (see also Stevenson, 1970). All of the individual actions involving the thumb getting to the mouth are followed by the consequence of sucking the thumb. The operant called "thumb-sucking" is an abstraction of features common to all of the different forms of the behavior. The common feature, of course, is that, all things being equal, they all produce the same consequence. This is not to say that Piaget's view and the behavior analytic view are indistinguishable, but it does indicate that Piaget's own observing behavior was under the control of the operant characteristics of behavior.

THE SENSORIMOTOR PERIOD OF COGNITIVE DEVELOPMENT

Piaget's sensorimotor period of cognitive development has been described as "the decline of egocentrism and the rise of the object concept" (Lamb & Bornstein, 1987, p. 250) to reflect the two major general changes that define this period of development. The first change, the decline of egocentrism, is that children's behavior is directed (behavior analysts would say controlled) less and less by their own bodies and more by the external environment. For example, many of the unconditioned reflexes (see chapter 5) that are prevalent at birth disappear after several months and are replaced by learned behavior that results from interactions with the environment. The second change, the rise of the object concept, is that objects in the environment begin to control more and more behavior; these conditions include occasions when objects are absent from view, but still seem to control responding. This latter phenomenon is called "object permanence" and is related to the object constancies discussed in chapter 6, in the sense that one aspect of the constancies of objects, in addition to their shape, position, and size, is their very existence.

The Substages of Sensorimotor Development

Piaget subdivided the sensorimotor period of development into six substages. The ages corresponding to these substages are not fixed, but the sequence is. This fixed sequence reflects Piaget's firm beliefs that a child's cognitive development represents qualitative changes in cognitive structures and processes and that earlier changes are required for later changes to occur. In what follows, we borrow heavily from a book we have already cited by Herbert P. Ginsburg and Sylvia Opper (1988), titled *Piaget's Theory of Intellectual Development*. This book provides a concise description and analysis of Piaget's theory.

Stage 1: Birth to 1 Month

The first sensorimotor substage may be called the stage of "reflex schemes" (Lamb & Bornstein, 1987); Piaget (1952) called it "The Use of Reflexes." As the title indicates, reflexes dominate this stage; experience, however, already begins to modify the inherited reflex activity. The sucking reflex provides a good example of the Piagetian view of the behavior of newborns. First, Piaget acknowledged that specific stimuli, such as a nipple or finger inserted in the infant's mouth, elicit the sucking reflex. Piaget also observed that sucking occurs at other times as well and in the apparent absence of any eliciting stimulus. In the attempt to explain this phenomenon, Piaget created his principle of *functional assimilation* which states that there is a basic (inherited) tendency to "exercise" structures to improve their functioning. We will not argue with Piaget's suggestion; however, we can point out that the only evidence for his principle of functional assimilation is the apparent absence of an eliciting stimulus for otherwise reflexive behavior. There are several alternative explanations. Either there is an eliciting stimulus that has been overlooked, the eliciting stimulus is internal, or there have been reinforcing consequences that have established the "feel" of the sucking movements as conditioned reinforcers (Stevenson, 1970). Ginsburg and Opper (1988) reject this last explanation on the grounds that "the extent of the association between pleasure and sucking was limited to such a short period of time" (p. 30). Piaget, however, did not control for the amount of learning that takes place during this first month; therefore, we simply do not know whether this conclusion is sound. We do know that the behavior of very young infants is susceptible to both operant and respondent conditioning and, consequently, these explanations must be experimentally, not logically, eliminated before we can accept Piaget's inference of functional assimilation.

Not only does the sucking scheme occur in the apparent absence of an eliciting stimulus, but it also occurs in the presence of other, novel objects, such as blankets or toys. Piaget called this "generalizing assimilation." Piagetians would say that because infants need to exercise their schemes, they also need objects to be used to satisfy the need. But this does no more than describe the observations without really explaining them.

The concept of stimulus generalization may help us understand Piaget's observations (Stevenson, 1970). Perhaps the most important aspect of reflexes during the first stage is that they become differentiated, which implies modification by contact with the environment. Piaget (1952) described this with his son as follows:

> [H]e bites the breast which is given him, 5 cm. from the nipple. For a moment he sucks the skin which he then lets go in order to move his mouth about 2 cm.

As soon as he begins sucking again he stops. In one of his attempts he touches the nipple with the outside of his lips and he does not recognize it. But when his search subsequently leads him accidentally to touch the nipple with the mucosa of the upper lip (his mouth being wide open), he at once adjusts his lips and begins to suck. (p. 26)

Piaget used the term "recognitory assimilation" to describe this primitive "recognition" by the infant. This discrimination or accommodation of the sucking scheme occurs only when the infant is hungry. Whatever we call it, Piaget could hardly have done a better job of describing a simple example of operant discrimination (see also Stevenson, 1970). The difference between the two accounts is that the operant interpretation follows from scientifically established principles; Piaget's interpretation is derived from observations only. As Ginsburg and Opper (1988) wrote in summarizing the first stage of sensorimotor development, "the sucking scheme has become elaborated and has developed into a fairly complex psychological structure which now incorporates the results of the infant's experiences" (p. 33). Behavior analysts would interpret the same observations as evidence for the operant conditioning and discrimination of sucking behavior. Whether operant sucking actually replaces reflexive sucking, however, cannot be determined from the observational data alone.

Stage 2: 1 to 4 Months

Piaget called this stage "The First Acquired Adaptations and the Primary Circular Reaction," which indicates that the most important advance during this stage is the appearance of *primary circular reactions*. This is the stage at which operant conditioning becomes obvious. For example, Ginsburg and Opper (1988) describe primary circular reactions as follows:

The infant's behavior by chance leads to an advantageous or interesting result; he immediately attempts to reinstate or rediscover the effective behavior and, after a process of trial and error, is successful in doing so. Thereafter the behavior and the result may be repeated; the sequence has become a "habit." (p. 34)

Notwithstanding the point made by Skinner (1989) that operant conditioning involves neither trials nor errors, this description of primary circular reactions is almost indistinguishable from an account of operant conditioning. Primary circular reactions are called *primary* because they are the earliest circular reactions. Behavior analysts would not make such a distinction between the operant conditioning observed during the first month and that observed during the next few months, but they would acknowledge the progressive complexity of the interactions. In any case, primary circular reactions are called *circular* because they are characterized by repetitions of chance discoveries. In the Piagetian account, the child "discovers" how two or more schemes can be put together or intercoordinated, and then "desires" to repeat the action that brought a pleasurable result. This type of description is common to the Piagetian approach. It implies that the infant's learning is active, but also that the activity occurs at another level—a cognitive level—beyond the observable behavior. Unfortunately, Piagetians often contrast their approach, which sees the child as an active learner, with a behavioral approach, which they misrepresent as viewing the child as a passive learner (Ginsburg & Opper, 1988). On the contrary, a behavior analytic approach does not view the child as passive; that would run counter to the nature of operant conditioning which describes changes in behavior as a function of *interactions* between behavior and the environment. A behavior analytic approach is selectionist; therefore, there is no reason to make the individual organism the originator of his or her actions or to cognitivize operant conditioning. Consequently, describing the infant as modifying his or her own behavior to conform to the environment is not seen as a productive way to understand the ontogeny of behavior.

Further similarity of the Piagetian and behavior analytic approaches is seen in Piaget's description of *primitive anticipations*. Let us look at the previous example of sucking by newborns. Newborns suck only when the nipple (or some other object) is placed in the mouth; however, older infants begin to suck when they are placed in their mother's arms. Ginsburg and Opper (1988) offer two possible ways of interpreting this observation. The first is that being placed in the mother's arms replaces the nipple as a cue for sucking which, they admit is similar to what has been called classical conditioning. The second possibility is that "the infant seems to show a primitive anticipation of feeding and that, as time goes on, this expectancy is evoked by fewer and more appropriate events than formerly" (Ginsburg & Opper, 1988, p. 37). From the perspective of the present book, the difference, of course, is that the only evidence for "expectancies" and "anticipations" is the very behavior they are said to reflect. What best explains the appearance of sucking *before* the actual nipple is placed in the mouth? Ginsburg and Opper admit that Piaget acknowledges the associations between sucking and the environmental stimuli that precede it, but that he rejects the notion that the associations are "acquired in a mechanical way." Ginsburg and Opper's (1988) account, however, leaves little doubt about what is really going on:

> [W]hen the infant nurses in the first few months he is almost invariably held in the same position, and the internal body sensations associated with this position become a part of the act of sucking. The body sensations and the move-

ments of the lips form a whole. Then, when the infant is placed in the position for nursing and the postural and kinesthetic sensations are activated, the whole cycle of the sucking act is released. (p. 37)

This would seem, as Ginsburg and Opper (1988) suggest, to involve classical conditioning, except that they add:

the association cannot be maintained if it is not consistently "confirmed" by the environment. That is, for postural cues to provoke the child's anticipatory sucking, the sucking must ordinarily be followed by milk. (p. 37)

They apparently overlook the possibility in this example that both classical and operant conditioning may be involved. Ginsburg and Opper do say that calling this anticipatory learning a conditioned reflex "omits much that is relevant" (p. 37). Although there may be some conditioned reflex functions involved in their example, it is probable that there is also operant discrimination going on, and that is what is "relevant."

Piaget also stated that during the second sensorimotor stage, the infant shows a new "curiosity" which is evidenced by the amount of time the infant spends looking at novel and familiar objects. Piaget said that such behavior is not required (presumably to sustain life) and, therefore, it is necessary to invoke the principle of functional assimilation to explain the behavior. Recall that functional assimilation was simply the tendency for infants to "exercise" already existing schemes. According to Piaget, infants seek out novel stimulation. We have already described how sensory (e.g., visual and auditory) changes function apparently as unconditioned reinforcers for human behavior (see chapter 5). These consequences shape and maintain the behavior Piaget referred to as curiosity and adequately explain such behavior without invoking functional assimilation.

Stage 3: 4 to 7 Months

Piaget (1952) called this stage "The 'Secondary Circular Reactions' and the Procedures Destined to Make Interesting Sights Last." The circular reactions in stage 3 are still considered to be circular because they involve repetition of previously learned behavior. But the circular reactions that occur during this stage are called *secondary* because they involve events and objects in the infant's external environment. As Ginsburg and Opper (1988) state, "[T]he secondary circular reactions describe the infant's newfound ability to develop schemes to reproduce interesting events that were initially discovered by chance in the *external environment*" (p. 43, emphasis added). The following excerpt from Piaget (1952) illustrates this progression of operant conditioning (he called it secondary circular reactions) from simpler instances:

> Laurent, from the middle of the third month, revealed global reactions of pleasure, while looking at the toys hanging from the hood of his bassinet.... He babbles, arches himself, beats the air with his arms, moves his legs, etc. He thus moves the bassinet and moves more vigorously.... I observe that when his movements induce those of the toys, he stops to contemplate them, far from grasping that it is he who produces them; when the toys are motionless, he resumes, and so on.... As Laurent was striking his chest and shaking his hands which were bandaged and held by strings attached to the handle of the bassinet (to prevent him from sucking), I had the idea of using the thing, and I attached the strings to the celluloid balls hanging from the hood. Laurent naturally shook the balls by chance and looked at them at once (the rattle made a noise inside them). As the shaking was repeated more and more frequently Laurent arched himself, waved his arms and legs—in short, he revealed increasing pleasure and through this maintained the interesting result.... The next day ... I connect his right hand to the celluloid balls.... The left hand is free. At first the arm movements are inadequate and the rattle does not move. Then the movements become more extensive and the rattle moves.... There seems to be conscious coordination but both arms move equally and it is not yet possible to be sure that this is not a mere pleasure reaction. The next day, the same reactions. (pp. 160–161)

Two days later, Piaget connected Laurent's right hand to the rattle and, after he shook the rattle once which "surprised and frightened" him, Laurent "swung his right arm ... with regularity, whereas the left remained almost motionless...." After six days of "experiments" with the right hand, Piaget attached a string to the left arm and observed that:

> [T]he first shake is given by chance: fright, curiosity, etc. Then, at once, there is coordinated circular reaction: this time the right arm is outstretched and barely mobile while the left swings.... This time it is therefore possible to speak definitely of secondary circular reactions. (p. 161)

We can interpret these observations according to Piagetian "principles" or behavior-analytic principles. The behavior analytic interpretation is simple enough. Right-hand movements increased in frequency in the presence of the attached string because they were followed by the movement of the celluloid balls and the sound of the rattles inside them. This effect of the sight of the moving balls and the sound of the rattles on the behavior is called reinforcement. When the left hand was attached, movements of it also increased; this is evidence for what behavior analysts refer to as *response generalization* or *response induction*. Response induction (or generalization) is the name given to the observation that reinforcement initially affects responses outside the limits of the operant class (Catania, 1992, p. 378). In this example, reinforced right-arm responses resulted in the increase in frequency of left-arm responses.

What is the Piagetian interpretation of Laurent's behavior? According to Ginsburg and Opper (1988), the learning demonstrated by Piaget's son consists of four steps:

> First, the infant's accidental movement produces an external result which is moderately novel and which therefore *interests* him. Second, the infant *perceives* that his actions are related to the external result…. Third, once the interest and the connection between act and results are established, the infant *desires* to repeat the interesting event…. The fourth step involves accommodation; the infant needs to learn the hand movements necessary for consistent reproduction of the result. (p. 45, emphasis added)

What is the evidence that the behavioral consequence "interests" the infant, or that the infant "perceives" the relation between his actions and the consequence, or that the infant "desires" to repeat the consequence, or even that it is "interesting"? The answer is that the only evidence for all of these cognitive inferences is the behavior, the consequence, and the increase in the frequency of that behavior under similar conditions, none of which require cognitive inferences or surrogates.

In fact, the observations by Piaget made with his son Laurent resemble the conjugate reinforcement procedure described in chapter 4 used by Rovee-Collier and her colleagues to study infant memory. You will recall that the concept of memory was not necessary to understand the resulting leg movements of the infants; and the concepts invoked by Piaget are equally unnecessary to understand the behavior of his son. There is, of course, no problem in calling these "secondary circular reactions" to distinguish them from "primary circular reactions," even though they are both instances of operant conditioning. However, the value of making such distinctions seems to be less than the disadvantages of classifying behavior according to structural characteristics (see chapter 2 for a similar argument).

In addition to secondary circular reactions, Ginsburg and Opper (1988) have pointed out other changes that occur during stage 3, such as "the infant's formation of classes or meaning." Consider Piaget's (1952) description of two observations of his daughter Lucienne:

> Lucienne perceives from a distance two celluloid parrots attached to a chandelier and which she has sometimes had in her bassinet. As soon as she sees them, she definitely but briefly shakes her legs without trying to act upon them from a distance…. So too … it suffices that she catches sight of her dolls from a distance for her to outline the movements of swinging them with her hand…. Thus, when seeing a doll which she has actually swung many times, Lucienne limits herself to opening and closing her hand or shaking her legs, but very briefly and without real effort. (pp. 186–187)

The Piagetian explanation is not parsimonious and involves many untestable inferences. The "abbreviation" of the behavior in this example is interpreted "as a behavioral precursor of *classification* or *meaning*" (Ginsburg and Opper, 1988, p. 46). Lucienne "does not choose to display the entire scheme when it would be quite feasible to do so," and:

> [T]he abbreviated behaviors show that Lucienne makes a beginning attempt at classification on the object. The brief kicking, for instance, is the first step toward thinking the thought, "That's the parrot; that's something to be swung." Her "understanding" is of course quite primitive and does not yet operate on a mental level. Nevertheless ... she displays behavior which indicates that the initial steps toward internalization of action are occurring. (Ginsburg & Opper, 1988, pp. 46–47)

In this example, Ginsburg and Opper seem to assume that the brief kicking is functionally equivalent to the verbal response of an older person who names the object and describes what can be done to it in order to produce a particular consequence. The evidence for this and all of the other inferences is simply the observable behavior in its context. The Piagetian explanation brings us no closer to an actual understanding.

The behavior analytic interpretation of the first observation would appeal to stimulus generalization. In other words, objects (celluloid parrots) that have in the past evoked behavior (leg shaking and arm swinging) because such behaviors have produced movement in the objects, now evoke the same form of the behavior, albeit briefer and less intense. This looks like a generalization decrement which might also occur in the early stages of discrimination training. In the second case, the diminished forms of the behaviors probably represent the effects of extinction.

Stage 4: 7 to 10 Months

Piaget (1952) called this stage "The Coordination of the Secondary Schemata and Their Application to New Situations." In addition to advances in imitation and object permanence, which we discuss separately below, stage 4 is characterized by what Piagetians call coordination of secondary schemes or secondary circular reactions. Simply stated, this means that two or more schemes that had been learned earlier are now observed to come together, that is, to be coordinated. Of course, the most important ingredient, which behavior analysts would stress, is that this increase in complexity produces the same consequences that previously were produced only by simpler actions. Consider Piaget's (1952) description in the following:

> I present Laurent with a matchbox, extending my hand laterally to make an obstacle to his prehension. Laurent tries to pass over my hand, or to the side, but he does not attempt to displace it. As each time I prevent his passage, he ends by storming at the box while waving his hand....

Piaget reported that the same reactions occur 8, 10, and 21 days later, but then 43 days later

> Laurent reacts quite differently.... I present a box of matches above my hand, but behind it so that he cannot reach it without setting the obstacle aside. But ... suddenly he tries to hit my hand as though to remove or lower it; I let him do it to me and he grasps the box—I recommence to bar his passage, but using as a screen ... a ... cushion.... Laurent tries to reach the box, and, bothered by the obstacle, he at once strikes it, definitely lowering it until the way is clear. (p. 217)

Piaget concluded that what Laurent has done is to "borrow from a familiar scheme: the scheme of striking" and to use this scheme, not as "an end in itself, but as a means." A behavior analytic interpretation of Piaget's observations is simple. Piaget nicely described the procedure of extinction, which occurred when he prevented Laurent from grasping the matchbox. Predictably, the behavior became more variable and, specifically, more intense. Then, Piaget permitted his son's hitting to move Piaget's hand out of the way, at which time Laurent grasped the matchbox. This example nicely illustrates the effects of extinction and the differential reinforcement of a slightly different form of Laurent's behavior. The Piagetian explanation, however, is not parsimonious. Piagetians would say that Laurent had the goal in mind from the beginning and that, when prevented from attaining it, he demonstrated some originality in utilizing schemes he developed in other situations. The result, of course, is the coordination of two schemes (Ginsburg & Opper, 1988). This is the first time that Piaget would attribute intentionality and intelligence to the infant.

In addition to the coordination of secondary schemes during stage 4, the infant establishes more complex relationships between objects and demonstrates more complex forms of anticipation. Ginsburg and Opper (1988) state that when Laurent removes Piaget's hand and the cushion to attain the matchbox (a goal), it is as if he "understands" that the obstacle stands in a certain relationship to the goal; the hand or cushion is *in front of* the matchbox, and it must be removed *before* the matchbox can be grasped.

To further illustrate the development of more complex forms of anticipation, Ginsburg and Opper (1988) cite another example from Piaget. Apparently, Piaget's daughter (Jacqueline) liked grape juice in a glass but not soup in a bowl. Consequently, when she saw or even heard the spoon coming from the glass, she opened her mouth; but when she saw or heard the spoon coming from the bowl, she closed her mouth. Ginsburg and Opper said that the child used a "system of meanings in the service of anticipation" (p. 53). The sight or sound of the spoon from the soup is called a signifier of the soup. The meaning for the infant is the unpleasant soup, and she closed her mouth not to the soup itself, but to its meaning (Ginsburg & Opper, 1988).

Again, these inferences are unnecessary, especially if we can account for this relatively simple set of relationships in a more parsimonious manner. In this case, a behavioral interpretation would suggest that the sight and sound of the spoon coming from the glass evoke opening the mouth because it has been followed in the past by getting juice, a reinforcer. Conversely, closing the mouth upon seeing or hearing the spoon coming from the bowl occurred because that behavior had been followed in the past by avoidance of the soup, also a reinforcer.

This hypothesis could be tested by selecting an arbitrary class of responses, such as head turning or leg kicking, and arbitrary stimuli such as differently colored lights. In the presence of the red light, head turns to the left are followed by juice and in the presence of a green light, head turns to the right are initially followed by the removal of the soup. As a result of this training, we would expect the red light to evoke left head turns and the green light to evoke right head turns. Such a demonstration would strengthen the plausibility of a discrimination interpretation. This interpretation does not require moving to a nonbehavioral level of *meanings* and *anticipations* in order to account for the behavior. The difference is that the behavior analytic interpretation is based on established principles of science, whereas the Piagetian interpretations are simply ways of rephrasing the actual observations. They are examples of reifications of the observed facts, or circular explanations.

Stage 5: 10 to 18 Months

This is the stage of *tertiary circular reactions*. They are called tertiary (third order) because, after the child causes something to happen accidentally, as in the primary and secondary circular reactions, he or she then deliberately varies the way in which the event is brought about (Lamb & Bornstein, 1987). Piaget (1952) subtitled this stage "The 'Tertiary Circular Reaction' and the Discovery of New Means Through Active Experimentation." Dworetzky (1993) describes an infant in this stage of development who, while sitting in her high chair eating oatmeal, drops a handful over the side again and again but each time in a different way. According to Dworetzky, the infant "learns that (1) things fall down, not up; (2) the force of the throw determines the radius of the splat; and (3) you can make an interesting pattern on the floor with oatmeal" (p. 247). The first two things the infant learns make it sound like she is a little physicist learning about the laws of gravity. The third reflects the reinforcing consequence maintaining the behavior, that is, the interesting patterns the oatmeal makes when it hits the floor. The more parsimonious account of Dworetzky's example is that complex behavior is more likely to produce variable consequences, which are more reinforcing in older children than in babies (Stevenson, 1970). Stevenson used the phrase "empirical groping" to describe the child's behavior of producing variations in consequences using objects, and counters a Piagetian interpretation by saying: "[T]he child does not 'try' to produce variation in the consequences of an act; behavior simply will not develop unless variable consequences are produced" (p. 105).

Stage 6: 18 to 24 Months

Piaget (1952) called this final stage of sensorimotor development "The Invention of New Means Through Mental Combinations." Stage 6 is considered a pivotal stage, because it forms "the transition to the next period of development in which the infant is able to use mental symbols and words to refer to absent objects" (Ginsburg & Opper, 1988, p. 61). The following example, in which Piaget puts a watch chain into a matchbox, is used by Piaget (1952), and later by Ginsburg and Opper (1988), to illustrate the beginnings of symbolic thought. According to Piaget (1952),

> I put the chain back into the box and reduce the opening to 3 mm. It is understood that Lucienne is not aware of the functioning of the opening and closing of the matchbox and has not seen me prepare the experiment. She only possesses the two ... schemata: turning the box over in order to empty it of its contents, and sliding her finger into the slit to make the chain come out. It is of course this last procedure that she tries first: she puts her finger inside and gropes to reach the chain, but fails completely. A pause follows during which Lucienne manifests a very curious reaction bearing witness not only to the fact that she tries to think out the situation and to represent to herself through mental combination the operations to be performed, but also to the role played by imitation in the genesis of representations. Lucienne mimics the widening of the slit.... She looks at the slit with great attention; then, several times in succession, she opens and shuts her mouth, at first slightly, then wider and wider! Apparently Lucienne understands the existence of a cavity subjacent to the slit and wishes to enlarge that cavity.... Soon ... Lucienne unhesitatingly puts her finger in the slit and, instead of trying as before to reach the chain, she pulls so as to enlarge the opening. She succeeds and grasps the chain. (pp. 337–338)

If we strip this observation of inferences and leave only the behavioral observations, we are left with the following. Within Lucienne's field of view, her father puts the chain inside the matchbox and opens the cover to 3 millimeters. Then she opens and closes her mouth. Then she puts her finger in the 3 mm slit and pulls, which results in the cover opening. The question is how to best interpret these actions. Let us assume that the opening and closing of her mouth is somehow functionally related to the barely open matchbox. We would have to assume a history in which other, perhaps similar, behaviors that have resembled the movements of inanimate objects have produced reinforcing consequences. If so, it is possible that in this case, her imitative behavior then serves as an S^D for her manual behavior of putting her finger in the matchbox and pulling open the cover. Without knowledge of her particular learning history, this interpretation requires significant inferences; however, the inferences are of potentially observable and testable events. According to a Piagetian interpretation, because the stage 6 child is not yet fully capable of representational mental thought, she can only think out problems by using overt behavior to represent the solutions.

To summarize, all of the observations that characterize cognitive development in the sensorimotor period of development can be parsimoniously explained according to the laws of behavior analysis without inferring hypothetical cognitive processes or making the infant the originator of his or her own actions. We have thus far omitted the topics of imitation and object permanence in our description of the six sensorimotor substages of development. Because Piaget considered the development of imitation and object permanence to be two of the most important repertoires that develop during the sensorimotor period, we will treat them separately.

IMITATION AND OBJECT PERMANENCE

Most developmental textbooks (e.g., Dworetzky, 1993), as well as standard textbooks on learning (e.g., Chance, 1993), describe learning in humans occurring as a result of three processes: operant and respondent conditioning, imitation (usually called modeling), and verbal rules. From a behavior analytic perspective, all of these represent function-altering operations in that they alter the control of behavior by stimuli (Schlinger & Blakely, 1994). Unlike other psychologists, behavior analysts interpret imitation and rule-governed behavior as operant behavior. In this section we present both Piagetian and behavior analytic views of the development of imitation in infancy. Specifically, we provide (1) a brief overview of Piaget's view of imitation, (2) a discussion of some of the literature on imitation in very young infants, and (3) a description of the role of learning, especially operant conditioning, in imitation in infants.

The importance of imitation for human learning cannot be overstated. As Meltzoff (1988) has written, imitation "provides for a kind of Lamarckian evolutionary change in humans. Imitation provides an efficient channel through which acquired behaviors, skills, customs, and traditions may be incorporated by the young" (p. 319) (see Figure 7.1).

FIGURE 7.1. A toddler imitates adult behavior. (Photo by H. Schlinger)

Piaget's View of Imitation

Piaget's view of the development of imitation is widely accepted by many developmental psychologists and, to be consistent with our treatment of his six substages of sensorimotor development, we will present it here. Rather than going through all six substages again, however, we will adopt Meltzoff's (1988) strategy for the purposes of abbreviation, and collapse the development of imitation during the six sensorimotor stages into three broad levels of imitative development. The first level of imitative skill is from birth to approximately 8 to 12 months of age when, according to Piaget, imitation is limited to the repetition of actions the infant has previously performed and is confined to elementary vocal and visual movements and to grasping (Ginsburg & Opper, 1988). Imitation during the early stages of this level begins only as functional assimilation; in other words, the infant does not yet reproduce the behavior of someone else, but merely continues (or exercises) his or her own behavior.

At about 12 months of age, level 2 imitation becomes possible. This includes the imitation of facial gestures such as tongue protrusion. For Piaget, the infant at this level can now imitate the movements of a model that she cannot see in herself, as well as imitate novel actions. Piaget (1952) described how he "alternately bent and straightened" his finger in front of his daughter (Jacqueline). The first time he did this, Jacqueline waved her hand. Seven days later, he did the same thing and this time Jacqueline imitated his actions using her whole hand. Piaget reported that three days later she correctly imitated the action. At this level, the infant is restricted only to movements that are similar to those she is capable of performing. In Piagetian terms, his daughter assimilated the novel behavior of her father (bending and straightening his finger) into an already existing scheme (bending and straightening her hand). A second restriction is that imitation is only approximate, that is, it rarely occurs perfectly on the first trial (Ginsburg & Opper, 1988). If the behavior changes on successive trials, then we can infer learning. Piaget might describe the learning as trial and error, even though this is probably not an apt description of the actual process.

The final level of the development of imitation emerges from about 18 to 24 months. At this time untrained, deferred imitation occurs (Meltzoff, 1988), or as Ginsburg and Opper (1988) describe it, the infant now has the "capacity to represent mentally an object or action which is not perceptually present" (p. 62). How do infants do this? According to Ginsburg and Opper (1988), "when faced with new models, the infant no longer needs to perform overtly trial attempts at imitation; instead, he now tries out the various movements mentally. Having made the necessary mental adjustments, the infant can then perform the correct action" (p. 62). As cited in Ginsburg and Opper (1988), Piaget (1951) described an example in which Jacqueline witnessed a friend of hers having a tantrum to get out of a playpen and then the very next day, "she herself screamed in her playpen and tried to move it...." (p. 63). Ginsburg and Opper (1988) assert, "[T]he internalization of the action is quite clear. The infant does not reproduce the scene at the time of its occurrence, but at some later period. Therefore, representation was required for the child to preserve the original scene for it to be evoked at a later time" (p. 63). Piaget's interpretation is similar to other interpretations of delayed imitation which also infer cognitive mediating mechanisms (e.g., Bandura, 1977). Once again, the only evidence for the mental representation is the behavior to be explained—the time lag between the model's behavior and the ultimate occurrence of the observer's behavior.

Based on Piaget's account of the development of imitation in infancy, we address two issues. The first is the accuracy of Piaget's interpretations concerning the capacity of infants for certain kinds of imitative behavior. The second issue concerns the role of learning in the development of imitative behavior. We will discuss vocal imitation in infants in chapter 8 on language.

Imitation in Infancy

Meltzoff and his colleagues have conducted a series of studies from which they concluded that very young infants are capable of imitation (Meltzoff, 1985; Meltzoff & Moore, 1977, 1983). In a recent summary of this research, Meltzoff (1988) reports that (1) 14- and 24-month-old infants reliably imitate the object-directed behaviors of a model, even after a 24-hour period during which the infants were not allowed to perform the imitative response; (2) 9-month-old infants reliably imitate a variety of arbitrary object-directed behaviors, even with a 24-hour delay imposed between the observation period and the demonstration period; (3) 2- to 3-week-old infants reliably imitate facial gestures, including lip protrusion, mouth opening, tongue protrusion, and sequential finger movement even when a brief delay was imposed between the modeled and imitated behavior; and (4) newborns (with a mean age of 32 hours) reliably imitate mouth opening and tongue protrusion gestures. According to Meltzoff (1988), these findings show that infants in the first 72 hours of life can imitate at least two facial displays. Although learning probably accounts for the variability seen in the imitative behavior of the older infants, it is difficult to infer learning as the determinant of the imitative behaviors in the neonates, if these findings are valid and reliable.

Although the findings and claims of Meltzoff and his associates have been challenged (see Dworetzky, 1993, p. 201; Poulson, Nunes, & Warren, 1989, for brief reviews), there does seem to be some form of imitation in human neonates. The major question concerning infant imitation is how to best account for the differences between individuals. It would not be earth-shattering to discover that there might be some inherited, perhaps reflexive, behavioral relations involving the imitation of facial gestures in humans. Recent longitudinal and cross-sectional studies conducted with infants under 6 months of age that show a decline in the imitation of mouth movements (see Poulson et al., 1989, for a review) suggest that these imitative relations may be reflexive. Even so, the research literature is not unequivocal. In other words, the broader imitative relation is not as inevitable as the sucking reflex or the pupillary reflex is; that is, there are significant individual differences in this behavior between infants. It is always possible that these individual differences are related to the development of the central nervous system mechanisms underlying such behavior. In any case, the more important issue surrounding imitation in infants is not whether there is some rudimentary form of imitation in neonates or even the normative course of specific imitative behaviors, but, rather, what are the determinants of the generalized imitative skills that permit children (and adults) to acquire so much novel behavior?

The Role of Learning in Infant Imitation

With respect to any behavior, we can ask three questions: what, when, and why (or how). The *what* question is an empirical question which simply asks: What behavior is observed under what circumstances? Concerning imitation, the question is: What do infants imitate and under what circumstances? The answers are likely to be determined by the maturational status of the infant's central nervous system and the past and present environmental conditions related to the particular behavior. The *when* question "is a developmental question, asking at what point infants exhibit imitative behavior...." (Masur, 1988, p. 301). In our previous discussion of imitation, we have followed the trend found in most developmental accounts and attempted to answer the *what* and *when* developmental questions of imitation. In fact, Piaget's most important contribution to the study of development in children is probably his careful observations and descriptions of the changes in his children's behaviors over time (Dworetzky, 1993). The question that is inadequately answered by developmental psychologists is the *how* question, or the processes by which imitative relations come about. This addresses the function of imitative behavior at different times in development (Masur, 1988). It is fundamentally about the genesis of behavior or *how* it comes to be, and the answers ultimately provide the scientific explanations for the subject matter. As we pointed out in chapter 2, developmental psychologists frequently assume behavior has been explained if the what and when questions have been answered. We also noted that in many cases the only way the how question can be answered is by experimentation. When the dependent variable consists of changes in infant behavior, however, it is often impossible to conduct an experimental analysis. This is because their behavior is constantly being changed as a result of interactions with the environment involving variables that researchers cannot control with any degree of confidence. Therefore, the experiments that can be conducted can only provide plausible answers or explanations. The plausibility of the explanations rests on the reliability of the findings and the soundness of the scientific principles used to interpret them. It is not possible to manipulate genes experimentally in order to test genetic explanations of imitation. Even if it were, a genetic explanation would not provide the whole answer. Therefore, the only independent variables at the disposal of psychologists are environmental ones.

Generalized Imitation

Behavior analytic accounts of imitation have centered around the concept of generalized imitation (Kymissis & Poulson, 1990). Imitation may be broadly conceptualized (i.e., defined) as situations in which the behavior of one person (the observer) is similar to the behavior of another person (the model) as a result of the former having observed the latter. The term *generalized imitation*, however, stresses the power of imitation as a learning mechanism and, thus, may permit psychologists to understand the acquisition of social, emotional, verbal and other behaviors (Poulson et al., 1989). According to Poulson and Kymissis (1988):

> Generalized imitation refers to behavior that (a) is topographically similar to that of a model, (b) is controlled by virtue of the fine-grained topography of the model's behavior, and (c) occurs in the absence of environmental consequences for its occurrence, or occurs under consequences that are reduced from those during training. (p. 325)

For the purposes of the present chapter, we will concentrate on the nature of generalized imitation and on experiments that have demonstrated it with nonvocal behaviors.

Although generalized imitation has been shown in mentally retarded children (e.g., Baer, Peterson, & Sherman, 1967); schizophrenic children (e.g., Lovaas, Freitas, Nelson, & Whalen, 1967); mute psychotic adults (e.g., Sherman, 1965); and normally developing preschool children (e.g., Baer & Deguchi, 1985), few studies to date have shown that generalized imitation in infants can be trained. One such study was conducted by Poulson and Kymissis (1988). Using a multiple baseline design across subjects, Poulson and Kymissis (1988) studied the effects of modeling and contingent praise on the motor response topographies of three 10-month-old infants. During some sessions, the infants' mothers modeled prescribed responses with randomly selected toys (see Table 7.1 for a list of infant response topographies with the toys), and during subsequent sessions the mothers praised the infants if they emitted responses that were topographically similar to their modeled responses. The effects of the modeling and praise were ascertained during nonreinforced probe trials interspersed among the training trials. The results showed systematic increases in the infants' response topographies as a result of modeling and praise, demonstrating that generalized imitation occurs in infants. Figure 7.2 shows the results for each of the three infants.

There are several implications of such a demonstration. First, by having mothers model behavior and praise their infants for imitating the same behavior, the Poulson and Kymissis (1988) experiment suggests a plausible explanation for the normal development of generalized imitation: that normally occurring interactions between mothers and infants consist of modeling and praise or other forms of attention for correct imitation. Second, these results suggest a plausible process for the acquisition of novel behavior in infants without moving to the nonobservable level of cognitive processes.

Table 7.1. Infant Response Topographies Trained by Poulson and Kymissis
(1988)

1. Toss ball into air	*24. Stack two small blocks
2. Push truck across table	25. Drop two blocks into box
3. Tap hammer five times	26. Pour ball out of bowl
4. Place shovel into bucket	*27. Put doll into crib
5. Pull up string to align toy	28. Lift and push plunger of top
6. Squeak rubber bear twice	*29. Drop cylinder into hole
7. Push the clown over	*30. Place clown onto stand
8. Raise book over head	31. Place doll into carriage
* 9. Hold horn with lips to mouthpiece	*32. Fit one box into another
10. Hold football up in air	33. Open and close pliers
11. Put pillow case on top of head	34. Place red barrel over blue
12. Hug pillow doll and swivel body	35. Place ring on upright pole
*13. Peer through tube at parent	*36. Fit cat onto ring on table
*14. Turn piano upright and play	37. Clap hands of floppy doll
15. Move airplane over head	*38. Hit ball with wrench
16. Toss paper ball into air	39. Touch finger puppet to head
17. Turn mirror over onto table	*40. Touch pony's tail to cheek
*18. Hold telephone receiver to ear	41. Uncover and hold block under cloth
19. Peer through plastic ring at parent	42. Lift ring by string
20. Tip cap onto head twice	*43. Place cylinder into cube
*21. Spin windmill rattle	44. Roll car across table
22. Pull helicopter by string	45. Squeak rubber apple twice
*23. Remove and replace puzzle piece	

Note. Asterisks indicate responses not producing praise during treatment.
Source: Reprinted with permission from Academic Press.

SEARCH BEHAVIOR AND OBJECT PERMANENCE

As we have already noted, when developmental psychologists speak of *object permanence* they usually refer to a theoretical construct that purportedly explains the behavior of continuing to respond to absent objects. The following is Ginsburg and Opper's (1988) description of the object concept problem for Piaget:

---→

Figure 7.2. Results of the effects of modeling and contingent praise on the motor response topographies of three 10-month-old infants by Poulson and Kymissis (1988). Shown are the percentages of 1 minute toy-presentation trials in which the infant emitted the targeted topographical responses over consecutive experimental sessions. Baseline sessions are shown with open circles on a line graph for the training trials and an open histogram for the probe trials. Model and praise treatment sessions are shown with closed circles on a line graph and a shaded histogram for the probe trials. (Source: Reprinted with permission from Academic Press.)

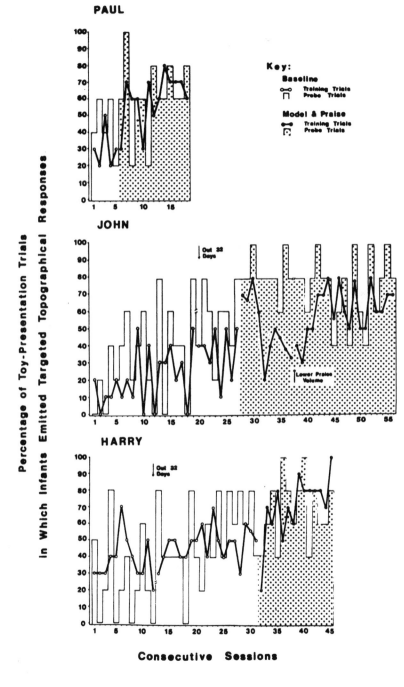

Consecutive Sessions

> An "object," according to Piaget, is something which the individual conceives of as having a reality of its own, and as extending beyond his immediate perception. For example, a man who has hung his coat in a closet *knows* several hours later that, in all likelihood, the coat is still there. Although he cannot see or touch the coat, he *knows* that it remains behind the closet door. The object, therefore, involves more than direct perception of external reality; the object is conceived to exist independently of a person's perception of it. (p. 41, emphasis added)

According to a behavior analytic view, the question of object permanence is whether an organism's behavior is still somehow controlled by stimuli associated with the absent object or not. The behavior analytic approach, that objects are sources of stimulus control over different kinds of behavior, is simpler than the cognitive version of objects as possessing their own reality beyond "immediate perception." The question, of course, is how best to account for behavior related to absent objects. It is clear that some of this behavior is quite different from behavior controlled by present objects. For example, a man will pick up his coat and put it on when it is within reach. When the coat is on the other side of the room, the behavior related to the coat may consist of walking toward the coat or talking about the coat. When it is absent, the man may talk about his coat, or he may walk toward the place where he last saw it. But he cannot pick it up or put it on.

According to Piaget, behavior related to absent objects develops over time as a result of interactions with the environment. As we have seen, the result of these interactions is that new cognitive structures—schemas— are formed that determine the infant's behavior that is called *object concept* or *object permanence*. As we have already noted, for Piaget, object permanence develops during the six substages of the sensorimotor period of cognitive development. In fact, Piaget considered the emergence of fully developed object permanence as the defining feature of the transition from the sensorimotor period to the preoperational period of development. Rather than describing the details of the changes in the object concept during the sensorimotor stage, we concentrate on the behavior of the infant during only one of the substages, stage 4, largely because Piaget himself considered this stage to be crucial in the development of the object concept and, consequently, many researchers have focused their research efforts on this stage.

Researchers have examined two types of search behavior in children. First, they have looked at infants' search behavior of hidden objects, behavior indicative of the classic problem of object permanence described by Piaget. Second, researchers have studied infants' search behavior of objects located in space either when the objects or the infants' positions are altered (Acreldo, 1985). Typically, cognitive psychologists describe the problems in terms of the infant's "understanding" of spatial relations or "the nature of the infant's hypotheses about the location of objects in space" (Acreldo, 1985, p. 119), as if understanding and hypothesizing are the real dependent variables. Although we devote our discussion to the development of the search behavior of hidden objects, we also briefly describe the development of spatial search behavior when it is relevant.

Object Concept during Stages 1 through 3

During stages 1 and 2, there is virtually no active search of objects that have moved out of sight; infants continue to look in the same place they did before the object disappeared. This is understandable because behavior has simply not yet come under the control of the stimuli reliably associated with the disappearance of an object. In stage 3, four new behavior patterns regarding object permanence emerge (Ginsburg & Opper, 1988). We describe the two that are most relevant for our current discussion. First, infants begin to show what Piagetians refer to as "visual anticipation of the future positions of objects" (Ginsburg & Opper, 1988, p. 48). This means, for example, that if a moving object passes behind a screen, infants will direct their gaze to the place where the object should reemerge. This behavior is similar to their behavior when they "play" peek-a-boo. Their following or continued looking is reinforced by the reappearance of the object, which thereby maintains future behavior in the absence of the object. It is not necessary to say that the behavior is based on the "appreciation of the permanence of objects." Also during stage 3, if an object is completely hidden, any previously object-directed behavior by the infant ceases. The second important advance that occurs during this stage is that if the object is left partially visible, the infant's object-directed behavior will continue. Harris (1987) has noted, however, that errors still occur even when the object is partially visible, and that these behaviors need to be included in any account of the development of search behavior. Once again, a behavior analytic interpretation adequately accounts for these behaviors. The stimulus characteristics of the partially visible object continue to control the infant's looking, reaching, and grasping. Those behaviors have not yet come under the control of the object being completely hidden.

Stage 4: The AB Search Error

Piaget described the occurrence of a simple "error" among infants in stage 4. If an object is hidden under a cloth at position A, infants will lift up the cloth and retrieve the object. If, however, while the object is still within sight of the infant, it is hidden under a cloth at position B, infants will continue to search under cloth A. This "error" is referred to as the "stage 4 AB search error." Of course, it is only an error from an adult's perspective. From a behavior analytic perspective, there are no errors in behavior: Behavior has causes, and the task for psychologists is to uncover them through experimental analysis. But, let us pursue Piaget's stage 4 error a little further.

Piaget described this error after having made observations of his own children. Interestingly, the stage 4 search error has become one of the most studied of the Piagetian phenomena. Based on what researchers have discovered, Piaget's initial conclusions regarding the stage 4 error have been substantially modified. For example, the presence of an interposed delay between the rehiding of the object at B and permitting the infant to begin searching for it has a profound effect on the outcome. If the infant is permitted to begin searching immediately after the object has disappeared, the error is eliminated, whereas if a delay of even one second is imposed, errors begin to emerge (Harris, 1987). Moreover, even with a delay, if the object remains visible, for example by using a transparent cloth, errors still occur, which means that "the disappearance of the object is not a precondition for error" (Harris, 1987, p. 169). The conclusion to be drawn is that the delay, not the visibility of the object, is the critical factor in producing search errors.

In addition to the presence or absence of a delay, search behavior is affected by the nature of the covers under which the objects are placed. Perhaps not surprisingly, if the cover over B is identical to the cover over A, errors are more likely, whereas if the B cover is distinctively different, errors decrease. The issue of different covers is discussed in terms of infants' use of landmarks to guide search behavior (Harris, 1987). Researchers have found that children between 6 and 12 months of age increasingly use landmarks to guide spatial responses (Acredlo, 1978; Acredlo & Evans, 1980). In fact, the findings from a variety of studies, including those involving visual tracking, reaching, and walking, show (1) a consistent improvement in these behaviors with age and (2) an increasing tendency for environmental stimuli associated with objects' spatial location to be related to accurate search behavior (Acredlo, 1985). Moreover, researchers have found different results when infants are studied in their own homes versus the laboratory, especially in studies which used training trials.

For example, Acredlo (1985) reported on her efforts to replicate a study by Bremner (1978) on infant spatial referencing. In studies on spatial referencing, infants are usually seated at a table and presented with an object permanence task in which an object is located either to the left or right of a midline. After training, infants are rotated to the opposite side of the table and then allowed to search for the object. Infants at about 9 months of age tend to be egocentric, that is, they tend to search for the object on the same side of the table in which previous searches were successful. Acreldo (1979) suggests that these perseverative responses occur either because they have become a "motor habit" or because they depend on "a spatial reference system centered on the body." Such a distinction does not recognize that the "spatial reference system" is really a context that controls the egocentric response because the response has been successful (i.e., reinforced) in the presence of that context. In his study, Bremner (1978) minimized the effect of the infant being exposed to many training trials simply by rotating the infants to the other side of the table after the object was hidden on the first trial. The result was that the proportion of infants emitting egocentric responses dropped. As Acreldo (1985) points out, however, Bremner's study was carried out in the infants' homes which might have confounded the results.

Acreldo (1978) replicated Bremner's study with infants at home, in a landmark-free laboratory, and in an unfamiliar landmark-filled office. Her results showed less egocentric behavior by the home-tested infants than infants in either the landmark-free laboratory or the unfamiliar landmark-filled office. Of the several interpretations of these results offered by Acreldo (1978), the one that seems the most logical from a behavior analytic position is that "having had a great deal of practice moving about the home and having repeatedly encountered the problems inherent in an egocentric system, the infant has developed sufficiently detailed knowledge of the spatial layout so that individual landmarks as direct cues are unnecessary" (p. 667). Such an interpretation, however, appeals more to the knowledge the infant has acquired than to the effects of the contingencies of reinforcement for accurate and successful behavior in a given context. In fact, Acreldo's (1978) results shouldn't be surprising to behavior analysts. From a behavior analytic perspective, infants don't "use landmarks" or develop knowledge; rather, the "landmarks" become S^Ds that evoke accurate spatial responding because they have been differentially associated with reinforcing consequences.

Harris (1987) has reviewed several "theories" that attempt to account for the data on the stage 4 error, one of which by Cornell (1978), he describes as "Skinnerian," although we may not entirely agree with him on this point. Harris criticizes Cornell's approach by asking why the infant searches under A on the very first trial before there has been any reinforcement for the behavior at that place before. The explanation seems to be that at this particular point in the infant's development, search behavior has been reinforced sufficiently at the initial place of disappearance. Thereafter, the AB problem seems to be one of discrimination. After search behavior has been reinforced at location A, searching at location B becomes more probable when there is no delay and when the cover is different. As infants grow older, the complexity of the contingencies with which their behavior interacts also increases. This complexity probably includes delays, not only between antecedent stimuli and behavior, but also between behavior and consequences.

In conclusion, let us mention a distinction suggested by Harris (1987) between search behavior and object permanence. Harris (1987) refers to search behavior "as a set of observations which require explanation" and to object permanence "as a theoretical construct which may or may not offer a convincing explanation for the development of search behavior" (p. 155). This is a distinction that behavior analysts should find appealing. On the one hand, we have the behavior of infants we call *search behavior* (which may include visual tracking, reaching, uncovering, and grasping). On the other hand, we have Piaget's construct of object permanence, the only evidence for which is the presence or absence of accurate search behavior. The behavior of searching is an objective, measurable behavioral datum; the concept of object permanence is a hypothetical construct. The general cognitive developmental approach, following from Piaget, is to make some general observations, summarize them with a term, and then transform the term into a theoretical or cognitive construct that has an existence of its own, for example, when the term is used to refer to something the child possesses. The next step is to use the term to account for the very behavioral observations made in the first place—a circular explanation. (Murray [1981] has made similar points concerning the Piagetian construct of conservation.)

The problem is that "the positing of hypothetical structures to account for behaviors which accrue and which are in a continuous state of change is at best gratuitous, particularly when the structures are essentially response-defined rather than tied to specific antecedents or manipulable stimulation" (Lipsitt, 1981, p. 36). Unfortunately, the "units" of analysis for cognitive developmental psychologists (e.g., schema, concepts, etc.) are not subject to direct measurement. The units of behavior analysis, in contrast, are objective and can therefore form the basis of an experimental analysis of behavior, which even nonbehavior analysts have called for (e.g., Harris, 1987).

SUMMARY

Most traditional developmental psychologists define cognition as internal processes that enable individuals to obtain knowledge of the world.

A behavior analytic view is to look at the behaviors from which such cognitive processes are inferred and to study them directly. This chapter focused on Piaget's sensorimotor stage of cognitive development. The chapter introduced Piaget's terms and concepts and then presented excerpts from his own writings illustrating these concepts for each substage of the sensorimotor period of development. Behavior analytic interpretations of these concepts supported the conclusion that, in each case, the behavior from which the cognitive concept was inferred was important in its own right as a variable of study, and that it was not necessary to infer cognitive structures and processes to understand or explain the behavior. The behaviors from which Piaget's concepts were derived can be parsimoniously explained according to the laws of behavior analysis. Because Piaget considered the concepts of imitation and object permanence to be especially important developmental milestones during the first two years of life, the chapter extended this same analysis to them.

8

Language Development

One of the first problems in discussing language development is to define what language is and what it is not. Of course, asking the question in this way is consistent with the common practice in psychology and philosophy of asking about the true nature of various human phenomena. For example, psychologists frequently ask whether some instance of behavior is truly language, or thinking, or a sign of intelligence, etc. Such questions are flawed because they are based on an essentialist approach to psychology (Palmer & Donahoe, 1992). With respect to behavior we call language, essentialism assumes, first, that there is a quality or essence that can be called *language*. One implication of this initial assumption is that this essence of language has an existence independent of the observed behavior. Once that assumption has been made, psychologists and philosophers begin looking for evidence of the presence of language. Following from the philosophical (i.e., Cartesian) traditions of psychology, essentialist scholars assume that the true essence of language is located somewhere in the mind. Unfortunately, because mental events are always inferred and never independently observed, psychologists must find other evidence for their existence. The only evidence for the existence of essentialist qualities in the mind is the behavior of individuals. This means that in the study of language acquisition, language theorists must take the gestural and vocal behavior of young children and ask whether some particular instance is really being "used" by the child as a symbol, or what the real meaning of an utterance is, or whether it is true language. This traditional approach to the study of language also assumes that language reflects an essential meaning, with the implication that the meaning has an existence separate from the observed behavior in its context. Unfortunately, the dictionary definition of language as "the expression or communication of thoughts and feelings by means of vocal sounds, and combinations of such sounds, to which meaning is attributed" (*Webster's New World Dictionary*, 1984) also reflects the essentialistic and fundamentally philosophical approach that has dominated the psychological study of language to date.

The present chapter uses the term "language" as Skinner (1957) did to refer to the verbal "practices of a linguistic community" (p. 2). By "practices" Skinner meant the contingencies of reinforcement in a given verbal community that are responsible for particular forms and functions of linguistic behavior. Skinner also noted that within a larger verbal community there exist more specialized communities or audiences, such as social or scientific groups, that control more specialized forms of linguistic behavior. In the present chapter, we are speaking of the behavior of individuals—primarily speakers—within verbal communities defined by the contingencies of reinforcement therein. Although "verbal behavior"—Skinner's (1957) term for the individual's language—can take many different forms (e.g., vocal, sign, writing), this chapter discusses only speech and follows the standard treatment of speech found in many developmental textbooks and other treatments of language development. As in previous chapters, we restrict our discussion to the development of language in infancy, during approximately the first two years of life, even though the word "infant," from the Latin *infans*, means literally "incapable of speaking."

The treatment of language development in this chapter emphasizes the function of language over its form. We consider the topics of speech perception, prespeech, and early speech production. As many developmental textbooks do, we include a discussion of the nature–nurture debate regarding language development. The chapter shows why Chomsky's analysis of language is flawed and points out the overwhelming evidence for the environment as the major determinant of language and for behavior analysis as a way to understand that relationship. Topics such as infant "preferences" for certain speech stimuli, including the possibility of prenatal learning, are covered in chapter 9 on social development and attachment relations.

SPEECH PERCEPTION

Psychologists and linguists often distinguish between producing and comprehending language. In this essentialistic fashion, language is dichotomized into expressive (productive) and receptive forms. It is often said that children can understand language before they can produce it, that is, that receptive language develops before expressive language. The evidence for this is that the behavior of children can be controlled by verbal stimuli (e.g., as S^Ds) before they can speak "meaningful words." For example, a child will pick up and drink a glass of milk when the parent says, "Drink your milk," before the child can say "milk." That receptive language develops before expressive language is not the only inevitable conclusion from such evidence; indeed, such evidence seems to strengthen the notion that there is an essence of language that develops. In fact, the control over behavior by linguistic stimuli enables cognitive psychologists to talk about language as a set of "symbols" whose "meaning" must be "decoded" in order to be "understood." The position taken in the present book is that language is not symbolic of anything. It has no meaning separate from the functional relations involving the behavior, so listeners do not need to "decode" anything.

Traditional language scholars know that children don't "understand" language immediately after birth; however, some authors contend that the foundations of linguistic understanding are not only present in neonates but are also innate. Studies on categorical perception (defined below) (e.g., Eimas, Siqueland, Jusczyk, & Vigorito, 1971) are said to provide support for this innateness hypothesis. More recent research, however, challenges these initial conclusions and argues for a greater role for experience in the perceptual behavior of speech sounds (Bates, O'Connell, & Shore, 1987).

Categorical Perceptual Behavior in Infants

"Categorical perception" is the name given to the tendency for infants to respond differentially to (i.e., discriminate) "categories" of phonemes. A phoneme is "the smallest unit of sound that signifies a difference in meaning in a given natural language" (Aslin, 1987, p. 68). In behavior analytic terms, phonemes are the smallest structural units that exert stimulus control over behavior. The first experimental evidence to suggest that humans are born with this ability for categorical perception came from a study by Eimas et al. (1971). In their study, Eimas and his colleagues used a high-amplitude sucking (HAS) procedure (see chapter 4) with infants from 1 to 4 months of age. The auditory stimuli consisted of the stop-consonant-vowel (CV) syllables *ba* and *pa*. In addition, the researchers also programmed a computer to generate synthetic speech sounds that could be varied along a stimulus dimension called "voice onset time" (VOT), which is the basis of the distinction between CVs like *pa* and *ba*. Voice onset time refers "to the point at which the vocal cords begin to vibrate before or after we open our lips" (Bates et al., 1987, p. 152). For sounds we experience as *b*, voicing begins either before or simultaneously with the consonant burst and in sounds that we experience as *p*, voicing begins after the burst (Bates et al., 1987). The computer can present stimuli along this VOT continuum from −150 to +150 milliseconds (ms) from burst to voice. Using the HAS procedure, infants show strong "biases about where the border between phonemes *ought to be*, resulting in a discontinuous change in perception when a particular VOT border is crossed" (Bates et al., 1987, p. 153). For English-speaking infants, the VOT boundary between *ba* and *pa* is at about +20 ms which is similar to that for English-speaking adults (25–30 ms). English-speaking adults and infants also do not respond differentially to VOTs that fall either significantly above or below the border. Thus, adults and infants are said to respond to differences between but not within perceptual categories. That infants show these perceptual discriminations in the first few weeks of life has been the basis for claims that discriminative behavior is inherited and not learned (Eimas et al., 1971).

Recent evidence challenges this conclusion (Aslin, 1987; Bates et al., 1987). The first of these challenges consists of experimental evidence showing that both adults and infants respond categorically to nonspeech (pure tone) and speech sounds (Pisoni, 1977; Jusczyk, Pisoni, Walley, & Murray, 1980), meaning that if there are innate discriminative repertoires, they are for nonlanguage sounds as well. The second line of evidence comes from studies showing the categorical discrimination of human speech sounds in nonhumans, such as chinchillas (Kuhl & Miller, 1975, 1978). A third challenge to the innateness of categorical perception comes from studies showing that adults who are reared speaking different languages respond to the same VOT in different ways. For example, the *ba* and *pa* VOT boundary in English-speaking adults is about 25 to 30 ms, whereas the same boundary in Spanish-speaking adults is much lower. Such findings indicate "that there must be plasticity in the formation of speech categories, including the possibility in shifts in boundary locations and the addition or subtraction of entire categories" (Aslin, 1987, p. 70). According to Bates et al. (1987):

> We rushed too quickly to the conclusion that the speech perception abilities of the human infant are based on innate mechanisms evolved especially for speech. The infant's abilities do indeed seem to involve a great deal of innately specified information processing. But we do not yet have firm evidence that *any* of this innate machinery is speech specific. We assumed that the human auditory system evolved to meet the demands of language; perhaps, instead, language evolved to meet the demands of the mammalian auditory system. This lesson has to be kept in mind when we evaluate other claims about the innate language acquisition device. (p. 154)

It is understandable why some researchers assume that differences between humans and other species are due to differences in genes. When the Eimas et al. (1971) study appeared in the early 1970s, Chomsky's "theory" of innate mechanisms of generative grammar dominated the study of language, at least in the United States. The finding of such consistencies in infants only a few weeks old is suggestive of inherited behavioral relations. In the case of speech perception, however, the demonstration that other species can also respond differentially to phonemic categories weakens this assumption. The position taken in the present book is that, in general, experiential (i.e., environmental) explanations must be ruled out before a specific genetic mechanism should be considered. In the case of speech perception, there is considerable evidence for learning. One example, mentioned above, is the differences in categorical perception between adult speakers of different languages. Another example involves the loss of early discriminative ability. It has been found that Japanese infants can easily discriminate *ra* and *la*, even though Japanese adults have difficulty with the discrimination even after extensive training (Bates et al., 1987). Aslin (1987) concludes that it is premature to classify infant speech perception as phonemic, although it does appear to become language specific beginning during the second six months of life. Thus, early infant categorical perception occurs solely on the basis of acoustic, not phonemic, properties. This conclusion by Aslin supports Bates et al.'s (1987) statement that language evolved to meet the demands of the mammalian auditory system, which evolved under environmental circumstances that were perhaps unrelated to communication.

A final issue to be raised in this discussion of infant speech perception concerns the nature of the processes that "mediate" phonemic categorization (Aslin, 1987). This book argues for an interpretation based on the principles of behavior analysis. In fact, many of the studies in this area, even though not conducted by behavior analysts, have used operant discrimination procedures similar to those found in the study of animal psychophysics (see Blough & Blough, 1977; for a recent review, see Aslin (1987).

THE DEVELOPMENT OF PRESPEECH

Because functional relationships probably exist between the infant's earliest vocal sounds and its later speech, we begin our discussion of speech production with the development of prespeech or prelinguistic behavior. Such behavior is vocal, although not yet considered to be "true speech." Prespeech includes primarily crying, cooing, and babbling.

It is difficult to disagree with claims that the orderly fashion in which prespeech behavior develops is a function primarily of maturational variables. This orderly development is seen in all normal, healthy infants at about the same time. Even children with hearing impairments exhibit these prespeech behaviors in the same order. Maturation, however, cannot be the whole story. Just as with other reflexive or inherited behaviors, once the behavior occurs and operates on the environment, especially if it produces changes in the environment, it begins to be changed. This interactive process between behavior and environment is what behavior analysts call operant conditioning. Recall that Piaget also mentioned behavior that initially appeared as reflexive but then was modified after interaction with the environment. The difference is that Piaget attributed the modification of the behavior to changes in the child's cognitive structures (i.e., schemas) in an effort to adapt to the environment, which resembles a Lamarckian approach, whereas a behavior analytic approach attributes changes in the behavior to the selective action of the environment, which resembles a Darwinian approach.

Crying

We begin our treatment of prespeech in general and crying in particular with a discussion of the form versus the function of behavior. Vocal behavior in general, and language in particular, has been classified largely according to its form. One reason vocal behavior, as opposed to nonvocal behavior, is so easily classified according to its form is because humans are capable of producing so many different and discrete forms. One problem that results from classifying behavior according to its topography or form is that it then becomes easy to treat instances of behavior as if they were either functionally distinct or identical when they are not. It becomes easier to invent unobservable mechanisms to explain the behavior because no objective functional relations have been discovered. With language, the unobservable mechanisms are the various "meanings" frequently invoked to explain it. A second, related problem with classifying behavior according to its form is that we might fail to distinguish between behaviors that are similar in form but have different causes. In other words, some behaviors are similar in form but different in function. Crying is a good example.

Dworetzky (1993) addresses this issue by asking the following question: "Is crying an unlearned reflex, a classically conditioned response, or an instrumentally learned (i.e., operantly conditioned) response?" (p. 195). The point of asking this question is that the form of the response is similar in all three instances, but the causes are different. So, in one instance, crying might occur as an unconditioned reflexive response (UR), like when the child has been without food. Crying might also occur as a classically conditioned response (CR). For instance, the sight of the pediatrician may evoke crying if at some previous time this person stuck the child with a needle. Finally, crying might occur as an operant. For example, the child might cry when put to bed, because in the past this brought attention from the parents.

We have made this point about the form versus the function of behavior by using crying as an example, but crying may not be the best example of this problem, because, as most caregivers will tell you, crying can take many different forms. Research seems to support parents' contention that they can tell the difference between cries which to the naive listener may sound the same (Zeskind & Marshall, 1988). This is not surprising. First of all, there is evidence to suggest that infants are born with several different reflexes each involving a slightly different form of crying as an unconditional response (UR), for example a "hunger cry," a "pain cry," etc. (see Figure 8.1). Second, even if infants were not born crying differently to different eliciting stimuli, operant conditioning is sufficient to differentiate responses that are similar in form. Thus, over time, crying that is followed by food could become discernibly different from crying followed by receiving attention (e.g., being picked up). Consequently, some language scholars have distinguished between undifferentiated and differentiated crying (Eisenson, Auer, & Irwin, 1963). Undifferentiated crying is reflexive crying which can be elicited by several different types of stimuli, such as hunger, pain, strong odors, or sudden loud noises. Differentiated crying is learned crying or, specifically, operant crying. As we have stated, once reflexive crying operates on the environment and produces consequences, the function of crying changes. Of course, it may be very difficult to distinguish reflexive crying from operant crying in any given instance, especially because both may be operating simultaneously. Nevertheless, the distinction is important, if for no other reason than to understand the different functional contributions of environmental variables to crying.

The First Languagelike Sounds

During the first few months of life, infants begin making a wide variety of sounds, many of which will ultimately be found in their mature language behavior. In the first two months of life, infants begin making cooing sounds. Some refer to this stage as the *phonation stage* (Dworetzky, 1993) because infants make quasi-vowel sounds like "ooh" and "aah." Also during the first few months of life, infants make sounds that are combinations of quasi-vowel sounds with hard consonants, like "goo." For the purposes of the present discussion, the really interesting prespeech development occurs with the onset of babbling at about 5 to 6 months of age. We describe some of the research on babbling and then offer a behavior analytic interpretation of the findings.

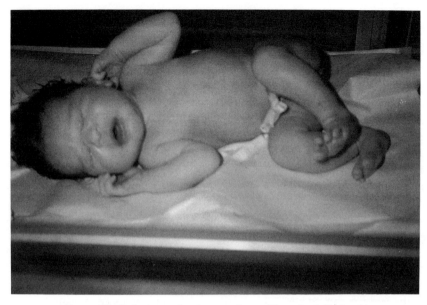

FIGURE 8.1. Reflexive crying in a newborn. (Photo by J. Gerhardt)

Babbling

Babbling consists mainly of the production of consonantal sounds which, partly because of the developing structure of the vocal system, are not physically possible before about 5 or 6 months of age (Lieberman, Crelin, & Klatt, 1972). Between 6 to 10 months, infants begin *canonical babbling*, which is "the systematic production of consonant–vowel (CV) sequences (e.g., 'ma' or 'dah')" (Bates et al., 1987, p. 156), and which may include echolalic babbling where the CV sounds are repeated. Although parents often, and understandably, interpret the infant's babbling or echolalia as meaningful speech, most language researchers agree that the onset of babbling or canonical babbling is not functionally related to environmental variables. Parents might mistake babbling for speech, because it has some of the pacing, rhythm, and intonation of the adult's language. The parent's delight at hearing these languagelike sounds no doubt has a reinforcing effect on its frequency, but the infant's vocal behavior does not yet show the kind of stimulus control we find in "true" speech.

Once babbling begins, there are several changing characteristics that suggest a strong causal role for environmental variables. For example, the intonation and segmenting of the babbling of hearing infants, as opposed to nonhearing infants, begins to match the language of their environment (Bates et al., 1987). Also, the phonemes of the native language become more prevalent while, at the same time, phonemic contrasts not heard in the native language begin to disappear.

It is not unusual to read that it is the infants who initiate or modify their own phonemes. For example, according to Dworetzky (1993), infants "increasingly narrow their use of phonemes" (p. 213), and Bates et al. (1987) write that "from 5 months onward, he (the infant) begins to shape or modify his own sound system to resemble the sounds produced by others—even though he does not appear to have any *insight* into the meaning or function of speech sounds" (p. 164, emphasis added). These accounts reveal that the observations and descriptions of the changes in the vocal behavior of language learning infants by developmental psychologists are under the stimulus control of a particular type of learning process, operant conditioning, probably because of the "purposive" nature of the behavior. These authors, however, attribute the changes to the infant rather than to the selective action of the consequences of the infant's vocal behavior. Perhaps one reason that language scholars fail to appreciate a behavior analytic account of the development of babbling is that they view reinforcement simplistically as something tangible that usually comes from another person (see chapter 5). For example, Bates et al. (1987) recognize "acquisition by operant conditioning" in describing an example of a child named Carlotta's vocal–gestural behavior, which they call "giving the raspberries" (i.e., an explosive sound caused by the rapid expulsion of air from the mouth which vigorously vibrates the lips). In their account, Bates et al. (1987) write:

> [T]he source of this particular game was not imitation of a conventional model. Instead, Carlotta had provoked an adult reaction of laughter when she hit upon the raspberries sound by accident; she repeated her performance, was reinforced again, and so the game continued. (p. 165)

In this case the reinforcer is clear: It is the adult's laughter. In fact, there is substantial evidence that infant vocalizations at different ages are sensitive to their consequences (e.g., Poulson, 1983, 1988; Rheingold, Gewirtz, & Ross, 1959; Sheppard, 1969; Todd & Palmer, 1968; Whitehurst, 1972). But what are the reinforcers for the changes in babbling toward matching the child's phonological environment? In other words, what are the processes by which the different and differentiated forms of babbling described above are acquired?

The answer seems to involve the role of conditioned reinforcing effects inherent in the phonological sounds the infant makes. There are two general steps in the process. First, from birth, or even before (see chapter

9), the infant constantly hears the phonological sounds of the language community. These sounds are heard when the infant is feeding, being held and caressed, and being played with, and also at times when the infant is not interacting with others. The effect of the constant correlation of these sounds with other stimulus events establishes the sounds as conditioned reinforcers. The second step is the shaping of the infant's own sound-making into the phonological sounds of the language community that he or she has been hearing for months. The only difference between this shaping and that which involves more direct tangible reinforcers is that the reinforcers in this case are automatic (see chapter 5; Vaughan & Michael, 1982). In the present example, when the infant makes sounds that resemble those that he or she has heard from the language community and that also function as reinforcement, it follows that the closer the sound match, the stronger the reinforcing effect. As Vaughan and Michael (1982) point out, this type of reinforcement also explains how children learn to speak with the accent or dialect of their parents, not to mention the actual sounds of the parents' voices. Just as in cases when the reinforcement comes from another person or source, it is not necessary when speaking of automatic reinforcement to make the child the initiator of his or her own actions or the modifier of his or her own behavior. We will return to the concept of automatic reinforcement later to understand other aspects of the acquisition of language.

The suggested role of direct and automatic reinforcement in the shaping of vocal babbling is strengthened by studies on deaf children and on children of deaf parents (e.g., Lenneberg, Rebelsky, & Nichols, 1965). For example, Bates et al. (1987) report studies where children of deaf parents, who themselves are native speakers of American Sign Language, apparently exhibit a kind of "manual babbling" as early as 5 months of age. Just like vocal babbling, this manual behavior becomes more like the environmental input of the specific language community and becomes language depending on the effects it has on the signers (i.e., the "speakers") in the community. Presumably this process is guided by automatic reinforcement, although in this case, it would consist of the visual match between the infant's hand movements and those he or she has seen produced by the parents. Finally, evidence suggests that infants who are congenitally deaf produce the same vocal sounds as hearing children until about the 6th month of life when the range of babbling sounds becomes more restricted for deaf infants (Lenneberg, 1970). This difference in babbling between deaf infants and normally hearing infants reflects, in part, the lack of automatic conditioned reinforcement for the babbling behavior of the deaf infants.

THE DEVELOPMENT OF SPEECH

Structural versus Behavior Analytic Views

We have noted throughout this book that many psychologists place a great deal of emphasis on the structure of behavior. Consequently, it is not surprising to find that discussions of language development proceed along a continuum from one-word to two-word mean-length utterances to sentences. Some divide this classification system into receptive and expressive development (e.g., Bates et al., 1987). Others distinguish between prespeech and "true language," which does not begin until the two-word stage (e.g., Chalkley, 1982). Some researchers make distinctions between different forms of speech, for example, between nouns and verbs, and devote extensive amounts of time to the question of which parts of speech are learned first and why (e.g., Gentner, 1982). Still others try to make a priori distinctions between forms of language that supposedly have different kinds of functions. For example, according to Chalkley (1982), the phrase, "Please don't do that " could be interpreted as a request or as an implied threat. Some authors have even devoted their time to studying the differences in and the development of one particular type of language function. Becker (1982) wrote an entire chapter on children's requests, classifying them according to what groups (e.g., parents, peers) are addressed by the request. What these and other language researchers share is the apparent belief that language behavior can be fruitfully partitioned according to various structural criteria before actually discovering functional differences. The view of this book is that very little understanding of the functions of language will come from such enterprises. At the most, structural classification schemes will give us narrow glimpses of the practices of particular language communities. Moreover, as we suggested in chapter 2, structural analyses of behavior have many disadvantages, not the least of which is the tendency to reify the structures, to create internal surrogates of them, and to use these inferred structures to explain behavioral forms.

Behavior analysts do not see language as inherently different from nonlanguage. Language, whether it be vocal, manual, or written, is behavior that operates on the environment, generates consequences, and is affected by those consequences. Perhaps the most important difference is that language operates solely on a social environment consisting of other people who mediate the consequences for the speaker. There are some properties of language, especially vocal language, that do seem to make it unique, but these unique properties seem to be a result of the mammalian auditory system in combination with the human vocal apparatus. As far as the varied forms of language behavior that seem to be interesting to language scholars, a behavior analysis would look to the functions of the behavior that produce those structures. On the one hand, many different forms of responding may still be functionally identical, such as when thirst (more specifically, fluid deprivation) evokes, "Water, please," or "I am thirsty," or " Will you get me something to drink?" On the other hand, several responses that are similar in form can be functionally different, such as when "fire" is evoked by seeing a fire, ordering troops to shoot, letting an employee go, etc. A structural analysis will not reveal these differences; a functional analysis can. And following from Skinner's work on language—*Verbal Behavior* (1957)—behavior analytic theory is poised to provide a functional analysis of the development of language in infancy and early childhood.

Single-Word Production

When we look at the first instances of single words in infants, it becomes tempting to classify them as nouns or verbs, or as requests or names. However, even if it were possible to make such structural distinctions, it would not help us to understand the function of the words or how the particular forms originated. The infant's prespeech vocal behavior is already functioning as operant behavior before the appearance of "true" words. For instance, suppose that when an infant is thirsty, she says "miwu" and the parent quickly provides milk. From now on fluid deprivation will evoke "miwu" as the result of operant conditioning. According to Skinner (1957, pp. 35–51), this is an example of a functional verbal unit called a *mand*. A mand is the name given to a verbal response that is evoked by a motivational variable because, in the past, under similar circumstances, the particular response form has produced that specific consequence. In an unchanging verbal environment, this response would always work when the infant wanted milk. However, the verbal environment is not unchanging; on the contrary, it is ever-changing. So, we would not be surprised to find that in a few weeks, the infant is saying "milk" when she is thirsty. If she says "miwu" anymore, it probably won't work in producing milk.

Traditional language scholars might debate whether this formal one-word utterance is truly language, whether it is a request or a demand, whether the infant *understands* what she is saying, whether she *intends* to affect the behavior of a listener, or whether she is *using* the word to communicate her desires, and so on. From a behavior analytic perspective, these are useful questions only if they refer to different behavioral relations. Otherwise, they detract from more important questions about the functional control of behavior. Suppose we revisit this little girl in a few months and find that when she is thirsty, she now says, "Milk, please," or even, "I want milk." While traditional language scholars may debate whether these are true sentences, behavior analysts are still classifying the function of the particular form of this behavior as a mand. Functionally, the different forms of the response, "miwu," "milk," and "I want milk" are identical, except for some possible small functional nuances, like "please." In fact, as an older child, when she says, "I would please like to have some milk, if you don't mind," behavior analysts would still speak of the utterance as a mand, albeit a more complex form. Traditional language scholars, however, might still debate the structure of this sentence. The difference is that in understanding the controlling variables of the operant, the behavior analyst is in a better position than the traditional linguist to understand the form of the behavior in its context.

Let us look at another example to understand the subtle differences between a functional and structural approach to language. Suppose, our hypothetical child walked into a room in which there was a table with a glass of milk on it and she said, "There's a glass of milk." This statement would probably be classified as declarative and described as an instance of naming by traditional linguists. A functional analysis might yield a somewhat different interpretation. Suppose the child is thirsty, especially for milk, and in her specific language community (i.e., family) in the past she has received milk and other things when this particular declarative form has been emitted. Even though her response, "There's a glass of milk," is partly controlled by the sight of the milk, it would not be an instance of naming, although it would still be considered declarative in form. This is a distinction that language scholars might not necessarily make based on the form of the response alone. Functionally, the sentence is a mand, and it is not much different than "miwu," or "milk," or "I want milk." Thus, although single words precede multiple words developmentally, their functions may be similar.

Naming

Many language scholars view single-word production as synonymous with naming (Bates et al., 1987). In fact, according to Bates et al. (1987), it is possible to describe "three different developmental moments" as forming the transition to "true naming." They are the following:

1. 9–10 months, when children first produce conventional sounds and show comprehension of at least a few words and phrases,

2. 12–13 months, when most children produce at least a few sound sequences that function like names from an adult point of view,
3. 16–18 months, when there is a sudden surge in vocabulary growth and an increased use of single words to convey combinatorial or essential meanings. (p. 170)

Unfortunately, Bates and her colleagues attempt to decide when the child has uttered her first "real" word or if a particular sound is intentional based on the form of the utterance alone. It may not be important from a functional standpoint to know when the first formal word has been uttered, although from a historical, sociological standpoint, the emission of the first formal word may be of some interest. From a behavior analytic perspective, a more important issue is the social contingencies that are responsible for particular forms of language behavior because these are the processes by which the behavior comes about. But again, this should be more of a sociological question about the reinforcing practices of verbal communities than a question about the child's intentions or developing cognitive structures.

Let us examine what nonbehavior analysts speak of as naming. Bates et al. (1982) describe an example in which a little girl named Carlotta first said "woowoo" in the context of a book reading game, in response to the adult's question of, "How does the doggie go?" This particular form is probably an example of what Skinner (1957, pp. 71–78) called an intraverbal, a verbal response evoked by a verbal (discriminative) stimulus that lacks point-to-point correspondence with the response. (A verbal response evoked by a verbal discriminative stimulus that is formally identical to the response is called an *echoic*.) According to Bates et al. (1987), by the time Carlotta was 13 months old, she was saying "woowoo" in the "presence of a whole class of dogs, in books and in real life, including the sound of a dog barking somewhere in the distance" (p. 172). Although identical to the previous form which we classified as an intraverbal, this form of "woowoo" is probably functioning differently. Rather than being evoked by the original question, the response is evoked exclusively by the sights and sounds of dogs. This functionally distinct response form is what Skinner call a tact (see Skinner, 1957, pp. 81–146). *Tact* refers to a verbal response that is evoked by the physical properties of nonverbal objects or events as a result of social reinforcement (e.g., praise). Saying "dog" when a dog walks in the room is an example of a tact if the response produced social consequences (e.g., praise) in similar circumstances. Traditional linguists would call it naming but, unfortunately, that practice has a lot of mental and cognitive implications. For example, Bates, Bretherton, Shore, and McNew (1983) define naming as: "The use of a symbol to recognize, categorize, identify or otherwise label a referent as a member of some known class of entities, or as an instantiation of a known unique individual" (p. 60). In this definition, there is only a vague reference to anything resembling the behavior of the speaker or the one doing the naming, and that is when the authors mention the "use of a symbol." What exactly are the actions of *recognizing, categorizing,* and *identifying*? Even though the only evidence of so-called naming is the behavior of the individual speaker in a particular context, cognitive psychologists ignore that in favor of reifying things at an unobservable level. Bates et al.'s (1983) definition of naming follows the traditional linguistic practice of considering language to be symbol use, where symbols (i.e., words) are substitutes for their referents. Nothing more than simple logic is needed, however, to realize that the word "chair" can in no way ever substitute for a chair. One cannot build, move, or break the word.

Another unfortunate result of the emphasis on naming can be seen in the following quotation: "However, names for food and water also appeared quickly in Carlotta's requests, and she soon began to collect names for toys, clothing, and other relevant objects in her world" (Bates et al., 1987, p. 172). Here, Bates and her coauthors are confusing tacts (names) and mands (requests). From their structural perspective, the mand, "I want water," includes the name for water. Functionally, however, unless there is a glass of water present that might partially control the form of the response, for example, "glass of" instead of simply "water," the response, "I want water," would be classified functionally as a mand if it is evoked by some motivational operation, like thirst because that form has been followed by water in the past. Classifying it as a name or as a request does not specify the controlling variables for the response. Finally, Bates et al. (1987) speak of names as if they were objects to be collected, and they implicitly attribute the developmental changes to Carlotta, instead of to her language community. This use of metaphor does little to further the scientific understanding of the variables of which language is a function.

So far in our discussion of the first words, we have implied that the first formal words are probably, functionally speaking, mands, that is, responses evoked by motivational variables because in the past the responses have produced the consequence they specify. For example, "water" is evoked by thirst, because it has produced water in the past; and "go" is evoked by the variables we describe as "wanting to leave," because in the past this particular form has resulted in being allowed to leave. Although it is difficult to trace precisely the functional development of early language behavior, it is likely that, after mands, the next functional units of language behavior in infants are tacts, or what traditional theorists would call names. Unfortunately, some discussions mistakenly focus on the acquisition not of naming, but of parts of speech, such as nouns and verbs. This is a mistake because both nouns and verbs can be mands, tacts, or intraverbals. In other words, classifying a word as a noun or a verb tells us nothing about the function of the word for the individual speaker. Even so, some textbook authors report that in acquiring nouns (or naming), children learn basic ones, like "dog," before learning subordinate nouns, like "dachshund," or superordinate nouns like "mammal." This ordering of learning has been called the "three-bears rule" (Gleitman & Wanner, 1984). In other words, the category "mammal" is too large, the category "dachshund" is too small, but the category "dog" is just right. Assuming that children do acquire tacts in this way, we must ask why this is so. The following is a typically cognitive answer:

> Basic words, such as "dog" or "chair," are perceptually accessible; they don't require abstract cognitive skills to comprehend. Children are simply more likely to be aware of what is easiest to perceive ... as children acquire language they continue to organize their experiences into categories in much the same way that they did when hearing their first verbal sounds.... (Dworetzky, 1993, p. 215)

A parsimonious explanation is one that accounts for a phenomenon with the fewest assumptions and points to potentially testable variables (see chapter 1). What does it mean to say that the terms "perceptually accessible," "abstract cognitive skills to comprehend," and "organize their experiences into categories" do not form parsimonious explanations? These ways of talking about the sequence in which nouns are learned are misleading and ultimately they tell us absolutely nothing about why children acquire certain tacts before others.

There is a simpler explanation for the behavior named by the "three-bears rule." Children learn "basic" (i.e., generic) tacts before subordinate and superordinate tacts simply because that is the convention established and followed by the language community. Parents and teachers speak that way, and, as a result, children tend to speak that way (White, 1982). When a dog is present, adults don't say, "Oh, look at the mammal. Can you say that, 'mammal?' " The reason is that classification at such a level does not easily permit discrimination between more subordinate levels. It is also less likely that they will say, "Look at the dachshund," unless the child is older and can already say "dog" to the class of mammals called dogs. Children do not "organize their experiences;" the verbal community organizes them by saying and responding to some classes of tacts before others. It is neither necessary nor parsimonious to make inferences about the child's perceptual capabilities or other cognitive processes in order to explain the three-bears rule. Moreover, if we encounter a child, such as a developmentally disabled child who lacks these verbal responses, we will not be able to effectively teach these repertoires by focusing on perceptual accessibility or abstract cognitive skills; they are not accessible to teachers. Effective teaching requires manipulating the independent variables of the behavior to be taught, and these variables lie in the environment.

One more point needs to be made regarding the "three-bears rule." Although it is called a rule, this does not mean that children follow such a rule when language behavior is learned. The rule, in this case, is an instance of the verbal behavior of linguists that describes the phenomenon and makes it familiar to students so that it is easier to identify and remember. But we need not use the rule to explain the behavior it described in the first place.

Extensions

When a particular name (tact) for an object has been learned, it may be evoked by other objects belonging to a larger conceptual class—called *overextension* by linguists—or it may not be evoked by an object deemed appropriate by adult standards—called *underextension*. Dworetzky (1993, p. 219) describes two examples of what developmental psychologists speak of as *overextensions*: In the first example, after a child was told that the moon was called "moon," she said "mooi." Then she said "mooi" when she saw a cake, and then again when she saw round marks on a window. In another example, a child was told that the sound a rooster makes was called "crowing." The child called it "koko." Afterwards, he said "koko" when he heard a tune played on the violin and then when he heard any music. Language researchers describe the child as overextending the meaning of these words.

Once again, from a behavior analytic perspective, overextensions are fairly simple to interpret. The initial occurrence of the tact to a stimulus not typical of adult categories is an instance of what behavior theorists speak of as *stimulus generalization*. Stimulus generalization is a useful scientific principle whereas overextension, although descriptive, is not, because it is usually restricted to only a few behavioral phenomena, namely, those related to language. The term "overextension" is appropriate only to the particular examples of naming; but the term "stimulus generalization" applies to any instance where stimuli similar to a stimulus in whose presence a response has been reinforced will evoke that response. The importance of this difference is perhaps nowhere more evident than in Collins and Kuczaj's (1991) description of research by Seyfarth, Cheney, and Marler (1980, as cited in Collins and Kuczaj, 1991) on communication behavior in vervet monkeys. These monkeys supposedly exhibited "overextension errors." Adult monkeys make a range of different calls evoked by the approach of a different predator. For example, they make the sound "rranp" at the approach of an eagle. Young vervet monkeys have been observed to make that sound to eagles, and any other flying object. Collins and Kuczaj (1991) explain that adult monkeys "ignore" the young monkeys' "rranp" sound to flying objects other than the eagle, and "the young vervets gradually learn to limit their warning sounds to the appropriate referents" (p. 183). This set of observations can be interpreted parsimoniously according to the laws of behavior analysis. The fact that all flying objects evoked the "rranp" sound in young monkeys is an instance of stimulus generalization. And the gradual restriction of this sound to approaching eagles as a function of the adult reaction nicely illustrates differential reinforcement and discrimination training. To consider the stimulus generalization to be an error is at the very least a misnomer, because if we assume that behavior is determined, there can be no errors, except of course, according to arbitrary social standards. And calling the behavior *overextension* is correct only insofar as it is another instance of stimulus generalization. What is most interesting about this example is not that stimulus generalization was observed in nonhumans—that is commonplace—but rather that the communication behavior of the young monkeys was shaped by the social consequences by the adults!

Once we understand that examples of so-called overextension are instances of stimulus generalization, then it becomes easier to reject the notion that the child (or the monkey) is the one doing the extending. It is more accurate to say that the behavior, which was initially reinforced in the presence of one stimulus, is now evoked by similar stimuli. The young vervets don't "learn to limit their warning sounds." Rather, the (social) environment selects particular sounds in the presence of particular stimulus conditions; this is discrimination training. Finally, the behaviors that are said to reflect overextension could be predicted simply on the basis of knowing about the principle of stimulus generalization. If we want to know why the child in the example above said "koko" the first time to a tune played on a violin, we need only look at the child's reinforcement history to similar stimuli, namely, to the rooster. If various music continued to evoke "koko" in the child, it would be a good guess that the adults in that child's immediate verbal community responded to the "overextension" with reinforcing attention. After all, when children do things like this, most adults think it is cute for a while and respond consistently.

Multiple-Word Production

The interest by psychologists and linguists in multiple-word production is consistent with their interest in a general normative, structural approach to language that stresses words, their number, their particular parts of speech, their meaning (semantics), and their organization (syntax). The occurrence of multiple words in a child's verbal repertoire is usually a precursor to the appearance of more formal conventional arrangements of words called sentences. This fascinating change in the structure of language behavior tempts language scholars even further away from the functional analysis of variables controlling language behavior into the almost purely structural world of sentence organization. In fact, as many linguists have shown in the last few decades, one can spend a professional lifetime dissecting and analyzing sentences, whether or not the sentences were ever spoken by anyone. This approach may tell us much about the formal structure of sentences, but little about how sentences originate or why anyone would ever say them in the first place. Nevertheless, because traditional treatments of language acquisition place a great deal of emphasis on syntax, we will briefly look at some of the more frequently discussed issues.

One-Word Period

Although we have already discussed single-word production, it is probably important to deal briefly with an issue found in many treatments of language acquisition, that of syntax. *Syntax* is the branch of grammar that deals with the arrangement of words and their relation to one another. (The other branch of grammar is called *morphology*, which deals with such things as prefixes and suffixes, which "build words and ... modify lexical 'roots'" and "free standing grammatical morphemes," such as, pronouns and prepositions, among others [Bates et al., 1987, p. 183].)

We begin with the time in the development of language in which one-word units dominate the child's repertoire—the one-word period. We use the term "period" instead of "stage" to indicate that it is a time *period* during which particular response forms dominate, and not a stage in the maturational sense of the word. For example, Bates et al. (1987) write that between about 16 and 20 months, children begin to "achieve productive control over verbs (e.g., 'play,' 'kiss,' 'go') and adjectives (e.g., 'pretty,' 'hot,' 'dirty')" (p. 177), and that this change reflects a "change in the meanings a child intends to convey—in particular, the emergence of predication" (p. 177). Once again, we have an explanation of language in terms of inferred constructs such as meaning and intention. Bates et al. (1987) relate the appearance of verbs and adjectives in the child's verbal repertoire to the appearance of different nouns. They cite the example of a child pointing to a pair of shoes and instead of saying "shoe," the child says "Daddy." Presumably the child means "daddy's shoes," or "Those are daddy's shoes." This behavior has been called a *holophrase*, which means that the meaning of an entire sentence has been expressed in one word. Collins and Kuczaj (1991) have suggested that these single word holophrases are actually Chomskian surface structures based on Chomskian "deep structures that represent complete sentences" (p. 187). It should be obvious to the reader by now that these accounts are based on fictitious mechanisms such as meanings and deep structures. Such explanations are not parsimonious because the proposed explanatory mechanisms can never be directly tested. Nor are these explanations even plausible, because the mechanisms to which they refer are not real events. Moreover, there is a more parsimonious account of the occurrence of the one-word units called holophrases.

When a child points to a pair of shoes and says, "Daddy," what are we to make of it? Rather than asking what the child really means, or what the deep structure of this one-word utterance is, it is more scientific to ask about the controlling variables of the response. The response "Daddy" evoked by a pair of (daddy's) shoes has become a tact, that is, a verbal response evoked by a nonverbal object because of social reinforcement. When a mother talks to a language-learning child we wouldn't be too surprised to hear her point to the shoes and say something like, "Are those daddy's shoes?" or "Those are daddy's shoes." The child immediately says, "Daddy?" (an example of imitation) and the mother says, "Yes, daddy's shoes." The next time the child sees the shoes, she says "Daddy," and the mother says, "That's right, daddy's shoes." Is the child intending to convey her understanding of the possessive case? Is there a deep structural meaning located in her mind that can only be expressed in one word because of an immature vocal system or undeveloped cognitive structures? Will this child ever be able to point to the shoes and say, "Daddy's shoes," or "Those are daddy's shoes"? Of course she will. In a language-learning environment, just as in all other functional environments, behavior–environment interactions change from simple to complex (Bijou & Baer, 1978). Whether the child says, "Daddy," or "Those are daddy's shoes," functionally speaking, these are both tacts, although the complete sentence is structurally more complex. To be fair, both Collins and Kuczaj (1991) and Bates et al. (1987) are aware of the criticism that the cognitive explanations outlined above involve methods of "rich interpretation." Bates et al. (1987) acknowledge that the "shift" in language seen in the second year might involve only an increase in complexity, as a behavior analytic view would suggest.

Two-Word Period

Traditional linguists are interested in the order and meaning of two-word units. Behavior analysts are interested in their function. For the traditional linguist, the increase in the number of words reflects changes in various cognitive or neural constructs. Remember, for the behavior analyst, the increase in the number of formal units (i.e., words) is a function of the increasing complexity of the verbal environment, which probably translates into increasingly finer discriminations, involving the controlling variables of the specific language and the speaker's own language.

As many authors point out, the particular words found in two-word utterances are not there by chance. Rather, they are the words that "convey the most meaning." Hence, two-word units usually include nouns, verbs, and adjectives, but exclude articles and conjunctions, as well as prefixes and suffixes. The resulting speech unit has been referred to as *telegraphic speech*, because it resembles the kind of messages sent by telegram where only the essential words are included (Brown & Bellugi, 1964). For example, it would not be uncommon to hear a child say, "Daddy car," or "Mommy home." The central question concerning telegraphic speech is how best to account for it. Of course, the parsimonious explanation is that, in many cases, these words are all that are necessary for reinforcement in the child's verbal community. Moreover, nouns, verbs, and adjectives are more variable than articles and conjunctions and the like. Thus, they are more likely to be associated with different contingencies of reinforcement. This difference means that in terms of the "communicative" value of the child's utterances the nouns, verbs, and adjectives will more likely be imitated by the child and then reinforced by adult listeners. The reader must remember that the child's language becomes more complex as the requirements of the verbal community do.

GRAMMAR AND THE PRODUCTION OF SENTENCES

Traditional linguists also infer cognitive explanations for the appearance of longer, more complex units, the transition to which usually occurs by about 36 months of age. For example, Bates et al. (1987) state, "The transition from single words to sentences seems to reflect cognitive reorganizations that transcend language proper" (p. 181). Of course, much of the evidence for the "cognitive reorganization" is the change in language behavior itself. And Collins and Kuczaj (1991) ask, "How do children accomplish this major developmental change?" (p. 191). It is certainly not the child who accomplishes the change; it is the variables controlling the behavior, whatever and wherever they are. At any rate, it is only when the two components of grammar—syntax and morphology—are finally evident in the child's language repertoire that most language scholars speak of "true language" (Bates et al., 1987). Bates et al. (1987) list four lines of evidence that are frequently cited to prove that grammatication is discontinuous with the rest of cognition. We will cite three of these lines of evidence for a different reason: They are often cited as support for nativistic (and also generally cognitive) theories of language development like the one proposed by Noam Chomsky (see below). These three lines of evidence are that (1) morphosyntactic behavior follows certain rules; (2) basic morphemes are acquired at a very fast rate; and (3) the nature and sequence of grammatical development across children and languages is very similar. We discuss each in the following three sections.

Rule-Governed Morphology

Perhaps the most common example of the presence of rule-governed morphological use is verb usage. Bates et al. (1987) report that English-speaking children go through similar "stages" in their use of verbs. First, they use the same form of the verb, usually the simple third-person singular form, for all tenses (e.g., "Daddy go"). Then, they begin to discriminate between past and present forms of the most frequently used verbs which are usually irregular verbs like go/went or come/came. It is also at this time that overgeneralizations (also called overregularizations) or overextensions of regular endings occur with irregular verbs. Common examples include "Daddy goed," or "Mommy comed." Eventually, these particular forms are replaced with the more appropriate forms.

For many psychologists, the occurrence of overgeneralizations of regular verb endings with irregular verbs seems to provide clues to the ways in which children acquire the rules of grammar (Dworetzky, 1993). The reasoning behind the assumption that language production is determined by rules is, on the surface, very simple: Children have learned a rule for the use of regular verb endings. That rule might be, "Whenever you use the past tense of a verb, add 'ed.'" In the case of plural nouns, the rule might be, "When a noun is plural, add 's.'" Of course, there are exceptions, such as foot/feet, man/men, etc. In fact, many linguists refer to overgeneralizations as errors. But they are only errors in that they do not match the conventional forms of adult speech. As we all know, most children will eventually learn to speak "correctly," that is, according to the conventional forms of accepted adult language. The rule interpretation accounts for the exceptions to the general rules for regular verbs and plural nouns with the same explanation. In these cases, it is said that the child learns an individual rule for each exception. First, we point out that Bates et al. (1987) probably reflect the position of many cognitively oriented psychologists when they say:

> [B]ecause children begin to produce overgeneralizations after a long period of producing the correct form, it is difficult to explain their behavior in terms of old learning principles like environmental frequency, practice, and reinforcement. The proliferation of rule-like behavior at 20–36 months of age thus provides grounds for the argument that the child is acquiring a new cognitive system.... (p. 184)

Interestingly, Bates et al. (1987) point out that there is reason to believe that language scholars overestimate the role of abstract rules in early morphological development. The alternatives they suggest, however, are still cognitive explanations with all of the problems we have previously pointed out.

Before turning to a behavior analytic interpretation of the overgeneralization of verb and plural noun endings, we should point out that, with the exception of reinforcement, the "old learning principles" mentioned in the above quote by Bates et al. are not behavior analytic principles. Even their use of the term "reinforcement" in this context leads us to suspect that it is not being used as behavior analysts would use it.

Our behavior analytic interpretation is predicated on the assertion that children go through a long period of producing correct forms of the most frequently used irregular verbs before they begin to make "mistakes" (Bates et al., 1987). First, we must recognize that the phenomenon here is not *over*generalization—that is redundant. Behavior either reflects generalization or discrimination. The linguists' concept of overgeneralization is an example of what behavior analysts speak of as *response generalization* or *response induction*. As we mentioned in chapter 7, response induction is the name given to the observation that the frequency of responses outside a particular operant class will increase as a function of the reinforcement of responses within the class. It is an instance of generalization. And if reinforcers are restricted to only certain responses, that is, the ones that will eventually define the operant class, then the generalized responses will extinguish.

In the case of irregular verb endings, it is possible for the correct ending to predominate early. But when adults begin enforcing reinforcement contingencies for correct regular verb endings, we would expect there to be a "spread of effect" to other responses that are similar, namely, endings on irregular verbs. Generalization, whether response or stimulus, is a natural byproduct of the initial reinforcement of a class of behavior. With differential reinforcement, however, the frequency of the reinforced response class (operant) increases relative to the frequency of nonreinforced responses. This is probably what happens when response differentiation and stimulus discrimination are involved in the acquisition of language behavior. The language community must make sure that the appropriate forms of behavior occur and that they are brought under the control of subtle properties of the environment, such as whether there is one or more than one instance of an object controlling a tact (i.e., plurality) or whether some action is occurring or has already occurred, in which case what may have been a tact for present action (i.e., a present verb) may change not only in its form (i.e., to past or future tense), but also in function from a tact to an intraverbal. For example, past or future verb forms would function as intraverbals if they were evoked by other (formally dissimilar) verbal stimuli instead of actual situations involving past or future events. In fact, we usually speak of past or future actions in the context of other verbal behavior, as for example when we say, "Yesterday as I drove to work, I saw an accident." The irregular verbs "drove" and "saw," are controlled by saying "yesterday" in addition to the broader context of describing events and actions that have already occurred. This explanation in terms of differential reinforcement for more specific forms of behavior brought under the control of subtle properties of the environment is more parsimonious than a cognitive explanation because it refers to established, confirmable principles. In fact, Bates et al. (1987) write that "figuring out the meaning and function of the contrasts involved in tense, aspect, case, number, person, and so on ... may be the most demanding aspect of morphological development from a cognitive point of view" (p. 185). Such a task, however, is unnecessary to explain aspects of changes in behavior.

Speed of Acquisition

A second type of evidence that cognitive psychologists and linguists use to support cognitive and nativistic theories of grammar is the apparent speed with which grammatization occurs. Bates et al. (1987) refer to the fact that this process is underway in 4 to 8 months as a "cognitive cataclysm"· (p. 185). Of course, speed of acquisition is in the eye of the beholder. Moreover, assessing the speed of acquisition of morphological characteristics of language behavior is relative. Let us assume, however, that the acquisition of correct syntactic and morphological forms of language behavior does happen more quickly than other behaviors. Is the only explanation for this difference some innate grammatical system? First of all, for a variety of reasons, innate grammatical systems, like other inferred constructs, are not scientifically valid explanations (Schlinger, 1993). As we have mentioned elsewhere in this chapter, such explanations are neither plausible nor parsimonious. Moreover, the explanation for speedy acquisition may be relatively simple. For example, once the child's vocal apparatus has matured, the effort involved in speaking, relative to the effort involved in almost any other type of behavior, is much less. Speaking does not require any support from the physical environment, a characteristic that lends vocal behavior some of its apparent discontinuity from other behavior. When this particular response system is combined with the rich and complex schedules of reinforcement for speaking, both from others in the language community, as well as from the automatic reinforcement inherent in the sounds themselves, the result is a fairly effortless, fluid, and highly reinforcable type of behavior.

Of course, it is also possible that if there is an apparent burst of language acquisition, this represents the cumulative effects of an intense period of differential reinforcement for similar and earlier forms of the behavior. The point is that there are other plausible, and more parsimonious, explanations of speedy language acquisition than invented, hypothetical constructs, whether they are cognitive or biological. Either way, these constructs must be plausible, that is, they must be about real structures or events, before we can seriously consider them as potential explanations.

Language Universals

A third type of evidence that has been used to support mainly a nativistic theory of language acquisition is that most of the important characteristics of language—for example, its grammar and the sequence of its appearance—can be found across all languages and cultures. It turns out, however, that language development is more variable than linguists once believed. Still, some language scholars will argue for some general language processes on the basis of commonalities across different languages. Consider that all languages have a grammar, that is, a structure including nouns, verbs, etc. What is the most parsimonious explanation of this structural similarity? Some would say that it represents a common inherited language structure in the brain. Although that is possible, it is not very plausible in light of the fact that such a structure has never been found, nor have its properties ever been suggested in biological terms.

Another possible explanation for a common grammar is that there are some very general principles that are not language-specific, which affect language learning in all humans. This is a position Bates et al. (1987) seem to support; however, their example points to a principle from Gestalt psychology. Although Gestalt psychology is an example of one of the numerous paradigms in psychology that have come and gone (Neisser, 1967, as cited in MacCorquodale, 1970), Bates et al. (1987) still seem to be on the right track. The general principles that result in any universality of language are probably those of operant (and respondent) conditioning. Moreover, not only are these learning principles the same for all humans (and for many nonhumans), but the environments of humans are also similar. For example, the simplest explanation of universality of nouns, verbs, and other parts of speech is that the environment consists of people (and other organisms) and other objects (nouns) that do things (verbs) to other things (predicates). The relationships of things to one another that control prepositions (e.g., in front of, behind) are properties of the environment; the colors, sizes, and shapes of things that control adjectives are properties of things in the environment. Plurality is a property of things in the environment. We cannot say with any certainty whether there are any innate language-specific mechanisms, but if we can parsimoniously explain language without appealing to such mechanisms, then inferring them is unnecessary (see also Bates et al., 1987, p. 191, for a similar argument).

We have shown a strong bias in the present chapter toward an environmental account of language behavior. At the same time, we admit that (1) the tendency for human behavior to be operantly conditioned is inherited; (2) the behavior of speakers involves a very complex vocal musculature system and depends on many characteristics of the human brain; and (3) some of the more complex aspects of language behavior (both speaking and listening) may be emergent processes resulting from a combination of (1) and (2).

The issue of the role of nature and nurture regarding language development has a long history in both philosophy and psychology. The most recent debate on these issues has been between generative grammarians like Chomsky and behavior analysts like Skinner (although these two never personally debated). Although Chomsky's views dominated the study of language by psychologists during the 1960s and 1970s, his influence has waned in the face of increasingly convincing evidence, some of which we reference in this chapter, of the effects of the environment on language acquisition and production. This evidence, however, has not come from behavior analysts (although behavior analysts have generated a considerable amount of support for the contention that reinforcement principles can account for language behavior). With these considerations in mind, let us look briefly at the nature–nurture debate regarding the acquisition of language behavior.

THE NATURE AND NURTURE OF LANGUAGE

Furrow, Nelson, and Benedict (1979) acknowledged that, "Whether or not the environment plays a significant role in language development has been a controversial issue for some time" (p. 423). At first glance, it would seem that the question of whether the environment is a significant factor in language development would be moot. The amount of casual, observational, not to mention scientific, evidence supporting a strong role for the environment in language acquisition would seem to be overwhelming. Over the last decade, most language researchers have acknowledged the important role of environment, even if they don't interpret it in behavior analytic terms. Despite the growing evidence opposing Chomsky's theory of language development, most developmental textbooks still describe Chomsky's theory in some detail (e.g., Bukatko & Daehler, 1992; Collins & Kuzcaj, 1991). The initial impact of Chomsky's ideas on the field of linguistics came in the form of perhaps his best known work, his review of B. F. Skinner's book *Verbal Behavior* (Chomsky, 1959). For a variety of reasons, rebuttals by behaviorists, including Skinner, were not immediately forthcoming (MacCorquodale, 1970). Moreover, contrary to popular opinion, Chomsky's was not the only review of Skinner's book (e.g., Andresen, 1991). There were several other reviews, many of them favorable (Knapp, 1992). For several reasons, however, it was Chomsky's review that was most influential and widely read.

Criticisms of Chomsky's Argument For a Universal Grammar

There are serious logical and factual flaws in both Chomsky's critique of Skinner's approach (MacCorquodale, 1970) and his own hypotheses about language (Palmer & Donahoe, 1992; Palmer, 1986). Palmer (1986) has presented a review of Chomsky's position that raises two major criticisms. First, Palmer challenges Chomsky's contention that specialized principles of organization specific to language, namely, a universal grammar, have evolved in the human species. Palmer (1986) notes Chomsky's own admission that the laws responsible for the evolution of these principles "are quite unknown." Palmer points out that such a contention "adds a further burden of proof" because, "[I]n addition to explaining the origins of grammar, he [Chomsky] must now formulate and explain the workings of the new evolutionary principles...." (p. 52). According to Palmer, Chomsky retreats to the position that perhaps this universal grammar arose as a byproduct of the evolution of other structural properties of the brain, such as "bigger brains, more cortical surface, hemispheric specialization for analytical processes" (Chomsky, 1980, p. 321). Except for these very general suggestions, then, Chomsky offers no information about the particular neurological structures or the relationship between them and a language structure. In short, Palmer (1986) criticizes Chomsky for claiming that a language-specific structure has evolved and then either ignoring or dismissing the very selectionist principles that would be necessary to explain how such a structure evolved.

The second and perhaps more fundamental criticism of Chomsky's claims for an innate language structure involves the environmental input necessary to trigger a grammatical structure in the brain. In particular, Palmer (1986) points out that, unlike the relationship between the stimuli and responses in behavioral reflexes, or in fixed-action patterns, the relationship between the environmental input (stimuli) and the grammatical output is an arbitrary one. As Palmer (1986) states:

> Languages vary from culture to culture and within a language there is no relationship between the sound of an utterance and its grammatical structure. Clearly there is no physical property of the stimulus that suffices to identify its part of speech. Nothing about the word "house" enables us to conclude that it is a noun, or that it might be a "subject." (pp. 54–55)

Thus, even if we assume that there is an innate language acquisition device that is responsible for taking environmental input and generating grammatical output, Chomsky does not specify the stimulus properties or the objective criteria by which such a device can recognize and "identify such theoretical entities" as sentences, subjects, verbs, etc. Palmer (1986) cogently concludes:

> Chomsky has been able to formulate precisely his theoretical ideas because they have remained abstract, but useful theories cannot remain abstract forever. If there is no way to use them to predict, control, or describe actual events, then they are empty. (p. 56)

The serious flaws in Chomsky's arguments for a specific brain mechanism for language acquisition could have been uncovered soon after he made them had anyone analyzed them in terms of Darwinian principles of selection. The onus of responsibility would then have been on Chomsky and his supporters to provide empirical support for his theories.

THE TREATMENT OF BEHAVIOR ANALYTIC VIEWS OF LANGUAGE IN DEVELOPMENTAL TEXTBOOKS

In the remainder of this section we present a brief discussion of the treatment of the behavior analytic approach to language by several developmental textbooks with the goal of presenting rebuttals to the various misrepresentations and criticisms.

Most developmental psychology textbooks include some discussion of different theories of language acquisition (e.g., Berndt, 1992; Bukatko & Daehler, 1992; Collins & Kuczaj, 1992; Dworetzky, 1993; Santrock, 1990; Vasta, Haith, & Miller, 1992). In most of these accounts, only brief attention is usually given to the behaviorist view—sometimes it is described as Skinner's view of language acquisition—but more attention is often given to Chomsky's view. Some actually present Chomsky's view of language acquisition as a biological theory (e.g., Santrock, 1990), despite the fact that neither Chomsky nor his supporters ever talked about real biological mechanisms or provided direct empirical evidence for them. In fact, although no developmental textbook recognizes this, the behavior analytic perspective on language behavior is much more biological than Chomsky's view is because the behavior change processes it involves do have specific biological correlates (e.g., Commons, Church, Stellar, & Wagner, 1988). Unfortunately, the behavior analytic view is almost never accurately represented, while at least some aspects of Chomsky's "theory" are presented as logically compelling, if not self-evident. Fortunately, recent editions of many developmental psychology textbooks present strong arguments for an environmental role in language development, and thus call into question some of Chomsky's claims about the innateness of specific language abilities. Many of these presentations, however, still inaccurately represent a behavior analytic view of language, and most do not cite the significant empirical contributions of behavior analysts to the study of language. For example, Santrock (1990, p. 188) incorrectly cites Skinner (1957) as arguing that language represents "chains of responses."

We will consider three frequently cited criticisms or misrepresentations of a behavior analytic interpretation of language acquisition: (1) reinforcement is insufficient to account for important changes in language behavior; (2) the child is a passive recipient of the environment; and (3) behavior theory cannot account for the creative aspects of language production, which linguists like Chomsky have referred to as the generative properties of language.

The Role of Reinforcement in the Acquisition of Language

Many accounts of the behavior analytic or Skinnerian view of language are inaccurate. Most authors report that reinforcement is the primary mechanism underlying the behavior analytic perspective on the acquisition of language behavior. Their criticisms, however, reveal a misunderstanding of the principle which, as we suggested in chapter 3, is one of the few examples of a scientific law in psychology. For example, Bukatko and Daehler (1992) claim that "there is little evidence that parents systematically tutor their children in producing grammatically correct speech or that they differentially reinforce grammatically correct and incorrect sentences with any consistency" (p. 296). The only part of this statement that is correct is that parents don't "systematically tutor their children," if this means that parents consciously try to teach their children how to speak. The suggestion that parents do not reinforce language beginning with babbling and continuing through grammatical sentences, however, is unfounded. Because no language researcher can realistically experiment with language-learning children, the best we can hope for is to conduct experiments that suggest plausible mechanisms of language learning.

There have been numerous studies suggesting that reinforcement is a plausible mechanism for learning language (e.g., Poulson, 1983, 1988; Sheppard, 1969; Whitehurst & Valdez-Menchaca, 1988). There have also been numerous studies showing that parents do respond systematically, although not necessarily intentionally or consciously, to their children's grammatical utterances (e.g., Bohannon & Stanowicz, 1988; Moerk, 1983; Penner, 1987). For example, some textbook authors describe "scaffolding," a term that refers to the many ways in which parents interact with their language-learning children and which result in increased vocalizations (Vasta et al., 1992, p. 393). Scaffolding involves turn-taking in which mothers talk to infants, infants babble in response, and the mothers then immediately respond back (e.g., Bloom, Russel, & Wassenberg, 1987). Scaffolding may also refer to the practice whereby parents continually ask questions of language-learning children, such as what, where, and who (e.g., Hoff-Ginsburg, 1990). Finally, scaffolding can refer to the practice of encouraging children not just to listen but also to talk during story-book reading time, which may include asking questions about what the characters in the story are doing, and then responding to the child's answer by repeating the child's answer, expanding on the answer, and praising both accurate and grammatical answers (Whitehurst, Falco, Lonigan, Fischel, DeBaryshe, Valdez-Menchaca, & Caulfield, 1988). Obviously, the term "scaffolding" as used by researchers encompasses both the evocative effects of parents' questions as S^{D}s for children's responses and the function-altering, that is, reinforcing effects of parents' repeating, expanding, and praising children's answers.

Behavior analysis is in an ideal position to explain the results of these research reports of the effects of the language environment on children's language. Moreover, it represents a plausible explanation of the general role of environmental variables on the learning of language. For example, "turn-taking" is a good example of parents' vocal behavior evoking vocal responses in their children which automatically produce reinforcing consequences when they occur. It would not be too difficult to test this hypothesis, as the process of reinforcement is observable and testable. What, where, and who questions function as discriminative stimuli to evoke verbal responses in children, and these responses can then produce consequences according to their content, truth value, or grammar. The reinforcers are not candy or even praise, although parents praise frequently. Reinforcers can be as subtle as simple continued responding or question asking, or smiles, or touches, and so on. Finally, during storybook reading, questions from parents again function as discriminative stimuli to evoke verbal responses in children that can then produce consequences along the same lines as the questions described above. These contingencies of reinforcement are observable and directly testable and can thus explain the effects of the environment on the development of all aspects of language behavior.

Unfortunately, the criticisms of reinforcement as a viable language learning process are based on misunderstandings of the concept itself. For example, no textbook ever mentions the possibility of automatic reinforcement (see Vaughan & Michael, 1982). Automatic reinforcement is a plausible process that is eminently observable and testable, because it points to the stimulus products of the speaker's own verbal behavior which acquire their reinforcing capacity by being correlated with other reinforcing events.

The Child as Passive Recipient of the Environment

According to some textbook authors, behavior analysts assume that the language-learning child "is merely a passive recipient of what the environment supplies" (Bukatko & Daehler, 1992), although no behavior analyst ever said this. In fact, Bukatko and Daehler (1992) call this criticism "one of the greatest limitations of the behaviorist perspective" (p. 298). Because such erroneous claims cannot possibly come from behavior analysts themselves—Bukatko and Daehler did not reference their conclusion—one wonders where such claims originate. Arguing for a strong environmental role in the development of any behavior does not automatically imply that the behaving individual is passive. On the contrary, reinforcement cannot operate on a passive individual; the individual must be active and behaving. However, the individual does not actively change his or her own behavior as most cognitive accounts would have us believe. For example, most authors claim that it is the child who overregularizes or overgeneralizes verb endings, but we have already demonstrated how behavior analytic principles (e.g., response induction and stimulus generalization) adequately explain this behavior. As a result, we need not credit (or blame) the child for making these "errors." Behavior analysts have also been criticized for being unable to explain overregularizations, a criticism we hope we have adequately put to rest. Cognitive psychologists, by contrast, have no scientific principles to support their claims (Andresen, 1991; Sidman, 1986).

Language as Inherently Generative (Creative)

The third major criticism of behavioral theories of language development is that they cannot account for the creativity of language. Hetherington and Parke (1986), for example, write that, "language affords an enormous degree of creative latitude," and "the vast majority of language utterances can in no way be directly predicted from specific 'environmental eliciting cues'" (p. 290). No behaviorist would deny that language is enormously varied and, thus, seemingly creative. However, all behavior is probably just as varied as language is, yet psychologists do not typically describe nonlanguage behavior, such as reaching, walking, sitting, etc., as generative. One difference may be that language seems to be more conspicuously variable than nonlanguage. This conspicuousness is enhanced by the fact that language is largely vocal and easily lends itself to transcription in systems of writing that can represent individual vocal sounds that differ only in very subtle ways.

The nature of operant behavior is that it is composed of classes of varied responses. What defines an operant class is the common consequence that each response, regardless of its form, produces. If we were to dissect any operant class, such as sitting in a chair, we would find that no two individual responses are identical, no matter how they look to the casual observer. We might say that sitting is creative, and we might then posit an innate sitting acquisition device that has evolved specifically to produce sitting. The point is that, beginning with Skinner (1957), behavior analysts have suggested that language is fundamentally like other operant behavior in that it is composed of various functional classes, each established and maintained by their common communicative effects (or reinforcers). This does not mean that related, and possibly emergent, processes that would help to provide a more comprehensive understanding of language might not be discovered (e.g., Sidman, 1986).

SUMMARY

This chapter argued for an account of language in terms of general principles of learning, namely, operant conditioning. The chapter also asserted that speculative cognitive or innate mechanisms were neither very plausible nor parsimonious explanations of language. The chapter began by citing evidence that infant perception of different phonemes may be a function of their acoustic, rather than their specific phonemic, that is, languagelike, properties. The conclusion, then, is that language evolved to meet the demands of the mammalian auditory system, not the other way around. The chapter then suggested that, even though maturation appears to influence the first appearance, and, perhaps, the order of prespeech sounds, like babbling, reinforcement principles account for the continuation and refinement of such sounds into those that may be called formal speech. The same argument was made for the first words, for multiple word production, for grammar, and for such phenomena as extensions and overregularization of verb endings. The behavior analytic view of language as presented in this chapter is that the form of language is shaped by the effects it has on the language community. Thus, its function is a more important clue to the controlling variables than its form. The behavior analytic view of language is that it is continuous with all other operant behavior and that selectionist principles best account for it. Finally, the chapter corrected various criticisms and misrepresentations of a behavior analytic view of language that are found in developmental textbooks. One of the more important corrections involves the nature of reinforcing stimuli found in language. Contrary to the view that reinforcers must involve conscious, systematic mediation by parents, this chapter pointed out that much of the reinforcement in language is automatic.

Social and Emotional Development I
Attachment Relations

Immediately after birth, the behavior of human neonates is affected increasingly by the behavior of other people. There is even evidence that the behavior of fetuses is affected by the stimuli arising from others, particularly the mother (DeCasper & Spence, 1986). From birth onward, infants and those around them, primarily the parents, engage in increasingly complex social interactions in which the behavior of parents affects the behavior of infants and vice versa, and the behaviors of both are changed as a result. The characteristics of the behavior of one person that affect the behavior of another person are called *social stimuli*; and the behavior that both produces these stimuli and is affected by them is called *social behavior*. As with other stimuli, social stimuli can have different functions depending upon the history of an individual. For example, the social behavior of others can produce eliciting stimuli (either USs or CSs), motivational stimuli (i.e., establishing operations or EOs), discriminative stimuli (S^{D}s), or reinforcing or punishing stimuli. As with the other forms of behavior we have discussed so far (i.e., memory, motor, perceptual, cognitive, and language), behavior we refer to as *social* shows a progressive complexity in terms of its interactions with the social environment. "Social environment" is the term used to describe all of the social stimuli that affect the behavior of an individual at a given time.

The area of psychology that deals primarily with social development includes a vast network of topics such as emotional development, infant attachment, social cognition, the self, achievement and independence, aggression, altruism and prosocial development, and moral development. Moreover, some perceptual behavior (see chapter 6) is social (i.e., under the control of social stimuli), and so, of course, is all language (see chapter

8). The area called social development has been partitioned by developmental psychologists into many formal categories. As we might expect, in many instances individual categories are treated as if they were each functionally distinct. Because we have restricted the discussion in this book to the period of development called infancy, and some of these categories have more import for older children, we will not deal with all of them in this chapter. As for those we do address, we honor the formal divisions of social behavior, only to conclude that, although they have descriptive value, they do not explain the behavior subsumed under them.

Specifically, we concentrate on social–emotional development in infancy. Social–emotional development usually denotes the development of attachment behaviors in both infants and caregivers, although the emphasis is usually on the behavior of infants. Topics in this area include emotional bonding, social referencing, stranger anxiety, and separation anxiety. We first present the most popular theory of attachment, that of John Bowlby. Following this, we consider some research areas that are frequently cited in support of his theory. Again, we attempt to show how behavior analysis is sufficient to explain the development of social–emotional behavior.

DEFINING ATTACHMENT

As it is used in most treatments of social behavior in infants, the term "attachment" refers to the close emotional ties between infants and their primary caregivers, usually the mother. Just as most researchers in the field of cognitive development followed Jean Piaget, most modern researchers in the area of social–emotional development have followed the lead of John Bowlby. Bowlby (1958, 1973, as cited in Shaffer, 1988) used the term "attachment" to refer to "strong and enduring affectional ties" between intimate companions. Thus, according to Bowlby, people (or other animals) who are attached will interact often, exhibit behaviors that result in their being in proximity to each other, and result in protest upon separation. Used this way, the term "attachment" defines a generally large area of psychology which now includes such phenomena as imprinting in nonhumans, the effects of early social deprivation or neglect, mother–infant bonding shortly after birth, social referencing, separation and stranger anxiety, dependence and independence, emotional behaviors such as smiling and crying, and so on. In this chapter, we discuss some of the behavioral relations that have been subsumed under attachment. The term "attachment" is, of course, a metaphor because organisms are not physically "attached." Thus, the term refers frequently only to certain formal behavioral relations, those initially between the behavior of infants and primary caregivers.

INTERPRETING BOWLBY'S THEORY OF ATTACHMENT

We should have no problem agreeing with the following description of attachment by one of the leading interpreters of Bowlby's view:

> Human newborns are capable of a variety of signaling behaviors that elicit caregiving and other social responses from adults and that provide feedback regarding the success of caregiving interventions. In the course of the first few weeks and months, these infant social behaviors become more complex and coordinated. At the same time, infants begin to direct them preferentially toward specific caregiving figures. (Bretherton, 1987, pp. 1061–1063)

For example, crying in newborns typically evokes both unconditioned and conditioned respondents and operants in adults. If the crying is elicited by hunger and the caregiver feeds the infant, crying stops. Over the course of weeks and months, crying changes from being almost entirely reflexive to learned—both respondently and operantly—and, thus, becomes more complex. In the operant case, if some adults reinforce the crying more often or more richly than others (i.e., differential reinforcement), then the crying will be more likely to occur when those particular adults are nearby.

As with memory, motor, perceptual, cognitive, and language behaviors, interaction with the environment is responsible for the transformation of social–emotional behavior from relatively simple, uncoordinated relations to more complex, coordinated ones. Bretherton's quote describes the development of infant social–emotional behavior in similar ways. Throughout the book, we have argued that interpreting development in terms of orderly, functional behavior–environment units of analysis is a sufficient explanation and that interpretations at nonbehavioral levels of analysis violate many of the criteria of science.

Bowlby's Evolutionary–Ethological Perspective

Bowlby's theory of attachment accounts for behaviors that involve proximity to a protective figure, such as approaching, crying or the lack of crying at separation from a caregiver, and the extent of exploratory/search behavior in the presence of the caregiver. Based on their observations of such behavior, Bowlby (1969, 1973) and other attachment theorists (e.g., Ainsworth, 1973) have proposed what they refer to as an evolutionary–ethological view of attachment. According to this view, over the course of the first two years of the infant's life, attachment behaviors become integrated into a behavioral–motivational system, called the *attachment system*, which is organized around a particular person or persons. This behavioral–motivational system "refers to a regulatory system hypothesized to exist within a person," whose "set-goal is to regulate behaviors that maintain proximity to and contact with a discriminated protective person, referred to as the *attachment figure(s)*" (Bretherton, 1987, p. 1063). The attachment system is said to regulate all aspects of attachment behavior, from its initial activation when either accessibility to a caregiver is possible or danger is perceived, to the actual production of the behavior. It is also said to monitor the whereabouts of the caregiver and to set limits on how far from the secure base the child will venture (Bretherton, 1987).

This system is called "evolutionary" because it "has fairly obvious survival value" (Bretherton, 1987, p. 1063). However, just because some behavioral relations may seem to have obvious survival value, doesn't mean that they necessarily have phylogenetic origins. In fact, not all characteristics of species exist because of their survival or adaptive value. Many characteristics, like the differences in scale numbers among related species of snakes may have no function, having evolved merely by genetic drift (Futuyma, 1979, pp. 433–434).

That some characteristics, like the behaviors that result in proximity to a caregiver, may seem to have survival value does not mean that they could not have ontogenetic origins. The behavior of precocial birds like ducks and geese of following a primary caregiver is a good example of behavior that has been misinterpreted as largely innate when there is very likely a strong learning component to it (Schlinger & Blakely, 1994). Even when behavior seems to have obvious survival value, it is incumbent on psychologists to experimentally rule out the possibility of learning before positing specific evolutionary mechanisms.

Bowlby's Concept of Internal Working Models

Bowlby's approach to attachment is based on his concept of internal working models of the self and attachment figures. Bretherton says that Bowlby's concept of internal working models was an attempt to rework some of the issues that have historically interested psychoanalytic theorists. Simply speaking, Bowlby, like Freud before him, has taken observable behavior–environment relations, constructed an internal model of these relations, and then used the hypothetical processes of the model to explain the original observations. Freud proposed an internal working of the personality in which different parts of the personality—id, ego, and superego—combine to produce the person's adjustment to reality and social morals. Except for the id, which Freud claimed was present at birth, he claimed that the development of the ego and superego originated in interactions with the real world and the social environment, respectively. Like Freud, Bowlby has proposed internal working models of the self and the principal caregivers. This internal system supposedly develops as a result of individuals' interactions with their environments, or in this case, with their principal caregivers. Bretherton (1987) offers an example of the types of possible internal working models that might develop given certain environmental experiences and how internal working models of the self develop as a function of interactions with the principal caregiver:

> [A] child who experiences—and hence represents—attachment figures as primarily rejecting may form a complimentary internal working model of the self as unworthy. Similarly a child who experiences a parental figure as emotionally available and supportive will most probably construct a working model of the self as competent and lovable. (p. 1067)

Once these internal processes are assumed to exist, Bowlby, like Freud, attributes to them the properties necessary to account for various attachment phenomena. This is not to say that a child who experiences constant rejection by a parent is not seriously affected by such treatment. The question is whether it is necessary, or even helpful, to posit internal models to account for the behavioral effects of the maltreatment. Bowlby's theory is little different than the other cognitively oriented theories of infant development we have mentioned throughout this book. Although Bowlby's theory is couched in ethological, evolutionary language, it is still a cognitive theory, because it infers unobserved and unobservable processes as explanations of behavior.

We return later to Bowlby's theory of internal working models, but first let us look at some of the specific attachment phenomena that developmental psychologists cite in support of Bowlby's theory.

ATTACHMENT BEHAVIORS

According to Bowlby (1969), attachment behaviors can be classified according to whether their effect is to bring the caregiver to the child, which he called *signaling behaviors*, or whether their effect is to bring the child to the caregiver, which he called *approach behaviors*. For obvious reasons, signaling behaviors, which include crying, smiling, and babbling, precede approach behaviors, which include actual approach behaviors and clinging, so we will consider signaling behavior first. As in previous chapters, we present the standard account followed by a comparison between cognitive and behavior analytic explanations.

Signaling Behavior

Evolutionary–ethological attachment theorists, like Bowlby, believe that we can find evidence for the aforementioned behavioral–motivational attachment system in the earliest days after birth. Obviously, actual approach behaviors, like clinging, do not begin to occur until the infant is mobile, although the existence of the grasp, Babinski, and Moro reflexes indicate that there are some unconditioned reflexes related to clinging. The crying reflexes, which are present immediately after birth, and the smiling reflexes seen shortly thereafter, are the bases for attachment theorists to posit an inherited behavioral–motivational attachment system. Just as Piaget felt that the earliest signs of cognitive development were seen in infant reflexes, which then became more coordinated after interaction with the environment, Bowlby believed that the earliest signs of attachment were seen in the same reflexes. Like Piaget, Bowlby believed that these attachment behaviors become more directed and complex after interaction with the social environment, although he did not specify the variables responsible for this increasing directedness. Because crying probably precedes smiling developmentally, we begin our discussion of signaling behaviors with crying.

Crying

Our discussion of crying in chapter 8 was primarily in the context of it being a precursor to verbal behavior. In the present chapter, we consider crying in general as a form of social behavior. Some developmental psychologists have said that crying is the most important form of communicative behavior present in newborns (Lester & Zeskind, 1982). But crying is also viewed as emotional behavior, usually indicating distress of some kind. That one particular form of behavior, like crying, can be classified as three presumably different types of behavior by developmental researchers—verbal, social, and emotional—reveals some of the problems with classifying behavior according to its form alone. One problem is that researchers might assume that each category is governed by a different set of psychological principles. A second problem is that classifying crying as an instance of communicative, emotional, or social behavior may hinder researchers in their attempts to accurately discriminate the controlling variables of behavior. We are not saying that there are no good reasons to distinguish crying on the basis of its form, but according to the behavior–analytic view in the present book, behavior is more fruitfully classified in a functional manner.

Crying in infants has been researched extensively. As mentioned in chapter 8, there seem to be at least three functionally different types of crying in neonates (Wolff, 1969). The first is the basic cry, which builds up slowly and consists of a rhythmical sequence of cry, pause, take in air, and pause. Although the basic cry is called a *hunger cry*, the term is misleading because this cry also occurs at other times (Wolff, 1969). The second type of cry is called an anger cry, and the third is called a pain cry.

Crying is a curious example of social behavior in humans because its initial appearance as reflexive behavior is not under the obvious control of social variables. If we consider crying in an evolutionary sense, however, it might be possible to speak of it as social behavior. Some research indicates that crying might be an adaptive response, which, at a physiological level, facilitates the reorganization of the cardiorespiratory system, improves pulmonary capacity, and helps maintain homeostasis (Lester and Zeskind, 1982). It makes sense to think about reflexive crying in newborns as an instance of phylogenetic social behavior, and it is not difficult to imagine how this behavior in particular might have evolved because of the effects it had on other members of a social group. Because crying is an unpleasant auditory stimulus, we do not have to interpret the mother's response to crying as an example of inherited behavior (see below) in order to account adequately for its occurrence. The stimuli arising from crying can be interpreted as motivational variables (EOs) whose termination reinforces any behavior that produces it. Anyone who has ever witnessed a parent trying to soothe a crying infant can attest to the fact that parents will try almost anything to stop the crying, even at the expense of inadvertently reinforcing the behavior, the results of which may not be seen or heard until some time in the future. Below we discuss the transformation of crying from reflexive to learned behavior, and the simultaneous effects of crying on the behavior of caregivers.

Maternal Responding and Infant Crying.   In a now famous and widely cited study, Bell and Ainsworth (1972) reported on patterns of correlations of maternal responding to infant crying across the four quarters of the first year of life for 26 mother–infant pairs. Their conclusion was that consistent and prompt responding by mothers to infant crying in the early quarters· was correlated with a reduction in the frequency and duration of crying in later quarters. Bell and Ainsworth suggested that these results contradicted the popular belief promulgated by learning theorists that contingent maternal responding increases infant crying and produces a demanding and spoiled child. According to Gewirtz (1977), some developmental authors uncritically accepted the Bell and Ainsworth findings and interpretations, and suggested that operant principles were not sufficient to account for important events in human behavioral development. The Bell and Ainsworth (1972) findings have even found their way into the popular press in the form of advice to parents about how to respond to the cries of their infants (Gewirtz, 1977). Because the Bell and Ainsworth (1972) study is still reported in many texts without citing its methodological and theoretical drawbacks (e.g., Gewirtz, 1977; Gewirtz & Boyd, 1977; Parsley & Rabinowitz 1975), we briefly discuss this study and offer a general behavior analytic view of crying, with supporting experimental (vs. correlational) evidence.

Because good methodological grounds exist for questioning the conclusions of the Bell and Ainsworth (1972) study (e.g., Gewirtz, 1977; Gewirtz & Boyd, 1977), our discussion will follow from a critique provided by Gewirtz (1977) about whether Bell and Ainsworth's conclusions are warranted from their data. Gewirtz (1977) makes two general points. The first is that alternative conclusions can be drawn from the Bell and Ainsworth data regarding the relation between infant crying and maternal responsiveness. Toward that end, Gewirtz (1977) enumerated several problems with the correlations calculated by Bell and Ainsworth. The first was that Bell and Ainsworth intercorrelated maternal responding and maternal ignoring, neither of which could occur until the infant actually cried. This meant that there was a unique type of dependence between infant and mother behavior and that scoring of only the mothers' behavior (i.e., responding to or ignoring crying) depended on the occurrence of the infants' behavior (i.e., crying). A second problem was the lack of statistical control of important antecedent and concurrent variables such as maternal responding and ignoring of crying both in earlier and later quarters in the study. Another problem was Bell and Ainsworth's conclusion that prompt maternal responding to infant crying decreased future crying, even though they did not present ongoing correlations of maternal responding and infant crying. Rather, the researchers based their conclusion on correlations of maternal ignoring and infant crying. According to Gewirtz (1977), Bell and Ainsworth treated maternal responding to crying as the inverse of maternal ignoring of crying. Gewirtz (1977) finds this especially troubling, because "Bell and Ainsworth defined as infant crying the frequency/ duration *only* of those episodes to which the mother *responded*" (p. 41). Gewirtz concluded that the Bell and Ainsworth data do not permit an answer to the question, "Does maternal responding really decrease infant crying?"

Gewirtz's (1977) second general point is that Bell and Ainsworth's data do not allow a functional analysis of the variables in question. This is because correlations between gross behavioral and environmental events, such as the ones calculated by Bell and Ainsworth, omit important details (e.g., the definition of the response class, the specific contingencies between maternal responding and crying) that would permit a functional analysis of the variables. Gewirtz (1977) demonstrates how a number of different outcomes regarding the frequency and duration of infant crying are possible depending upon the specific contingencies of reinforcement between mother and child. The important point here is that a behavior analytic interpretation of crying is not the simplistic one frequently implied, namely, that attention to crying increases the future frequency of crying. In fact, Gewirtz discusses how the Bell and Ainsworth results could, themselves, have resulted from operant conditioning. According to Gewirtz (1977):

> One responsive mother may shape effectively her infant's loud, lengthy cries by ignoring both short, low intensity cries, and by responding expeditiously only to high-intensity, long-duration cries. A second responsive mother may shape the short low-intensity cries of her infant by ignoring both the precursors of crying and lengthy, loud cries, while she responds rapidly and decisively only to short, low-intensity cries. In yet another contrast, a third responsive mother may foster behavior incompatible with her infant's crying; she may respond with dispatch only to short, low-intensity precursors of her infant's crying and/or to noncrying responses, to rear a child who cries rarely (and then mainly when painful events elicit crying). (p. 43)

Each of these three interactive patterns could contribute to a positive correlation between infant crying and maternal ignoring.

In closing, let us briefly discuss the operant conditioning of infant crying. Although some attachment theorists suggest that infant crying is not very much affected by operant conditioning, experimental research demonstrates that crying is susceptible to reinforcement, extinction, and stimulus control (e.g., Etzel & Gewirtz, 1967; Hart, Allen, Buel, Harris, & Wolf, 1964). Experimental evidence also shows that other social emotional responses in infants are susceptible to operant conditioning, for example, smiling (e.g., Brackbill, 1958; Etzel & Gewirtz, 1967); eye contact (e.g., Etzel & Gewirtz, 1967); and vocalizations (e.g., Rheingold, Gewirtz, & Ross, 1959). If we accept that all crying is reflexive at birth, then we must be able to suggest a plausible mechanism for the transformation of crying from reflexive to learned. Behavior analysis possesses the basic laws and principles to offer a plausible account of such a transformation. Our conclusion is that nonreflexive crying is the result of ontogenetic, selectionist principles of reinforcement and stimulus control.

We have considered crying in infants as an instance of signaling behavior, in part to illustrate how crying may be classified as early social emotional behavior in infants. Under other circumstances, crying has been used as a criterion for attachment, for example, when the caregiver departs or a stranger approaches. Therefore, we will return to crying when we discuss these attachment relations.

Smiling

Most developmental psychologists agree that the earliest smiles of the infant are not social smiles, largely because they are elicited by a variety of nonsocial stimuli, such as changes in brightness or visual patterns, and they are often seen during sleep. It is said that *social* smiles are seen around 3 weeks of age. At this time, the smile is evoked by the sound of the female voice. Later on, the sight of a human face, particularly the eyes, evokes a smile. Bowlby and his followers stress that the infant's smile is evoked by social events and itself evokes attachment behavior in other people. Hence, Bowlby (1969) refers to social smiles as a form of "signaling behavior."

Dworetzky (1990, p. 156) has described the infant smile as "intrinsically satisfying" to the parents. This implies that a behavioral–motivational attachment system is operating for adults. After all, it would be useless for an inherited attachment system to be present only in infants. That infant smiles evoke certain behaviors in most adults, however, does not automatically prove the existence of an innate attachment system. An argument for such a system becomes stronger, however, if we can eliminate other plausible explanations.

Although the origins of the onset of social smiling are unclear, once social smiling in infants begins to occur, its occurrence may be a powerful reinforcer for the behavior of adults. When infants smile others will usually smile back, talk to the infant, and so on. Moreover, the eye and mouth movements of the adults, which may become exaggerated, are correlated with these consequences. The movements of the adult's eyes and mouth are important because they are part of the stimulus complex that evokes infant visual fixation and, thus, what psychologists speak of as facial recognition (see Aslin, 1987, for a brief review of face perception).

The consequences of infant smiling increase its frequency, and they also result in the discrimination of such behavior. In other words, the sight of the primary caregivers will evoke more smiling than the sight of other, less "familiar" people. For developmental psychologists interested in attachment, this discriminated smiling is one of the earliest signs of attachment (Shaffer, 1988). Many developmental psychologists attribute the response differentiation and discrimination of smiling to maturing cognitive processes, such as the infant's memory, or to certain neurological structures (e.g., Bukatko & Daehler, 1992). However, a behavior analytic account that appeals to the operant principles of response differentiation and discrimination offers a plausible and more parsimonious explanation of smiling.

Because smiling is evoked by social stimuli, and because it produces such strong and immediate effects on the social environment and is strengthened in return, a more parsimonious interpretation would account for the increasing complexity of smiling relations in terms of the principles of behavior–environment interaction, that is, of operant and respondent conditioning. After all, the operant conditioning of smiling in infants has been reliably demonstrated in numerous experiments (e.g., Brackbill, 1958; Etzel & Gewirtz, 1967). In chapter 8, we saw that the operant conditioning of infant vocalizations has been demonstrated experimentally. As we have already seen, the operant conditioning of infant crying has also been demonstrated experimentally. These demonstrations increase the plausibility of a behavior analytic interpretation of infant smiling and other emotional responses. There are no such data demonstrating functional relationships between proposed cognitive independent variables and the dependent variables of attachment behaviors.

Some correlational evidence also supports a behavior analytic interpretation of smiling in infants. For example, Kuchuk, Vibbert, and Bornstein (1986) studied individual differences in 3-month-olds' preferences for smiling at pictures of female faces in various degrees of smiling, from less to more intense (as defined by the researchers). The infant preferences were measured by visual fixation to the stimuli in a laboratory setting. The results of the laboratory measurements were then correlated with observations of infant–mother interactions in the home setting. Kuchuk et al. (1986) found that infants who looked at the more intense smiling stimuli had mothers who encouraged more attention to themselves when they were smiling. In other words, there were positive correlations between the laboratory findings and the observations at home. The authors concluded that the perception of smiling by infants is strongly affected by their experience at home.

These results are easily interpreted within a behavior analytic framework. Mothers evoke visual attention in infants through such behaviors as smiling, talking, etc. When their infants are looking at their faces, the mothers' smiling changes because the mouth and eyes move, and the mothers also continue to talk to their infants. All of these events are contingent upon the infants' visual gazes. In fact, because these stimuli are visual, the infants' gazes are necessary for smiles to be produced. It is not surprising that such extensive experience with single caregivers results in infants who prefer to look at smiling faces, usually of females, and more specifically of their mothers.

Approach Behaviors

For Bowlby (1969), some behaviors (e.g., seeking and following) bring infants to their mothers, while other behaviors (e.g., clinging) keep the mothers present. Obviously, any behavior we call "true approach" requires mobility. For Bowlby, approach behaviors, like signaling, become goal-directed and "goal-corrected." The process by which this occurs has been called the attachment process. Attachment theorists, by definition, are interested in "the process of becoming attached [and] how infants and their companions establish these close emotional ties" (Shaffer, 1988, p. 105). Rather than describing the many specific types of approach behaviors in detail in this section, we discuss them in the broader perspective of proximity-establishing and proximity-maintaining behaviors, as well as behaviors that result when proximity to a significant other is lessened (separation anxiety) or when proximity to non-significant others is increased (stranger anxiety). Thus, we will discuss approach behavior in terms of functional response classes.

Proximity-Establishing and Proximity-Maintaining Behaviors

Attachment theorists, following Bowlby, believe that attachment behavior in infants, regardless of its form, brings proximity to the primary attachment figure, usually the mother, as its predictable outcome (Bowlby, 1969). For Bowlby, this helps to explain and unify a great deal of data regarding infant behavior. For example, if there is a behavioral–motivational attachment system, then it might be reasonable to assume that the infant's developing ability to respond differentially to the mother's voice, face, etc., is mediated by this attachment system. Such a system would also explain the "goal-correctedness," as Bowlby (1969) calls it, of signaling and approach behaviors. The purpose of the present treatment is not to dispute the presence of these attachment behaviors but, rather, to offer a plausible explanation of them, without postulating a cognitive organizing system.

Frequently, standard textbook treatments of attachment present several, usually mutually exclusive, theories of attachment. For example, Shaffer (1988) presents a psychoanalytic theory, a learning theory, a cognitive–developmental theory, and an ethological theory. Although these theories are often based on systematic observations and attempt to order the observations in an effort to explain them, they are not "scientific" theories in the natural science sense of the term because their methodologies do not allow for the discovery of functional units of analysis and, consequently, scientific laws. Although the learning theory that is typically presented is the most empirically based, it is an old learning theory. It does not represent behavior analysis which, in the view of this book, combines features of an ethological and learning approach in the context of known units of behavior analysis.

The first part of our discussion of proximity establishing and maintaining behaviors will focus on attachment in nonhumans. Even though this is a book on human development, we present a discussion of attachment in nonhumans for several reasons. First, Bowlby (1969, p. 223) concluded that there was a parallel between human and nonhuman attachment processes. More recently, Petrovich and Gewirtz (1991) have argued that the data on imprinting in nonhumans would provide to the developmental psychologist "an expanded data base across species" that could lead to a more complete understanding of the processes involved in the behavioral development of humans. We will summarize the treatments of imprinting in precocial and altricial animals. The term "precocial" is used to refer to animals (e.g., ducks, geese, goats) that are relatively mature at or soon after birth or hatching. The term "altricial" is used to refer to animals (e.g., cats, dogs, some primates, and humans) which are more helpless and, thus, more dependent on parental care to survive after birth or hatching (Fantino & Logan, 1979, p. 364).

Attachment Behaviors in Precocial Animals: Imprinting

"Imprinting" (the English translation of the German, *pragung*) is the term the ethologist Konrad Lorenz used to denote the behavior of precocial birds of following the first large, moving object seen soon after hatching. Most students of psychology have seen photographs of Lorenz being followed by newly hatched goslings. As Bowlby (1969) pointed out, the term "imprinting" is used in at least two distinct ways. In its most narrow usage, imprinting refers to a learning process that occurs in precocial birds within a brief critical period soon after hatching when moving objects are in close proximity and begin to evoke following. In its broader or more generic usage, the term "imprinting":

> refers to whatever processes may be at work in leading the filial attachment behaviour of a young bird or mammal to become directed preferentially and stably towards one (or more) discriminated figure(s). (Bowlby, 1969, p. 167)

Stated this way, we might easily include the human social attachment behaviors discussed so far as instances of imprinting. While this may be a matter of semantics, many human attachment theorists see important differences between imprinting behaviors in precocial animals and attachment behaviors in altricial animals (Bowlby, 1969; Petrovich & Gewirtz, 1991). Although ethologists such as Lorenz (1935), Hess (1973), and Sluckin (1965) emphasize innate mechanisms, some psychologists have focused more on environmentally based processes (e.g., Gewirtz, 1961; Hoffman & Ratner, 1973). Despite the various theoretical interpretations of imprinting phenomena, the one thing that most recent researchers agree on is that some form of learning is involved, with changes in social relationships as the outcome (Petrovich & Gewirtz, 1991). Before we consider the possible role of operant and respondent conditioning in imprinting, let us look briefly at the standard experimental demonstration of imprinting.

In the standard experimental preparation, a moving object is presented to a newly hatched duckling. Soon thereafter, the moving object evokes following, snuggling, and vocal behavior by the duckling. The removal of the object will evoke "distress" calls and "searching" behavior, and at a later time it will continue to evoke approach and following if represented. The presentation of a novel object at this time will evoke avoidance behaviors in the duckling. Ethologists and psychologists alike have attempted to understand these observations of imprinting in precocial birds in both naturalistic and laboratory settings. The evidence from these types of studies suggests that there is a strong interplay between species-specific mechanisms of behavioral acquisition and more general mechanisms of conditioning.

Gewirtz (1961) and Hoffman and Ratner (1973) have proposed reinforcement models of imprinting that are based on a precocial bird's innate disposition to be affected by exposure to certain kinds of stimulation soon after hatching. For the purposes of the present book, the important thing about imprinting is that, while we can describe the learning as specific to certain species of precocial birds, what appears to be learned is not the particular behavior but, rather, the functions of a particular stimulus. Hoffman and Ratner (1973) have noted that specific properties of the imprinted stimulus, for example, its movement, will evoke or suppress certain responses in the duckling, such as distress calls. Those properties will also evoke or suppress approaching and following the imprinted stimulus. Although it is difficult to separate the inherited and environmental effects of exposure to a moving object, it appears that at some point the imprinted stimulus takes on a reinforcing function. Thus, behavior should increase in frequency when presentation of the imprinting stimulus is contingent upon that behavior and decrease in frequency when removal of the imprinted stimulus is contingent on the behavior. Several researchers have reliably demonstrated such operant functions of the imprinted stimulus consistent with this prediction (Bateson & Reese, 1968; Hoffman, Searle, Toffey, & Kozma, 1966; Hoffman, Stratton, & Newby, 1969; Peterson,

1960). Peterson (1960), for example, showed that exposing young duck-lings to a particular stimulus (e.g., a moving yellow light source) soon after hatching, established that stimulus as a reinforcer. This stimulus function was evidenced by demonstrating that movement of the imprinted stim-ulus could be used to condition an arbitrary response such as pecking a plexiglass disc. Skinner (1974, p. 41) speculated that presentation of the imprinted stimulus could also increase the frequency of moving away from the stimulus, whereas removal of the imprinting stimulus contingent on approach behavior could decrease the frequency of such behavior. Such a demonstration would lend support to the suggestion that it is not a specific behavior that is inherited but, rather, a tendency for behavior to be strengthened by certain properties of the imprinted stimulus. In this way, the process that results in attachment behavior in precocial birds can be classified along with other stimulus functions as an operation that alters the behavioral functions of some stimulus (Schlinger & Blakely, 1994).

The one inescapable conclusion from all the studies on imprinting is that precocial birds are capable of being relatively permanently affected by some types of early experience. Because ducklings and goslings are capa-ble of locomotion soon after hatching, this early process is most conspicu-ously manifested in their behavior of following. Hence, it is no surprise that following is the attachment behavior studied most in precocial birds.

Attachment Behaviors in Altricial Animals

By definition, altricial animals are not capable of locomotion soon after birth, but they are capable of nonlocomotor behaviors, for example, sucking, clinging, cooing, crying, and snuggling, which seem to serve the same function as following in precocial birds, namely, increasing or main-taining contact with caregivers (Petrovich & Gewirtz, 1991). Perhaps the most famous example of the study of attachment behaviors in altricial animals is the set of studies by Harry Harlow and his colleagues with infant rhesus monkeys.

Most students of psychology are familiar with Harlow and Zimmer-man's (1959) study in which they compared the clinging of infant rhesus monkeys to two surrogate monkey mothers, one made of wire mesh and one covered with cloth. Except for the time spent feeding, the monkeys who fed on the wire mother spent a majority of their time clinging to the cloth mother. These results are usually presented as refuting the "feeding theory" of some early learning theorists, because although the infants were fed by the wire mother, they clung to the cloth mother.

The description of Harlow's study, at least in some developmental textbooks, presents at least two problems. First, even Harlow and Zimmerman (1959) admit that feeding is important in attachment behavior, although it is by no means the only important variable. Second, their (1959) study is flawed in at least one way: The two surrogate mothers are not identical (see Figure 9.1); the cloth covered mother has a realistic head, whereas the wire mesh mother has an unrealistic head. Why is this important? In one of his studies, Harlow and his colleagues showed that infant monkeys learned to press a lever if the consequence was the sight of the cloth surrogate or a real monkey, but not if the consequence was the sight of the wire mother (see Harlow, 1967 for a description). For a control group raised with no mothers at all, however, the rate of lever pressing was higher when they could see a real monkey as opposed to either surrogate. These findings suggest that some visual characteristics of the real monkey will apparently function as reinforcers without any history with real monkeys. Thus, the infant monkeys might have clung in part to the cloth mother, because it more closely resembled a real monkey.

Irrespective of these problems, how may we interpret the findings by Harlow and his colleagues? First of all, they do not refute any behavior analytic prediction or theory. On the contrary, they fit nicely and simply into a behavior analytic framework, because "contact comfort," like the proximity or movement of the imprinting stimulus for precocial birds, is a potent reinforcer for behavior that produces it. In the case of precocial birds, the behavior that normally produces proximity is following; for altricial rhesus monkeys, the behavior that normally produces and maintains warmth and softness is clinging. In both cases, however, if we could separate the consequences from the behavior that naturally produces them, we could presumably condition any arbitrary behavior (see Peterson, 1960).

The results of the imprinting studies and Harlow's studies have as yet unknown implications for humans, despite the temptation to generalize based on the form of the behaviors, that is, following primary caregivers and clinging to them, both of which may be observed to occur in human infants.

DEVELOPMENT OF "FEARFUL" BEHAVIORS

In one of Harlow's studies, when infant monkeys were presented with a strange object, they ran and clung almost exclusively to the cloth-covered surrogate mother. Only after a period of time would the infants leave the cloth mother and venture toward the strange object. According to Harlow (1967), "The analogy with the behavior of humans requires no elaboration" (p. 104). Indeed, one of the most extensively studied attach-

Figure 9.1. Infant rhesus monkey feeding on wire mother while clinging to cloth mother. (Photo courtesy of Harlow Primate Laboratory)

ment relations in humans is that between a fear-producing situation and the behavior evoked by it. The two "fear-producing" situations that have been most extensively studied in human infants are those that have produced what attachment theorists call "separation anxiety" and "stranger anxiety."

Separation Anxiety

The term "separation anxiety" is used when infants begin to show "signs of discomfort when separated from their mothers or other familiar companions" (Shaffer, 1988, p. 127). In nonlocomoting infants the "signs of discomfort" mostly include crying, whereas in locomoting infants, running and clinging may also occur. For the behavior analyst, "separation anxiety" is not a thing to be studied and understood, but rather a verbal response in attachment theorists evoked by the occurrence of crying or running and clinging in an infant upon the departure or absence of his or her mother. In other words, it is a name for these behavioral relations. The question for any science of behavior is how the behavioral relations can be most parsimoniously explained.

Shaffer (1988) presents three theories of separation anxiety: the conditioned anxiety explanation, the ethological viewpoint, and the cognitive–developmental viewpoint. The conditioned anxiety position is that infants learn to associate periods of discomfort with the absence of a caregiver. The ethological viewpoint is that separation anxiety is an innate reaction that helps to protect infants from harm by increasing the chance that caregivers will not stay away. The cognitive–developmental viewpoint posits that Piagetian schemata develop with respect to different kinds of departures and absences by the caregiver, so infants are most likely to protest separation when they cannot understand where the caregiver has gone or when they will return. According to Shaffer (1988), a study by Littenberg, Tulkin, and Kagan (1971) supports the cognitive developmental explanation. This study found that 15-month-old infants showed little separation protest when the mother departed through a doorway she used often but showed considerable protest when she left through a door that she used infrequently. Absent from Shaffer's list of possible explanations is a behavior analytic one.

According to Gewirtz (1976), infant protests increase in frequency because mothers respond contingently to them. Because mothers respond contingently more often in the presence of stimuli associated with their departure or absence, infant separation behaviors come under the discriminative control of those stimuli. The implication and the prediction is that when maternal behaviors are no longer made contingent on those discriminated infant responses, the S^Ds associated with maternal departure or absence should no longer evoke the infant protests. This prediction is consistent with scientific predictions in general, because it is precise and suggests relations between observable, manipulable independent variables and behavioral dependent variables (see chapter 1). The cognitive–developmental hypothesis, in contrast, does not permit the direct manipulation of variables. How, for instance, can we directly manipulate the infant's schemata?

The behavior analytic interpretation described by Gewirtz (1976) also has other important implications for separation anxiety in particular and attachment in general. First, Gewirtz points out that the stimuli associated with a caregiver's departure or absence that evoke protest behavior are no different functionally than the stimuli associated with a caregiver's entrance or presence that evoke infant orienting or smiling. In other words, they both probably function as S^Ds. Thus, unless there is some innate relation between separation and protest behavior, it may be misleading to classify separation protests separately from other infant behaviors controlled by caregivers. Such an interpretation challenges the use by attachment theorists of a single index of attachment such as crying or separation protest (Gewirtz, 1976). A second implication is that the discriminated protest behavior "would no more need to connote affective states like those termed unhappiness, distress, or despair than would such cued responses as smiles, orienting, approaching, or vocalizing need to connote joy, satisfaction, or pleasure" (Gewirtz, 1976, p. 148).

The term "separation anxiety" denotes events, namely anxiety, occurring at a nonbehavioral level. The anxiety must be inferred from the very behavior it is said to explain; if no crying occurs upon the departure of the mother, for instance, no anxiety is inferred. A more parsimonious and scientific explanation attempts to relate the infant's behavior to objective variables. For example, the findings of the above-mentioned study by Littenberg et al. (1971) can be more easily explained according to the behavior analytic interpretation offered by Gewirtz (1976). If infants respond differently depending on which of two doors their mothers use to leave the room, then we must ask what the mothers have done differently when using those doors in the past, such that the departure through a particular door would evoke protest behavior. Are the mothers more likely to respond to their infants' protests with contingent attention when exiting through a rarely or never used door? Have the mothers stopped responding in similar ways when they exit through often used doors? These questions specify variables that can be observed, potentially manipulated, and, thus, tested.

Scientific interpretations of behavioral relations are strengthened when scientists demonstrate experimental control over similar behavior (see chapter 1). Gewirtz and Pelaez-Nogueras (1991a), for instance, showed experimentally that infant protests can be brought under the stimulus control of a mother's departure and brief separation. Using an A-B-A repeated-measures design, Gewirtz and Pelaez-Nogueras (1991a) had mothers provide attention contingent on their infants' protest behaviors. After the mothers had shaped discriminated protest behavior in their infants, two experimental conditions were programmed. In the noncontingent condition (A), mothers responded to their infants' behavior on a differential reinforcement of other behavior (DRO) schedule in which any behavior other than protest behavior was contingently responded to. As a result, mothers responded to their infants after periods of time during which protest behavior did not occur. In the contingent condition (B), mothers responded to their infants' protest behavior on a continuous reinforcement (CRF) schedule. The cued trials were the same for both the contingent and noncontingent conditions, and consisted of the mother saying, "Bye, bye, Mommy will be right back," while looking at her infant. The responses by the mothers were also the same for both conditions and consisted of the mother saying, ' "It's all right; Mommy will be back soon"; "What's the matter?" "Don't worry!" ' The results (see Figure 9.2) clearly showed that infant protests were higher during the CRF condition than during the DRO condition. The A-B-A (reversal) design used by Gewirtz and Pelaez-Nogueras (1991a) is a powerful demonstration of experimental control that does not require any interpretation, statistical or otherwise, on the part of the experimenters regarding the relation between the independent and dependent variables. The results of the Gewirtz and Pelaez-Nogueras (1991a) study strongly support the plausibility of a behavior analytic interpretation of separation protest behavior, whether we call it separation anxiety or not. Moreover, as Gewirtz and Pelaez-Nogueras (1991a) note, such a demonstration can also "identify procedures that parents might employ to minimize separation difficulties by precluding their children's protests in these settings" (p. 124). Nonbehavior analytic attachment theorists have not been able to offer any comparably reliable demonstration of the plausibility of their proposed attachment mechanisms.

Stranger Anxiety

Attachment theorists use the term "stranger anxiety" to refer to protest behaviors (e.g., crying, turning away) by infants when an unknown or "strange" person enters or approaches. Developmental psychologists used to believe that stranger anxiety represented a true developmental milestone that was displayed by infants at a particular time during the attachment process (Shaffer, 1988). Since the initial groups of studies, which argued for the universality of stranger anxiety or wariness (e.g., Schaffer & Emerson, 1964), it has become clear that wariness of strangers is neither universal nor even necessarily common (Rheingold & Eckerman, 1973). In fact, after reviewing the literature, and on the basis of their own research, Rheingold and Eckerman (1973) showed that, in many instances, strangers evoke positive responses, such as smiles and touching from infants. Rheingold and Eckerman also criticized many of the nonexperimental (e.g., longitudinal) studies for not providing a clear picture of the infants' actual responses to strangers. They wrote:

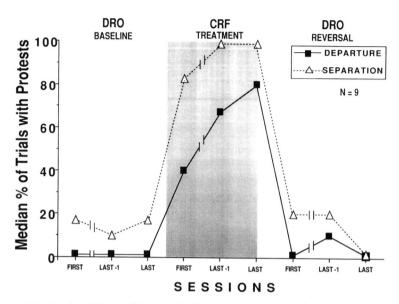

FIGURE 9.2. Results of the conditioning of infant separation protests by Gewirtz and Pelaez-Nogueras (1991a). A composite conditioning curve for the nine infant subjects, representing Median Percent Protest Trials Per Session, across the First, Last-1 (i.e., next to last), and Last session score under each of the three successive treatment conditions. (SOURCE: Reprinted with permission from Lawrence Erlbaum Associates, Inc.)

> The infant's response is lost in composite scores, ratings, and such general labels as shy or anxious.... (and) even if an adequate behavioral description were available, the research literature lacks the information necessary to ascribe the behavior to the person's being a stranger. (p. 204)

Of course, even one exception to the stranger anxiety rule would invalidate the claim of universality. The fact that infants do not respond negatively to strangers in many instances should put the matter to rest. These observations notwithstanding, there are situations in which infants respond negatively to strangers and these need to be explained. As Rheingold and Eckerman (1973) point out, however, it is just as likely that infants would respond negatively to parents or positively to strangers. Such a conclusion might influence attachment theorists to cease their search for a universal, underlying attachment mechanism that generates fear of strangers. Nevertheless, many textbook authors still provide a treatment of stranger anxiety, giving the impression that it is a separate attachment phenomenon worthy of separate consideration (e.g., Berndt, 1992; Bukatko & Daehler, 1992; Shaffer, 1988).

For behavior analysts, the important question is not why infants have stranger anxiety or at what age they show it, but rather why and how the presence of another person evokes certain behaviors in an infant. For the behavior analyst, the answer lies in the history of the interaction between that infant's behavior and the stimuli arising from the behavior of other persons. As Gewirtz (1976) has suggested, both positive and negative infant responses evoked by strangers occur because of their reinforcing consequences. Following from Gewirtz and Pelaez-Nogueras' (1991a) demonstration that infant separation protests can be brought under the discriminative control of stimuli associated with the mother's departure by providing contingent maternal attention under those circumstances, we suggest that infant protest behavior can also be brought under the discriminative control of other stimulus conditions, including the appearance of a stranger (or a familiar person for that matter). Rather than representing a separate *phenomenon* from other attachment relations, as many attachment theorists would have us believe, the protest behavior sometimes evoked by strangers may not be any different functionally than any behavior that is evoked when parents leave or unfamiliar people enter. Following from Bowlby (1969), many attachment theorists have found in stranger and separation protest behavior confirmation of their "theories" of attachment. Such a deductive approach might work if these theorists had discovered basic, functional units of analysis first and then induced more general laws and principles. Based on the evidence, however, we must reject the existence of any universal fear or anxiety in infants.

A BEHAVIOR ANALYSIS OF
SOCIAL–EMOTIONAL DEVELOPMENT

Throughout this chapter, we have maintained that social stimuli can have the same basic, behavioral functions as nonsocial stimuli. In other words, social stimuli can function as unconditional or conditional elicitors, discriminative stimuli, and reinforcers and punishers. For example, we have already cited a study by Gewirtz and Pelaez-Nogueras (1991a) that showed that stimuli associated with a mother's leaving and absence can evoke infant protest behavior, because such behavior produced maternal attention. But while evidence of the behavioral functions of social stimuli may be unquestioned by behavior analysts, other psychologists may not be convinced, or they may find that a "deeper" analysis is necessary. Thus, in this section, we provide two specific examples of the behavioral functions of social stimuli. In the first, we will discuss the work of DeCasper and his associates showing that various auditory stimuli, including the sound of the mother's voice and the sound of the intrauterine heartbeat, can assume reinforcing functions as a result of prenatal experiences (e.g., DeCasper & Fifer, 1980; DeCasper & Sigafoos, 1983; DeCasper & Spence, 1986). In the second example, we offer a behavior analytic interpretation of the phenomenon called *social referencing* by illustrating how the mother's facial expressions can become discriminative stimuli for an infant's motor behavior.

Social Reinforcement

Reinforcement is the term given to the observation that consequences of behavior actually increase the frequency of that behavior under similar conditions. The "similar conditions" refer to the establishing operations and discriminative stimuli that are present when reinforcing consequences occur. Some behavior analysts have described reinforcement as altering the evocative function of the EOs and S^Ds such that the momentary frequency of the behavior is greater in their presence (Schlinger & Blakely, 1994). The term "reinforcer" is used regardless of the source of the consequence or of its formal properties. Reinforcers can arise from nonsocial or social environments. For the purposes of the present chapter, the term "social reinforcer" refers to stimuli resulting from the behavior of one person that, when occurring contingent on the behavior of another person, increase the frequency of that behavior under similar circumstances.

In a series of clever studies, DeCasper and his colleagues have shown exposure to certain stimuli prior to birth can result in those stimuli acquiring reinforcing functions after birth (e.g., DeCasper & Fifer, 1980; De-Casper & Sigafoos, 1983; DeCasper & Spence, 1986). In one of the most frequently cited studies in the developmental literature, DeCasper and Fifer (1980) showed that neonates preferred the sound of their mothers' voice to that of the fathers or of other women. But what do they mean by *prefer*? DeCasper and Fifer (1980) took neonates under 3 days of age and placed a nonnutritive nipple in their mouths and headphones over their ears. The experimenters then arranged for each infant to hear the sound of its mother's voice when the infant's pattern of sucking included longer intervals between individual bursts (interburst intervals or IBIs) of sucking than were observed in a baseline condition. When the pattern of sucking included shorter than baseline IBIs, each infant heard the sound of a different woman's voice. The findings showed that longer IBIs increased relative to baseline and shorter IBIs decreased, thus demonstrating the reinforcing function of the sound of the mothers' voices.

The logical question, of course, was whether the sound of the mothers' voices acquired reinforcing functions prior to birth or in the short

3-day period after birth. To test this question, DeCasper and Spence (1986) had mothers read the Dr. Seuss story, *The Cat in the Hat*, aloud to their fetuses during the last 6½ weeks of pregnancy. After birth, the infants were given the nonnutritive nipple and their sucking behavior produced the mother reading either *The Cat in the Hat* or another poem with a different meter. The results showed that the sucking pattern that resulted in hearing *The Cat in the Hat* increased relative to the pattern that resulted in hearing the other poem. In other words, the sound of the mother reading *The Cat in the Hat* functioned as a reinforcer for longer IBIs.

Nonbehavior analytic accounts of these findings allude to cognitive explanations. For example, Hepper (1989, p. 290) writes that the infants "learned and remembered something about the acoustical cues" of the specific story read to them before birth. Dworetzky (1990, p. 122) writes that the results demonstrate "the presence of a functioning memory." A behavior analytic account is simply that as a result of the prenatal experience, the sound of the mothers' voices had acquired reinforcing functions.

DeCasper and his associates have also demonstrated that the sound of the intrauterine heartbeat can function as a potent reinforcer for the behavior of neonates (DeCasper & Sigafoos, 1983). In addition to supporting the assumption that behavioral functions of stimuli can be altered prior to birth, these findings by DeCasper and his colleagues also provide indirect evidence that at a certain point in development fetuses can hear (DeCasper & Sigafoos, 1983). The findings by DeCasper and his colleagues also provide a partial explanation for other related findings. Wahler (1967), for example, found that mothers' verbal responses and smiles functioned as more potent reinforcers for smiling in 3-month-olds than the same actions by unfamiliar women. Although the infants in the Wahler (1967) experiment were 3 months old, the findings by DeCasper and his colleagues indicate that the reinforcing function of the sound of the mothers' voices may have been established before birth. DeCasper and Prescott (1984) have also shown that the sound of the father's voice does not function as a reinforcer for the sucking patterns of newborns even though the newborns could discriminate their father's voice from other male voices. If the finding of prenatal learning is indeed as valid as it appears to be, then it may in part explain the features of early attachment that lead attachment theorists to infer innate mechanisms of attachment (Gewirtz & Pelaez-Nogueras, 1992a).

Social Discriminative Stimuli

We have already provided examples of the experimental demonstration of social S^Ds. However, one more demonstration should help to strengthen our behavior analytic interpretation. We take a traditional developmental concept, social referencing, and describe both a behavior analytic interpretation and an experiment that strengthens that interpretation.

Social Referencing

In a section of Shaffer's book *Social and Personality Development* titled, "Recognizing Emotions: Can Babies Read Faces and Voices?", he writes that:

> At about the same time that infants are beginning to recognize emotional expressions in photographs, they are becoming quite proficient at reading their mothers' emotional reactions to uncertain situations and using this information to regulate their own behavior. (1988, p. 107)

Shaffer is referring to the "phenomenon" of social referencing. The above quote nicely illustrates all we have been saying about the drawbacks of a generally cognitive interpretation of a behavioral relation. For instance, there is no mention of actual behavior. Moreover, rather than describing the direct effect of the stimuli resulting from the mothers' behavior on the behavior of infants, infants are said to "use information" and, finally, to "regulate" their own behavior. In short, infants read the mother's reaction, and then use the information contained therein to determine their own behavior. Shaffer's description is not unique. Other developmental authors have discussed social referencing in similar terms. For example, Lewis (1987) has written that infants "obtain information … indirectly" (p. 476), and Emde (1987) has written that when "confronted by a situation of uncertainty … the infant is observed to seek out emotional information from another.…" (p. 1310). Even though most of these authors acknowledge the effects of the social environment on the behavior of infants, it is rarely, if ever, the datum of interest. Indeed, Barrett and Campos (1987) write that infants' "reactions … are shaped by the *meaning* of the emotional expression" (p. 560, emphasis added). For Lewis (1987), it is infants' schemas, not their behavior, that is important.

Although several studies have apparently demonstrated social referencing, we will briefly describe a representative one by Sorce, Emde, Campos, and Klinnert (1985). In their study, Sorce et al. (1985) used a visual cliff (see chapter 6). They placed infants on the shallow side of the visual cliff and asked the infants' mothers to show expressions of either happiness or fear when their infants began to venture toward them approaching the "deep" side of the cliff. Not surprisingly, the researchers found that infants were more likely to crawl over the deep side of the visual cliff when their mothers had happy expressions on their faces than when they showed fearful expressions. We have already noted the traditional cognitive descriptions of these and similar findings in which a mother's expression affected the behavior of her infant in an "uncertain" situation. Now let us look at a more parsimonious, behavior analytic interpretation.

Gewirtz and his colleagues have taken this attachment phenomenon and demonstrated experimentally the plausibility of a parsimonious, behavior analytic interpretation. In an experiment by Gewirtz, Pelaez-Nogueras, Diaz, and Villate (1990, as cited in Gewirtz & Pelaez-Nogueras, 1992b), infants sat at a table on which there was a puppet theater. Eight covered boxes, each containing a set of eight objects unfamiliar to the infants, were located out of sight behind the puppet theater. At the beginning of a session, the infant's mother was asked to select one of the eight boxes and, for each trial, individual objects covered by a white cloth were presented to the infant in random order. The cloth was removed by the experimenter after the infant turned back to the object after first looking at the mother—social referencing.

FIGURE 9.3. Mother displays a closed fist-to-nose facial expression with the covered object in front of the infant. (SOURCE: From Gewirtz and Pelaez-Nogueras [1992b]. Reprinted with permission from Plenum Press. Photo courtesy of Martha Pelaez-Nogueras.)

FIGURE 9.4. Mother displays a palms-to-cheek facial expression with the covered object in front of the infant. (SOURCE: From Gewirtz and Pelaez-Nogueras [1992b]. Reprinted with permission from Plenum Press. Photo courtesy of Martha Pelaez-Nogueras.)

The mothers were trained to provide two distinct and arbitrary cues to their infants. If the infant reached for an object after the mother displayed a closed fist to the nose (see Figure 9.3), one of three alternating loud sounds was heard. If the infant reached for the object after the mother displayed a palms-to-cheeks sign (see Figure 9.4), a musical baby melody was played. The mothers were instructed to maintain neutral facial expressions at all times and to say nothing to their infants. During baseline, all infants reached about equally often in the presence of the two maternal cues, but by the end of the treatment condition all infants were reaching 100% of the time (median percentage of reaching) after the positive cue (palms-to-cheeks, S^D or S+) and only 20% of the time after the negative cue (fist-to-nose, S delta or S−).

The results of this experiment show that responses by infants in unfamiliar situations can be brought under the stimulus control of maternal cues; Figure 9.5 shows the sequential details of the social referencing process. Such a demonstration makes a strong case for the plausibility of behavior analytic interpretations of social referencing. Perhaps most importantly, these findings add to the argument in the present book that the formal classification of infant behavior can obscure functional similarities

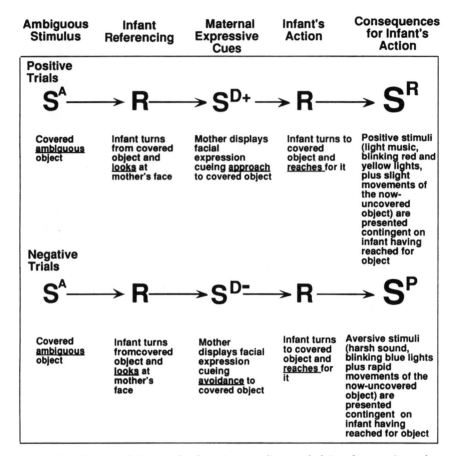

FIGURE 9.5. Elements of the social referencing paradigm underlying the experiment by Gewirtz and Pelaez-Nogueras (1992b). (SOURCE: Reprinted with permission from Plenum Press.)

between apparently different behavioral phenomena. The formal classification of infant behavior can also result in positing different explanations for functionally similar but formally different behaviors.

SUMMARY

This chapter demonstrated how the development of behavior–environment relations termed "attachment" may be interpreted parsimoniously according to behavior analytic principles. Such relations include infant crying and smiling, proximity-establishing and proximity-maintaining behaviors, and fearful behaviors. The chapter provided examples of the experimental demonstration that these behaviors, like all others, can be brought under the control of reinforcement contingencies. These demonstrations not only strengthen the plausibility of the behavior analytic interpretations, but they also suggest practical ways for parents and teachers to change the behavior of children.

10

Social and Emotional Development II
Moral Behavior

As infants grow older and their interactions with others increase in number and complexity, newer types of social relations emerge. These new social relations involve more than just proximity-establishing and proximity-maintaining behaviors. To understand the nature of these new social relations, consider the following hypothetical situations. In the first, several infants are isolated from normal society and left to develop on their own, and we observe what interactional patterns emerge and evolve. We compare that group to a second group of infants who grow up in two-parent families comprising several siblings and who attend well-supervised day care programs followed by preschool, etc. Most people would probably agree that we would observe significant differences in the interactional patterns between both groups.

The first group would probably exhibit much more interperson aggression and overtly selfish behavior, and much less of what we would call prosocial or moral behavior. In fact, we would not be surprised to observe a lot of what we would call amoral behavior. Moreover, their language (if any) would probably mirror their nonlanguage behavior. For example, there would be much less in the way of "moral reasoning." They would probably not have evolved a verbal system of rules in which the rights of individuals are maintained and enforced. In contrast, children in the second group would exhibit more helping, sharing, and nurturing behaviors, and fewer selfish and aggressive behaviors. Their verbal behavior would probably correspond to their nonverbal behavior; that is, they would be able to reason about why they should share, help, and take care of others; and they would be able to state rules concerning moral conduct.

Our conclusion would have to be that there is something about the social community that determines the type of interactions that we consider moral. Of course, in our society we can witness behavioral interactions that span the moral continua, from selfish to altruistic behaviors, from social to antisocial or asocial behaviors, from hurting or nonhelping to helping behaviors, and from aggressive to nonaggressive conflict resolving behaviors. All of these behavioral interactions are inherently social in nature and fall under the structural category that developmental psychologists refer to as moral development. As with the other types of behavioral relations we have discussed so far in this book, traditional treatments of moral development attempt to make both structural and functional distinctions between such aspects of moral development as prosocial, altruistic, and antisocial development. The present book views behavior that we call moral like other behavior, that is, operant behavior that is established and maintained by contingencies of reinforcement in the environment, in this case, in social communities.

Much of what is interesting about moral behavior is not present until the child is older than 2 years of age and begins to exhibit a fairly sophisticated verbal repertoire. However, because we have restricted our discussion in this book primarily to development in the first 2 years of life, this chapter will focus largely on moral behavior that is not related much to the child's own verbal behavior. We discuss the development of prosocial behaviors that developmental psychologists refer to as helping, sharing, cooperation, altruism, and empathy. We juxtapose a behavior analytic interpretation of developmental trends and research findings with the more traditional cognitive orientation that still dominates most discussions of moral development.

VIEWS OF MORAL DEVELOPMENT

The traditional, and generally cognitive, view of moral development is replete with subjective and nonscientific descriptions. In fact, the actual behavior of children usually comprises only a small component of this total view of morality. Just as with other types of behavioral relations we have discussed, such as language, the traditional view of morality is an essentialistic one in which some essence called morality is said to exist in each of us. Hence, our behavior, whether nonverbal or verbal, is only a reflection of this moral sense. This essentialistic view is seen clearly when cognitive developmental psychologists present word problems to children and then ask them about their moral reasoning. Presumably how they reason about the particular problem reflects their underlying sense of morality. The behavior analytic view, by contrast, views morality as a term that is evoked in people by a wide range of behaviors in social contexts. The behaviors reflect not some underlying or internal sense of morality but, rather, the cumulative effects of social contingencies of reinforcement and punishment (and respondent conditioning).

A Traditional View of Moral Development

According to Shaffer (1994), young adults view morality as a set of principles that enable people to distinguish right from wrong, to act on that distinction, and to experience corresponding emotions. He refers to these three components as an affective component, a cognitive component, and a behavioral component. Shaffer points out that the three major theories of moral development—Freudian psychoanalytic, cognitive-developmental, and social-learning and social-information processing—focus on these three components of moral development respectively. In this way, morality or moral development is subdivided into three structural components, each presumably requiring a different theory. Once again, we see how traditional developmental psychologists take a theoretically eclectic approach to understanding development. The overriding question regarding each of these theories should be the extent to which each satisfies the criteria of proper science described in chapter 1.

What then are the important issues for traditional developmental psychologists regarding moral development? First, traditional treatments of moral development focus on developmental (i.e., normative) trends in which changes in various aspects of moral development are correlated with changes in age. A second question of interest for traditional developmentalists is whether some particular aspect of moral development is stable across time and situation or not. Of particular interest is whether particular forms of moral behavior in younger children are correlated with similar forms of the behavior later in life (e.g., Waters, Hay, & Richters, 1986). A related issue involves the degree of correspondence between what children say about moral behavior and how they act in ways consistent with their moral reasoning. A fourth question for traditional developmentalists is whether there are gender differences with respect to different types of moral behavior or thinking (e.g., Maccoby, 1986). Once again, this is a question that can probably only be answered with correlational research methods. Of course, developmental psychologists are interested in whether, and to what degree, moral development is influenced by inheritance and environmental variables. The environmental influences are usually considered in a molar fashion. For example, developmentalists might ask about the extent to which the culture or the family influences aggressive behavior.

A Behavior Analytic View of Moral Development

A behavior analytic approach does not view the questions posed by developmental psychologists as unimportant. It is difficult to imagine any good behavior analyst who does not value correlational research; for example, research on the prevalence of aggression in different cultures, or on the relation between the educational level of the parents and patterns of prosocial behavior in children. For the behavior analyst, however, the more important question about moral behavior is not what happens, or when it happens, but, rather, how it happens, that is, the variables that determine the behavior. In other words, behavior analysts are interested in the processes responsible for the behavior. Because much of the standard research in moral development points to a strong environmental component, behavior analysis is in an ideal position to offer a unitary account of the behavior without speculating about or inferring hypothetical unobservable events and processes.

It is difficult to speak of moral development in infancy because much of what psychologists speak of as moral behavior does not appear until humans can talk and reason, which further permits such concepts as self-control, etc. This does not mean that some infant behavior isn't under the control of interpersonal variables that we might speak of as moral. In what follows, we take a look specifically at the development of prosocial behavior (including altruism) and empathy in infants.

THE DEVELOPMENT OF PROSOCIAL BEHAVIOR

The Problem of Definition

Developmental psychologists are concerned with defining terms such as "prosocial behavior" or "altruism." Just as with some of the other topics we have considered (e.g., language, cognition, etc.), developmental psychologists writing about prosocial behavior frequently fall into the essentialism trap when confronted with the task of defining their terms. Their definitions imply that there is some essence or nature of prosocial and altruistic behaviors that can potentially be discovered to make defining the terms easier. Consequently, some authors present the debate among developmental psychologists over the true essence of altruistic behaviors (e.g., Eisenberg, 1982).

According to Eisenberg (1982), altruism has been defined as an intentional act that is usually, but not always, motivated by the desire to benefit another and can, depending on which author one reads, either include or not include the effects of external rewards on the behavior. For some authors, behavior is altruistic only if it costs something to the behaver; for others, altruistic behavior must be motivated by moral convictions or beliefs. Authors like Eisenberg (1982) end up debating such irresolvable issues as whether a behavior is intentional or not and whether it occurs because of various internal motivations or not.

As Palmer and Donahoe (1992) have pointed out, this kind of approach to definition is essentialistic because these terms are defined formally before orderly relations involving behavior are discovered experimentally. Of course, if we assume a priori that there is some essence of altruism, then it does make sense to try to find behavior that reflects that essence. If the essence is internal, however, the possibility of discovering it and distinguishing it from other related essences is impossible. The approach to definition taken by many developmental psychologists can be described as essentialistic because they formally categorize (i.e., define) behaviors which, as Palmer and Donahoe (1992) point out, may never reflect any real distinctions in nature.

When the term "prosocial" is used, most authors include behaviors that are generally labeled as helping, cooperating, sharing, caregiving, taking turns, friendliness and affection, and empathy and sympathy (Rheingold & Hay, 1980). These distinctions, however, are strictly formal, and even Rheingold and Hay (1980) admit that the definitions "represent a combination of those given by the dictionary, those proposed by others, and those based on our own intuitions" (p. 94). To their credit, the definitions of Rheingold and Hay are based solely on the observable behavior of the child and not on hypothetical internal intentions, emotions, or motivations. Nonetheless, from a behavior analytic perspective, it is entirely likely that the functional distinctions, if any, do not map precisely onto the formal distinctions.

The issues have to do with the verbal behavior of psychologists who study these behaviors. In order to understand what developmental psychologists are interested in, we may ask first about the circumstances that lead someone to call one behavioral relation "helping" and another "sharing." Also we may analyze the functional similarities and differences between the various "types" of prosocial behavior according to already established, functional units of analysis to see whether the formal distinctions have any merit.

Toward these ends, let us look at the development of prosocial behavior according to developmental researchers. Instead of considering all of the formal categories of prosocial behavior listed above, we focus on those called sharing, helping, cooperating, and empathy, with the understanding that these verbal categories are not mutually exclusive. For example, there are many instances when the term "sharing" is used interchangeably with cooperating or helping. Finally, to be consistent with the previous chapters in the book, we restrict our discussion of prosocial behaviors to approximately the first 2 years of life.

Formal Categories of Prosocial Behavior

Sharing

Instead of presenting a priori various definitions of sharing, this chapter describes some of the behavioral relations that developmental researchers use the term "sharing" to describe. Rheingold (1977, see also Rheingold, Hay, & West, 1976) has used the term for three behavioral relations involving infants and others in their immediate environment. The first is *showing*, which consists of infants pointing to an object or holding the object up for another person (see Figure 10.1). The second relation is *giving*, which consists of bringing the object from a distance, placing it in the other person's hand or lap, and releasing it. The third type of sharing relation is *playing* with an object while it is in contact with another person.

Rheingold et al. (1976) looked at these and other behavioral relations in 18-month-old infants and their mothers. The mothers were seated in chairs placed against the center of one wall of a large room. They faced a wall with doors to smaller rooms which contained toys and other objects. The mothers were instructed to remain "passive," that is, if and when their infants showed a toy from a distance or brought the toy to them, the mothers could respond with a nod or slight smile or could say, "Thank you." The results showed that all infants engaged in at least one sharing behavior, and 17 of 24 exhibited all three sharing behaviors. In a second study, the researchers compared trials in which the mothers were instructed to respond to their infants' sharing with more enthusiasm, just as they would if they were at home, and trials in which the mothers were instructed to respond "passively," as they did in the first study. The results showed that although more children exhibited each sharing behavior, the mean frequencies of all three behaviors between the two trials were comparable. In further trials, Rheingold et al. (1976) showed that the infants also shared with their fathers and with unfamiliar persons.

The results of studies like those of Rheingold et al. (1976) demonstrate that behavioral relations called sharing are present in infants as young as 18 months old. Rheingold et al. (1976) point out that although these behavioral relations are probably found in even younger infants, 18-month-old infants were used, because they were physically more mature and thus more proficient in locomotion, etc. Other researchers (e.g., Hay, 1979) have

FIGURE 10.1. A young child holds up a crayon
for another person. (Photo by H. Schlinger)

observed instances of showing and giving in 12-month-old infants, although higher frequencies of these behaviors were observed in 18- and 24-
month-old infants. As we noted, the researchers found only minor differences between groups in which mothers more actively encouraged sharing
behavior and those in which the mothers were more passive. However, we
must remember that the word "passive" was used by the researchers and
may not have accurately reflected the actual effect of mothers' "passive"
responses on their infants' sharing behaviors. For example, it is likely that
simply nodding, smiling, or saying "Thank you," was sufficient to function as reinforcement for the preceding sharing responses. A better control
condition would have had the mothers be completely passive. This would
mean that they could have made no acknowledgement of their infants'
sharing behaviors, that is, no eye contact, no hand movements, no smiling,
and no verbalizations. Notwithstanding these points, the results of the
Rheingold et al. (1976) study show that by 18 months of age, the behavioral
repertoires of infants include a number of so-called sharing relations.

Unfortunately, Rheingold et al. (1976) asked what the children "intended" by their sharing behaviors. We might rephrase the question in
terms of the origins of such behavior, as Rheingold (1977) does elsewhere.
As we mentioned previously, studies like Rheingold et al's (1976) answer

what and when questions concerning behavior, but do not answer why or how. Rheingold (1977), however, does point to some possible general processes responsible for the development of prosocial behaviors like sharing. First, she points out that there are thousands of times that infants observe others pointing to, bringing, and giving things to them. Second, infants begin to imitate these behaviors. Third, all of these prosocial behaviors produce effects on others, which is part of what leads us to call them social. These prosocial behaviors are adaptive; the behaviors are selected by the social environments in which they occur. In other words, these behaviors are operant. Let us look more closely at pointing, one of the behaviors that Rheingold and her associates call sharing.

Pointing. Pointing may be considered an instance of sharing if sharing is defined as one person granting to another the use, enjoyment, or possession of a thing (Rheingold et al., 1976). Pointing may serve that function. Relatively few studies have looked at pointing (e.g., Jeung & Rheingold, 1981; Murphy & Messer, 1977). Like many studies on the development of prosocial behavior, these studies on pointing have been strictly observational in nature. Their purpose seems to be nothing more than demonstrating either the age at which mothers' points reliably evoke some behavior (e.g., looking) in the infants or the age at which pointing behavior is observed in infants. Let us look at one of these studies in more detail.

Jeung and Rheingold (1981) compared pointing behavior in infants ranging in age from 10.5 to 16.5 months. The infants sat in a high chair in a room with posters on the walls and objects placed throughout the room. Each infant's mother, who was seated next to her infant, was instructed to respond to infant vocalizations, points, and reaches as she normally would. During separate trials, the mothers were instructed to point to the various stimulus objects while saying, "Look" or "See." The results showed that although only 1 of 8 infants at 10.5 months of age pointed, more than half of the infants at 12.5 months of age pointed, and all of the infants at 16.5 months pointed. The results also showed that vocalizations and looking at the mother accompanied the points, indicating to the researchers that pointing was indeed a social gesture. However, as in the study by Rheingold et al. (1976) described above, the study by Jeung and Rheingold (1981) on pointing answered only what and when, but not how. Let us, therefore, offer a behavior analytic interpretation of pointing.

Like all operant behavior, pointing can be described as a stimulus and a response class. We may use an analogy of language to make the point. The person doing the pointing may be called the *speaker*, and the person whose behavior the point has an effect on may be called the *listener*. As a stimulus, pointing affects the behavior of the listener in one important way: As an S^D, the point evokes orienting and looking by the listener. The probable reinforcers are what is immediately seen or heard, although initially a parent may use praise to establish the operant. In many cases, the consequence of looking which is itself evoked by someone's point functions as reinforcement, because it then enables further behavior, such as reaching, grasping, or simply further looking. The establishment of pointing-evoked behavior in listeners is analogous to what is termed receptive language. Pointing is functionally equivalent to the verbal S^Ds, look, see, or listen. In the presence of these discriminative stimuli, some behavior is more successful than in their absence; as a result, the occurrence of these stimuli evokes the behavior (see Michael, 1980).

But what about the behavior of the *speaker* or pointer? It is unlikely that parents shape the behavior of pointing through physical or verbal prompts and fading of the prompts, although it would indeed be possible to do so. More likely, children have seen others point and the stimuli arising from those behaviors have evoked imitative behavior. Once the behavior occurs for the first time, even if it is imperfect, the social community reinforces it. In fact, Jeung and Rheingold (1981) indicate that the mothers in their study looked at or verbally acknowledged an average of 88% of their infants' points. It would not be too difficult to conduct a within-subject A-B-A design to demonstrate the reinforcing control of mothers' responses to pointing in infants.

Unfortunately, other researchers have not been as parsimonious when interpreting pointing. For example, Murphy and Messer (1977) have acknowledged that there is some uncertainty as to "the age at which the infant understands that a point is a social signal designed to attract one's attention to a specific object" (p. 325). If this type of understanding were a prerequisite, then many adults would probably fail to respond to a point. Is it really necessary to talk about something as simple as pointing in this way? Of course, we must remember that, in general, many psychologists use a nontechnical vocabulary. Because psychologists have not discovered functional units of analysis enabling the discovery of laws and principles and have no formal vocabulary tied to those laws and principles, it is no wonder that the vocabulary of psychologists is often indistinguishable from that of the layperson.

As we have already noted, one problem in the traditional literature on the development of prosocial behavior in infants is that researchers often define their subject matter a priori and then proceed to look for instances of it. For example, researchers frequently define sharing in a particular way and then, based on their own definition, conduct research to discover at what age such behaviors occur. Unfortunately, in many cases, researchers end up debating over formal parts of their definitions instead of trying to discover the variables of which the behavior is a function. Sometimes, traditional researchers come close to a behavior analytic approach. For example, Hay, Caplan, Castle, and Stimson (1991) say that "it is important to examine closely the various social and physical situations in which children share" (p. 987). However, although researchers sometimes manipulate variables, they usually do so only to demonstrate that some behavior occurs.

For example, Hay et al. (1991) were interested in the extent to which spontaneous sharing by toddlers (24 and 48 months old) with peers was affected by the resources present, in particular, the number of toys. Their research question was couched in terms of "rational decision making" following from evolutionary and political/economic models of altruism. With regard to sharing, rational decision making would mean that the sharer recognizes that, even though in the short run it is easier not to share and to seek personal gain, in the long run it is more profitable to be cooperative (Hay et al., 1991).

In the study by Hay et al. (1991), three children were placed in a room at one time with either six toys (ample resources) or two toys (scarce resources). For half of the groups, the toys were duplicated so that sharing meant that another identical toy was still available to the sharer. The results showed that although spontaneous sharing occurred in all children, sharing "under pressure" from peers occurred more frequently in the 1-year-old children than in the 2-year-old children. Even though the researchers concluded that "all the experimental variables together influenced spontaneous sharing" (p. 987), there was no attempt to isolate control by any of the variables. Moreover, there were other variables, for example, the presence of the infants' mothers, that were not controlled for. So, what can we conclude about the functions of sharing from such a study? Are 1- and 2-year-old children rational? As you might guess, we cannot conclude much that is useful about this question from the Hay et al. (1991) study. Although the effects of some of the variables may be of interest, the results don't really tell us much about the origins or functions of sharing. The experimental circumstances were contrived based on concepts derived from rational decision theory, but we still don't have even a primitive account of why the children shared at all.

In summary, behaviors that many developmental psychologists would call sharing have been observed in infants as young as 12 months of age in a variety of circumstances. Although no study cited here reported any experimental analysis, the findings of several studies do suggest that the occurrence of sharing is affected by imitative stimuli (e.g., Hay & Murray, 1982) and contingent consequences.

Helping and Cooperating

Helping. The term "helping" has been used to refer to "giving aid or support to another person" (Rheingold & Hay, 1980, p. 98). But, specifically, what behaviors evoke these terms in developmental researchers? Bar-Tal, Raviv, and Goldberg (1982) conducted an observational study of helping behaviors in children between the ages of 18 and 76 months of age. For these authors, helping included sharing, giving, aiding, and comforting. In aiding, one child alleviates another child's "nonemotional needs through verbal or motor behavior" (Bar-Tal et al., 1982, p. 397); and in comforting, one child alleviates another's emotional needs. Once again, there are difficulties in making formal distinctions between behaviors before actually understanding their functions.

Nonetheless, in the Bar-Tal et al. (1982) study, children were observed in free-play settings on three separate occasions. In addition to coding behaviors according to whether they were instances of sharing, giving, aiding, or comforting, the authors coded the helping behaviors in terms of four "reinforcement conditions." These "reinforcement conditions" included instances of the behavior when no reward was offered for the helping act, when tangible or intangible social rewards were offered, or when a threat was made. Notice that these observations only included whether a reward was offered or not, not whether a consequence was actually made contingent on the helping behavior. If anything, these authors were looking at the effects of antecedent operations (e.g., promises of rewards or threats), not consequences, on the occurrence of helping behaviors. Behavior analysts will certainly find this type of methodology faulty in terms of analyzing the effects of consequences on helping behaviors. In any case, the results for the children under 30 months of age showed that about 20% of all social contacts between children were coded as helping acts. The results also showed that the infants under 30 months of age had more social contact with the teachers than did older infants (see also Eckerman, Whatley, & Kutz, 1975). Finally, the results indicated that the younger children engaged in more giving, but less aiding and comforting, than the older children. Results from studies such as these are valuable as very gross indicators of the histories (both genetic and conditioning) that combined to produce the children's current repertoires; however, they tell us nothing about the ontogeny and very little about the details of the stimulus control of the behaviors.

Rheingold (1982) observed children ranging in age from 18 to 30 months old to see whether and to what extent they would help or assist their parents accomplish a variety of everyday household chores in a laboratory situation. She found that more than 50% of the 18-month-old children helped their parents on at least half of the tasks and all of the 30-month-old children helped. Rheingold also observed that even among the youngest children, their helping behavior was accompanied by statements describing their behavior. For example, the 18-month-old children made statements such as, "Sandy sweep," or "Fold clothes," whereas the 30-month-old children made statements such as, "I'm going to pick up these books." Rheingold also noticed that by 30 months of age, the word "help" was appearing in their statements. Of most interest, however, were the parents' behaviors. Rheingold observed that the parents also made verbalizations as they performed their tasks, most of which included labeling their own and their children's behaviors. Not surprisingly, Rheingold observed that on about three-fourths of the tasks, parents praised their children's helping behaviors. Of course, we don't always have to identify external consequences as the reinforcing consequences for behavior. It is likely that simply performing the same behaviors that children see their parents perform functions as automatic reinforcement for the particular behavior (see chapter 3).

So far, we have presented the results of several observational studies of young children's prosocial behaviors. Although none of the studies conducted any experimental analyses of the behaviors, we have strongly suggested that the behaviors are operant and, as such, are shaped and maintained by their consequences.

Because it is difficult to demonstrate conclusively that prosocial behaviors are indeed operant behaviors, behavior analysts must rely on plausibility experiments. As Gelfand and Hartmann (1982) have written:

> Charitable and helpful behaviors that are maintained by praise may be attributed incorrectly to altruistic motivation. Therefore it is important to determine whether fairly subtle incentives such as praise *could* reinforce children's helpfulness. (p. 169; emphasis added)

A reinforcement interpretation would gain support through experiments in which various types of "altruistic" behaviors are shown to be shaped and maintained by reinforcement (e.g., Gelfand, Hartmann, Cromer, Smith, & Page, 1975; Grusec & Redler, 1980).

Using a within-subject reversal (i.e., ABAB) design in which baseline frequencies of children's prosocial behavior were measured before any independent variables were manipulated, Gelfand et al. (1975) investigated the rates at which young children would donate pennies to other children while playing a game. Young children individually played a marble-drop game in which they could earn pennies as prizes. Periodically, each child was given the opportunity to donate pennies to another child who was supposedly having trouble earning pennies on the same game in a nearby room. The two-thirds of the children who did not donate pennies in the baseline condition (A) to the other child were then used as subjects. In the second condition (B), the children were verbally prompted to donate and were praised when they did so. The next two conditions repeated the first two. The results showed quite clearly that the prompting followed by praise increased donation rates by the children. Although there is some question regarding the relative roles of prompts and praise on the frequency of donations, it would be easy enough to separate experimentally the effects of those two variables.

Cooperating. The term "cooperating" has been used to describe one person "acting with another to a common end or to produce an effect jointly" (Rheingold & Hay, 1980, p. 98) (see Figure 10.2). Although it may seem obvious that behavior called cooperating, as an instance of prosocial behavior, has its genesis in the contingencies of reinforcement present in the social environment in which the behavior is observed, not all authors agree with this. In fact, some authors explicitly exclude the direct rewarding of prosocial behavior in their definition (e.g., Mussen & Eisenberg-Berg, 1977). Such an exclusion is an oversight because, for these authors, rewards are defined formally, and not functionally. In such cases, it is more important than usual to distinguish between what people call "rewards" and what behavior analysts call "reinforcement."

That a researcher calls some event a reward says nothing about its possible effect on a child's behavior. Reinforcement, in contrast, is defined not a priori, but only after a functional relation between its occurrence and some behavior is established. We have already pointed out that reinforcers need not be extrinsic, if that means tangible events like money, food, or praise. The principles of behavior analysis suggest that any number of stimuli, including the stimuli associated with the form of behavior itself, may assume reinforcing functions.

Mussen and Eisenberg-Berg (1977) acknowledge that the origins of prosocial behavior are located in the culture in which the child is reared:

> To understand cultural differences in these tendencies, we need precise descriptions of the socialization techniques to stimulate or restrict the development of prosocial behavior. (p. 55)

But instead of examining the contingencies of reinforcement that form the basis of all socialization practices irrespective of culture, Mussen and Eisenberg-Berg (1977) claim that

FIGURE 10.2. A brother and sister act to produce an effect jointly. (Photo by H. Schlinger)

What is needed is a detailed and focused examination of precisely how the norms and approved responses are communicated and inculcated, how children learn them, and how they are generalized to new circumstances. (p. 57)

But, of course, norms are not "communicated" to children; they are statistical devices employed by developmental psychologists. Neither are "approved responses" "communicated" to children; operants are reinforced or punished. Mussen and Eisenberg-Berg (1977) make no reference to the extensive experimental contributions toward the understanding of the acquisition of behavior through operant conditioning (including the effects of modeling), how such behavior comes under motivational and stimulus control, and how reinforcement contingencies determine the generalization of such behaviors. As a result, Mussen and Eisenberg-Berg (1977) are forced to conclude that:

> [C]hildren are likely to develop high levels of prosocial behavior if they are raised in cultures characterized by (1) stress (from parents, peers, and other agents of socialization) on consideration of others, sharing, and orientation toward the group; (2) simple social organization or a traditional, rural setting; (3) assignment to women of important economic functions; (4) members of the extended family living together; and (5) early assignment of tasks and responsibilities to children. (p. 63)

Unfortunately, these cultural characteristics are defined structurally and not functionally. Moreover, they allude to sociological–anthropological, and not behavioral, units. As a consequence, there is simply no way to understand prosocial behavior without understanding operant conditioning in all of its subtlety. Unfortunately, prominent authors in the field, like Mussen and Eisenberg-Berg (1977) make no mention of it (Gewirtz & Pelaez-Nogueras, 1992).

Nonetheless, let us provide the outline of a functional account of behavior called cooperation and competition, including references to some experiments that demonstrate the plausibility of a behavior analytic interpretation. Before 1972, there already existed numerous experimental demonstrations of the operant conditioning of cooperative behavior in rats and monkeys and in normal, schizophrenic, and retarded humans (see Hake & Vukelich, 1972 for a partial review). Behavior analysts such as Hake and Vukelich (1972) solved the problem of definition relatively easily by isolating a functional unit of analysis, namely, "at least one cooperative response and one reinforcer," that is, "the minimal response requirement for reinforcement" (p. 333). Of course, more than one cooperative response usually occurs over time.

Having identified a basic unit of analysis for cooperative behavior, Hake and Vukelich (1972) classified the different experimental procedures used to investigate this unit. For example, Hake and Vukelich (1972) identified procedures in which (1) an individual's reinforcers are completely to partially dependent on the behavior of a partner; (2) the distribution of reinforcers between two or more individuals is unequal or equal; and (3) the cooperative behavior is controlled exclusively by social or nonsocial variables. The research summarized in Hake and Vukelich's (1972) review, in combination with more recent research (e.g., Hake, Olvera, & Bell, 1975; Hake, Vukelich, & Olvera, 1975), suggests that cooperative behavior can be shaped and maintained by a variety of procedural variations on the basic analytic unit suggested by Hake and Vukelich (1972) and that it is sensitive to a variety of subtle environmental manipulations.

You will recall that one criterion of a scientific theory is its utility (see chapter 1). A behavior analytic theory of prosocial behavior, based as it is on functional relations between objective variables, can suggest ways to generate such behavior in individuals lacking the behavior. Indeed, behavioral analysts have shown that prosocial behaviors in a variety of human populations are sensitive to operant principles (e.g., Hingtgen, Sanders, & DeMyer, 1965; Hingtgen & Trose, 1966; Lindsley, 1966; Schmitt & Marwell, 1968). For example, in the 1960s, Hingtgen and his colleagues (Hingtgen, Sanders, & DeMyer, 1965; Hingtgen & Trose, 1966) demonstrated experimentally that cooperative responses in pairs of young children, who were diagnosed with early childhood schizophrenia, could be shaped and maintained with completely nonverbal operant conditioning procedures. Interestingly, the experimenters found that the frequency of physical interaction between the pairs of children also increased during the cooperative interaction in other settings. In a second study, the experimenters directly reinforced social responses, such as touching and vocalizations, and found that such behaviors increased relative to baseline. Moreover, there were anecdotal reports that some of the children actually exhibited vocal and touching behavior at home, a place where these behaviors had rarely been observed before. These two experimental demonstrations lend support to the plausibility of a behavior analytic interpretation of behaviors we call cooperation.

EMPATHY

Much of the interest in prosocial behavior by traditional developmental psychologists is not in the behavior per se, or in the circumstances in which it occurs, but rather in the underlying motivation for such behavior (e.g., Hoffman, 1982). In the case of many of the behaviors we have already discussed such as sharing and helping, plus those we can call protecting and nurturing, the underlying motivation is said to be empathic feelings, or empathy. Because empathy, as an unobservable state, is inferred solely from behavior it is said to explain, authors who write about it represent a straightforward cognitive approach to prosocial behavior. Recall that cognitive psychologists are by and large interested in overt behavior as a reflection of usually unobservable, internal events or processes. In the area of prosocial development, some authors even acknowledge the problem. For example, Lamb (1991) writes:

> Some researchers have concentrated on prosocial behaviors as indicators of the beginnings of empathic responding, simply because empathy has been so difficult to define and even more difficult to observe. (p. 172)

Nonetheless, authors like Lamb (1991) still speculate about processes that apparently have no objective reality. Some authors attempt to develop models that use inferred qualities to explain other inferred qualities. For example, Hoffman (1982) writes that he has been more interested in altruistic motivation than in altruistic responses and that he has been working on a developmental model that "does not depend on reinforcement and imitation, but on the interaction between affective and cognitive processes that change with age" (p. 281). Such a model utilizes hypothetical and inferred constructs such as affect and cognition, which supposedly change with another construct, time, to explain another inferred construct, empathy.

Approaches that infer underlying motivational states to explain prosocial behavior, however, suffer from the same problems as other cognitive approaches in developmental psychology. First, the only evidence for the underlying motivation—empathy—or the lack of it, is the very behavior the empathy is said to explain. Second, the empathy itself can never be tested directly; rather, it must always be inferred from other, more direct data. Third, research into other, potentially more rewarding avenues of inquiry is stymied. Nevertheless, because so much of the prosocial literature deals with empathy, we must attempt to discover what developmental researchers mean by it, that is, what behaviors evoke their use of the term, and then try to provide a more parsimonious interpretation of the behaviors.

Defining Empathy

Rheingold and Hay (1980) have used the term "empathy" to refer to "the capacity for participating in or experiencing another's emotions," whereas "sympathy" is used to refer to "behavior" to alleviate the discomfort of another (p. 97). In contrast, Hoffman (1982) used the term empathy to refer to a vicarious, affective response, that is, "an affective response that is more appropriate to someone else's situation than to one's own situation" (p. 281). In fact, despite his overtly cognitive leanings, Hoffman's (1982) approach is more objective than is apparent at first glance. For example, his model focuses on "empathic distress—the empathic response to another person's pain or discomfort...." (p. 282). Hoffman's (1982; see also Rheingold and Hay, 1980) definition of empathy focuses more on affective components of empathy, whereas other definitions stress cognitive components.

The cognitive components consist of a person's "ability to cognitively assume the psychological role of another" (Thompson, 1987). Of course, this description of cognitive ability is vague. To have any understanding of what such language means, we need to observe the behavior of individuals that cognitive theorists describe this way. We would probably find the individuals talking to themselves about what another person might be feeling (or thinking) in a given situation. For example, many parents talk about the feelings of others to their young children, and these behaviors are positively correlated with the children's own verbal references to the feelings of others (Dunn, Bretherton, & Munn, 1987).

Defined in these ways, it becomes easier to discover what developmental theorists mean when they speak of empathy. Many authors agree that empathy has been and can be defined in many ways (Barnett, 1987; Thompson, 1987). As we have indicated, definitions differ according to whether affective or cognitive components are stressed. However, definitions also differ according to whether the empathic response of one person directly matches that of another person, and according to the specific cues of a person to which an empathic observer responds (Thompson, 1987). Rather than endlessly debating these formal, structural, definitional issues, a behavior analytic approach is to look at the behavior of individuals when they are said to be behaving empathically.

Based on Hoffman's (1982) and Rheingold and Hay's (1980) use of the term, many different forms of behavioral relations may be classified as "empathic distress." Thompson (1987) has described several behavioral relations that developmental researchers speak of as empathy. They are (1) reactive crying in newborns; (2) affective synchrony in mother–infant play; (3) interpreting facial cues of emotion; and (4) emotional sharing and prosocial motivation.

Reactive Crying in Newborns

Reactive crying refers to the tendency for the cries of a newborn to elicit crying in another newborn. In one study, Sagi and Hoffman (1976) presented taped recordings of infant cries, or synthetic cries, to neonates who averaged 34 hours of age. The authors reported that infants cried significantly more to the real cries than to the synthetic cries or silence, which led them to refer to newborns' cries in response to other newborns' cries as "empathic distress," regardless of whether the cries represented unconditioned or conditioned reflexes. Hoffman (1982) concluded that "infants respond to a cue of distress in others by experiencing distress themselves" (p. 283), but such a conclusion is an inference based solely on the infant's observable behavior evoked by another infant's cries.

Of course, that a neonate's crying is elicited by other real cries does not explain why this is so. It could be that it is part of a specific unconditioned reflex or part of the more general startle reflex.

Affective Synchrony in Mother–Infant Play

Some researchers have devoted much time to studying what parents have known for a long time, that is, that beginning around the second or third month of life, parents, especially mothers, engage in face-to-face interactions with their infants which are described as play exchanges or nonverbal conversations. Unfortunately, developmental psychologists have taken this relatively simple type of behavioral interaction and complicated it by the way they talk about it. For example, Thompson (1987) has summarized other researchers' descriptions of the face-to-face interactions between mother and baby as "the mutual sharing of positive arousal during which infants manifest the excited, engaged sociability that adults find rewarding" (p. 127). He has also said that "the hypothesized goal of these exchanges is the *positive affective synchrony* between mother and baby" (p. 127), hence, the title of this section.

Although the terminology about how mothers and infants share positive arousal is easily understood, these ways of talking about the interactions are not very useful scientifically. For example, many researchers in this area are interested in the infants' behaviors only insofar as they permit the researchers to infer underlying emotional states (e.g., Stoller & Field, 1982). Moreover, complicated hypothetical models involving invented internal mechanisms and processes have been developed to account for behavioral data (e.g., Fogel, 1982). Traditional developmental psychologists don't look for orderly relationships between behavior and objective events; instead, they seem more interested in such hypothetical constructs as "arousal," "basic feeling experiences," "fluctuations of stimulation," or "tension release" (Stoller & Field, 1982). Let us, therefore, look at mother–infant face-to-face interactions and why they are labeled as instances of empathy.

Several studies have shown that the behavior of very young infants is sensitive to (we would say controlled by) differences in their mothers' facial expressions, especially those that are said to be associated with certain types of affect (Cohn, Campbell, Matias, & Hopkins, 1990; Cohn & Elmore, 1988; Cohn & Tronick, 1983; Fogel, 1982; Haviland & Lelwica, 1987; Stoller & Field, 1982; Tronick, Ricks, & Cohn, 1982). Of course, the opposite is also true: The behavior of mothers is sensitive to (controlled by) the behavior of their infants (Frodi, Lamb, Leavitt, & Donovan, 1978; Gewirtz & Boyd, 1976; Lewis & Rosenblum, 1974). Let us look at one of the more common methodologies that developmental psychologists employ to show that the behavior of young infants is sensitive to differences in their mothers' facial expressions.

If we suspect that the behavior of infants is affected by face-to-face interactions with their mothers, then it would make sense to manipulate the mothers' behavior as an independent variable in a face-to-face interaction with their infants. Toward that end, several investigators have had mothers either imitate their infants' facial expressions, remain still-faced, or "keep their infants' attention" (Stoller & Field, 1982). The results showed the following: (1) Infants spent more time gazing at their mothers when the mothers imitated the infants' facial expressions; (2) infants tended to avert their gaze when mothers became more active; and (3) during the still-faced manipulation, infants initially repeatedly looked at their mothers while vocalizing and occasionally reached toward them. After a while, the infants averted their gaze from their mothers. These manipulations seem straightforward and they might have been suggested by a behavior analyst interested in understanding face-to-face interactions between mothers and their infants.

A crucial difference between behavior analysis and traditional cognitive psychology can be seen in the respective interpretations of these manipulations. Consider first the general, cognitive interpretation. Some researchers have suggested that the still-face manipulation upset the infants, because it violated their expectancies, or that, in Piagetian terms, the infants were unable to assimilate the discrepant event (see Stoller and Field, 1982, for a summary). Stoller and Field (1982) discussed one of the more popular models of infant emotion, that of Stroufe (1979, as cited in Stoller & Field, 1982). Stroufe's model is a tension-release one in which the infant experiences increasing tension with "increasing attention to a stimulus in an effort to process stimulus content" (p. 59). As tension increases, infants can do one of two things. Either they can assimilate the event and experience a decrease in tension, which is pleasurable for them and evidenced by smiling or laughing, or they cannot assimilate the stimulus, in which case the tension builds up to the point where they become distressed, as is evidenced by an increase in gaze aversion, fussiness, and crying. Stroufe's model, therefore, seems to be a combination of a Freudian hydraulic tension-release model and a Piagetian cognitive adaptation model. Stroufe's is not the only model proposed to account for the data resulting from mother and infant face-to-face interactions. The other models, however, are really no different from Stroufe's tension-release one. For example, Field (1981, as cited in Stoller & Field, 1982) has proposed a model of activation (i.e., arousal). Although talking about the behavioral relations with these terms is easier because they are terms with which most people are familiar and well acquainted, the proposed causal mechanisms are problematic.

How do these models of infant emotion as expressed in the mother–infant face-to-face interplay hold up to the criteria of science described in chapter 1? First of all, the models fail the criterion of testability, mainly because the proposed mechanisms—for example, expectancy, assimilation, tension, and arousal—are not plausible. These processes are not independently observable; in other words their existence must be inferred solely on the basis of the observed behavior (Schlinger, 1993). For example, if no gaze aversion is observed, then no violation of expectancy would be inferred. Second, these models fail the criterion of external validity. Remember that external validity involves being able to make accurate predictions based on specifying objective independent and dependent variables.

Interestingly, those who study mother–infant synchrony manipulate clear independent variables—the mother's behavior—but their models make almost no mention of these as causal variables. Instead, the models infer internal, unobservable, and ultimately untestable entities and processes. Thus, any predictions based on these unobservable events will always be less than accurate and always subject to alteration after the fact (Schlinger, 1993). Finally, these models of mother–infant synchrony are not parsimonious. You may recall from chapter 1 that parsimony dictates that of two or more explanations of behavior, the one that accounts for a body of data with the fewest number of hypothetical statements and assumptions that are testable is to be preferred.

A behavior analytic interpretation of mother–infant face-to-face interactions is simple, but not simplistic. Consider the results of the three manipulations carried out by researchers as described above. First, when mothers imitated their infants' facial expressions, the infants spent more time gazing at their mothers. This result suggests that the mothers' contingent imitation of the infants' facial behaviors increased the frequency of those behaviors as well as the infants' gazing behavior. Certainly gazing under such circumstances is reinforced by being able to engage in other behavior whose consequence is the mothers' contingent imitation. This reinforcement interpretation is strengthened by the results of the other two manipulations.

In the second manipulation, the mothers were instructed to get and keep their infants' attention which, according to Stoller and Field (1982), resulted in the infants becoming "less attentive." We can only assume that "less attentive" means that the infants gazed less at the mothers. These results suggest one of two possibilities. Either the mothers' behavior functioned as a stimulus in whose presence the infants' gaze behaviors were not contingently responded to or the mothers' attempts at keeping their infants' attention functioned as noncontingent or response-independent reinforcing consequences. Even nonbehavior analysts have shown that response-independent consequences will not sustain behavior (e.g., Watson & Ramey, 1972).

During the third manipulation—the still-face—infants at first repeatedly looked at their mothers while vocalizing and occasionally reaching toward them, but eventually averted their gaze. This seems to demonstrate clear operant extinction. In this procedure, a stimulus that has already been shown to be a reinforcer for a particular behavior is withheld. The effect is twofold: First, there is an increase in behavioral variability, including what has been referred to as emotional behavior, and second, the frequency of the behavior eventually decreases. In the present example, the first effect of the mother becoming still and silent while looking at her infant was to increase not only the infant's gazing behavior but also other behaviors, such as reaching and vocalizing, which are not necessarily an important ingredient of the face-to-face interactions. The increase in the frequency of these behaviors is also a predictable outcome of operant extinction and has been called "resurgence" (Epstein, 1983, 1985). It is likely that reaching and vocalizing are behaviors that produced the mother's attention in the past, and they now occur again when the contingent attention for gazing is withheld. Eventually, however, as predicted by the principle of operant extinction, the infant's gaze behavior at the mother decreases in frequency.

Stoller and Field (1982) wrote that the "silent, still face of the mother has a predictable effect upon the infant" (p. 58), but they could not have predicted this effect before the manipulation. A behavior analyst could have accurately predicted the effect based on the principle of extinction. Moreover, a behavior analytic interpretation would likely permit additional manipulations involving a detailed component analysis of the relation between a mother's and infant's behavior in the face-to-face interaction.

Interpreting Facial Cues of Emotion

In chapter 9, we discussed the phenomenon of social referencing in which stimuli arising from the mother's face (e.g., smiles or frowns) control the behavior of the infant. The phenomenon has been studied using the visual cliff apparatus (see chapter 6). When the infant is placed on the "shallow" side and coaxed onto the "deep" side, he or she is more likely to crawl if the mother is smiling (Sorce et al., 1985). Unfortunately, traditional researchers account for this phenomenon in terms of the infant interpreting the emotional signals of the mother, rather than in the more parsimonious terms of stimulus control and reinforcement.

These and similar findings have been discussed in terms of emotional communication. It has been said that "infants respond affectively to the mothers in ways that suggest resonant emotion" (Thompson, 1987, p. 128). In addition, some of the questions asked by traditional researchers are not the kinds of questions that can be answered in terms of objective independent and dependent variables. For example, with respect to social referencing, Thompson (1987) asks, "When do infants begin to attribute emotional meaning to different facial expressions" (p. 129)? There are several problems with this seemingly simple question. First, it assumes that what the infant does is to "attribute meaning," when the only observable evidence is that the infant behaves in various ways. For example, on the visual cliff, the infant either crawls or does not crawl depending on the mother's facial expression. Second, Thompson's question implies that the infant initiates the action, which neglects the evocative (discriminative) effect of the mother's facial expression on the infant's behavior.

Social referencing is one example of what developmental psychologists call "emotional communication" in which there is an "active effort by infants to obtain emotional cues from others to assist in their own assessment of an uncertain situation" (Thompson, 1987, p. 129). Notwithstanding the problems with describing the mother's facial expressions as "emotional cues" or the infant as using these cues to assist in assessing uncertain situations, social referencing may suggest how this so-called emotional communication takes place. We have already provided a parsimonious interpretation of the behavioral relations between mother and infant called social referencing (see chapter 9), and this behavior analytic interpretation can be used to understand other types of behavioral relations between mother and infant that may be labelled empathic responding.

Emotional Sharing and Prosocial Motivation

Very young infants have been shown to respond to other infant cries, to facial expressions of their mothers, and to a number of different forms of distress exhibited by others (Zahn-Waxler & Radke-Yarrow, 1982; Zahn-Waxler, Radke-Yarrow, Wagner, & Chapman, 1992). For example, Zahn-Waxler and Radke-Yarrow (1982) trained mothers both to observe and report on their children's responses to others' emotions (e.g., anger, fear, sorrow, pain, affection, and pleasure) and to simulate emotions in the children's presence. The children in the study ranged in age from 38 to 134 weeks of age. The researchers concluded: "The distress of another person is a remarkably compelling stimulus for children in the first years of life: Distress elicits some form of response on between 80–90% of all occasions in which it occurs" (p. 118). In the Zahn-Waxler and Radke-Yarrow (1982) study, the form of the children's responses changed as they got older: The younger children showed more orientation, distress cries, and seeking out of the caregiver, whereas the older children exhibited more forms of (prosocial) interventions on behalf of the victim. Children at all ages were observed to imitate the distress behaviors of the victims. Interestingly and perhaps not surprisingly, the forms of intervention behavior also changed over time. Zahn-Waxler and Radke-Yarrow (1982) reported that the earliest forms of intervention consisted of "relatively undifferentiated positive physical contacts with the victim" (p. 122), such as touching and patting, whereas later forms of physical contact included hugging and kissing, as

FIGURE 10.3. A brother and sister demonstrate prosocial intervention by hugging.
(Photo by H. Schlinger)

well as more sophisticated verbal responses of reassurance (see Figure
10.3). Based on the dictionary definition of altruism, Zahn-Waxler and
Radke-Yarrow (1982) concluded that many of the prosocial behaviors of
young children may be said to have elements of altruism.

Having demonstrated early forms of prosocial behavior such as helping, comforting, empathy, and altruism, the next logical question concerns
the variables that control the behaviors. Zahn-Waxler and Radke-Yarrow
(1982) correctly note that it is not viable to posit such hypothetical, inferential mechanisms as adoption of specific value systems, adherence to norms
of reciprocity and responsibility, or careful balancing of cost and gain
when considering the origin of altruistic behaviors in very young children.
Even though some authors acknowledge the role of environmental factors,
such as child rearing practices, in the development of prosocial or altruistic
behaviors (e.g., Zahn-Waxler & Radke-Yarrow, 1979), many authors still
attribute changes in children's empathic and prosocial behavior to changes
in inferred cognitive and affective processes (Hoffman, 1982; Zahn-Waxler
et al., 1992).

A behavior analytic view of older children's reactions to the distress
of others follows from Rheingold and Hay's (1980) formal distinction

between empathy as the vicarious experiencing of another's emotions, and sympathy as the behavior that results in the alleviation of another person's discomfort. As the title of this section implies, there is something about the experience of another person in distress which motivates the behavior of the sympathizer. We would want to understand all of the possible behavioral effects on a viewer of situations in which another person is subjected to distressed circumstances. Based on the taxonomy of behavioral effects of environmental events as described in chapter 3 (e.g., Michael, 1993a; Schlinger & Blakely, 1994), we might predict that person A's distress, as a CS, elicits sympathetic, autonomic responding in person B. This might be what Thompson (1987) means by "emotional sharing." Moreover, this distress evokes sympathetic helping behavior in person B as a motivational variable (i.e., establishing operation), in that it establishes the alleviation of person A's distress as a reinforcing stimulus for person B. This is probably what Thompson (1987) means by "prosocial motivation."

The Origins of Empathic Responding and Prosocial Behavior

The distress of others, including the circumstances in which it occurs, evokes smooth muscle and glandular responses in observers that can be called empathic distress, and this probably originates through direct respondent conditioning and/or observations that produce similar function-altering effects. However, what a person does when they experience such empathic distress, often referred to as altruism or prosocial behavior, is operant behavior and must be analyzed as such. Such behaviors might include saying something to the person in distress, hugging, or touching, etc. Interestingly, and unlike other areas of development we have considered, many researchers do implicate learning principles in the acquisition of prosocial behaviors. Some authors with a behavior analytic orientation point to reinforcement and imitation as the processes by which these behaviors are learned (e.g., Rheingold & Emery, 1986; Rheingold & Hay, 1980), whereas other authors point more to structural experiences such as secure versus insecure early attachment, parental affection, encouragement of the perception of similarity to others, or discouragement of excessive interpersonal competition (e.g., Barnett, 1987).

Although some behavior analysts have provided behavior analyses of moral behavior in general (e.g., Bijou, 1976; Gewirtz & Pelaez-Nogueras, 1991b), none has tackled the specific problem of empathy and prosocial or altruistic responding. Aronfreed's (1970) analysis of the socialization of altruistic and sympathetic behavior has probably come the closest to a behavior analytic interpretation. We will present his analysis, including a description of an experiment he and his colleagues conducted, which demonstrates the plausibility of a behavior analytic interpretation of empathy and prosocial behavior.

You may recall that some developmental researchers are not willing to call behavior altruistic if there are obvious external rewards for such behavior. Even though we may not find the distinction between internal and external rewards to be useful, it is true that much behavior appears to occur in the absence of obvious reinforcing consequences. Although the controlling variables may be unclear, it may still be operant behavior. Nevertheless, the issue of the internal versus external control over behavior is a recurrent one and must be dealt with in any analysis.

Aronfreed (1970) suggests that sympathetic behavior in response to another person's distress (as Rheingold and Hay, 1980 speak of it) is partially under the aversive control of internal events that Aronfreed (and perhaps Hoffman, 1982) describes as affective distress. In behavior analytic terms, the affective distress evoked in the observer, in combination with the obvious distress cues displayed by the other person, function as establishing operations by evoking behavior which in the past has produced a reduction or termination of such cues. Aronfreed points out that sympathetic behavior is often established and maintained, at least in part, by externally mediated reinforcers, such as praise. Sympathetic behavior, however, may be described as altruistic to the extent that it is independent of such externally mediated consequences (Aronfreed, 1970).

According to Aronfreed (1970), the socialization of altruistic and sympathetic behavior requires two classes of phenomena that we would describe as function altering. According to Aronfreed, "The first class establishes the child's capacity for affective experience" (Aronfreed, 1970, p. 111). Here, the cues arising from the distress of others acquire an evocative function over the child's affective responses. In other words, one person's distress causes another person to feel similarly. It is unclear exactly how this process occurs, although Aronfreed suggests that initially there must be some temporal contiguity between the social cues arising from one person's distress and the distressful events that directly evoke affective responses in the other person.

The second basic class of phenomena is the actual socialization of altruistic and sympathetic behavior through contingencies of reinforcement. In the first case described above, the cues indicating another person's distress, in combination with the affective responses produced in the child, become motivational operations that establish their own reduction or termination as a form of reinforcement. In this case, the consequence of the sympathetic or altruistic behavior is the reduction or termination of the distress cues in the other person or of the affective responses in the child. Of course, we can only speculate about the actual process whereby the reinforcing value of these consequences is established and, whereby, the behavior is actually conditioned. It is also possible to design experiments that might demonstrate the plausibility of these general interpretations.

Aronfreed (1970) describes an experiment he conducted (Aronfreed & Paskal, 1965, as cited in Aronfreed, 1970) that lends plausibility to his interpretation and to a general environmental interpretation of altruism, even though the subjects were not infants. In the first phase of the experiment, 6- to 8-year-old girls' positive, empathic affectivity was conditioned to the expressive cues of an adult; and in the second phase, the altruistic value of a particular behavior that would result in the adult's positive, expressive cues was established. In the first phase of socialization, the adult demonstrated to the child the operation of a choice box which contained two levers. When one lever was depressed, a small candy was delivered; when the other lever was depressed, a 3-sec red light came on. Over 20 trials, the adult operated both levers showing no reaction when the candy was produced. When the light was produced, the adult smiled and uttered exclamations in an excited tone of voice such as, "There's the light!" while at the same time smiling at and hugging the child. In the two control groups, the adult either showed positive expressions without physical affection toward the child or displayed physical affection without showing positive expressions.

In the second phase of socialization, the child operated the choice box. The red light was deactivated under some pretext, but now the adult sat directly across from the child facing the rear of the box. The adult could now see another red light that was only visible to her, and the child was told about this red light. The child was also told that she could keep and eat all of the candy she earned by pressing one of the levers. When the child's lever press produced either no outcome or the candy, the adult remained passive. When a lever press turned on the red light, the adult smiled and exclaimed, "There's the red light!" Thus, the child was in a position where she could produce either candy for herself or pleasurable consequences—the red light—for the adult.

The results showed that children were more likely to sacrifice the candy for the red light, if they had previously experienced the adult's affection (smiles and hugs) than if they only saw the adult's positive, expressive cues without physical affection and vice versa. In general, however, the children responded more often to produce the red light for the adult than they did to produce candy for themselves. These results suggest that the adult's expressive cues had acquired some conditioned reinforcing value as well as some empathic affective value for the children (Aronfreed, 1970).

In another experiment by Aronfreed and Paskal (1966, as cited in

Aronfreed, 1970), the socialization of children's sympathetic behavior was studied using a similar procedure, which produced similar results: Through observation, children's empathic, affective responses and sympathetic behavior—behavior that reduces another person's distress—were conditioned.

Even though some developmental psychologists question the utility of experimentation as a way of understanding the behavior of children (Trevarthen, 1977), the experiments described by Aronfreed (1970) suggest plausible mechanisms for the development of altruistic and sympathetic behavior in children and point to potentially testable variables. Moreover, they are consistent with reports of naturally occurring interactions between parents and children regarding altruistic behavior (Grusec & Dix, 1986).

SUMMARY

This chapter demonstrated how the development of behavior–environment relations called "moral" may be interpreted according to behavior analytic principles. These relations include prosocial behaviors such as sharing, helping and cooperating, altruism, and empathy. As in other chapters throughout the book, this chapter argued that the most parsimonious approach is to look at the specific behaviors from which these concepts are inferred and to ask about their controlling variables, rather than to endlessly speculate about inferred, hypothetical processes. This chapter in particular—and the book in general—has made a case that a behavior analytic view of the concepts in the field of developmental psychology is both scientifically logical and valid.

References

Acreldo, L. P. (1978). Development of spatial orientation in infancy. *Developmental Psychology, 14,* 224–234.

Acreldo, L. P. (1985). Coordinating perspectives on infant spatial orientation. In R. Cohen (Ed.), *The development of spatial cognition* (pp. 115–140). Hillsdale, NJ: Erlbaum.

Acreldo, L. P., & Evans, D. (1980). Developmental changes in the effects of landmarks on infant spatial behaviour. *Developmental Psychology, 16,* 312–318.

Ainsworth, M. D. S. (1973). The development of infant–mother attachment. In B. M. Caldwell & H. N. Ricciuti (Eds.), *Review of Child Development Research* (Vol. 3, pp. 111–136). Chicago: University of Chicago Press.

Ainsworth, M. D. S., Blehar, M. C., Waters, E., & Wall, S. (1978). *Patterns of attachment: A psychological study of the strange situation.* Hillsdale, NJ: Erlbaum.

Allesi, G. (1992). Models of proximate and ultimate causation in psychology. *American Psychologist, 47,* 1359–1370.

Andresen, J. (1991). Skinner and Chomsky 30 years later or: The return of the repressed. *The Behavior Analyst, 14,* 49–60.

Aronfreed, J. (1970). The socialization of altruistic and sympathetic behavior: Some theoretical and experimental analyses. In J. Macaulay & L. Berkowitz (Eds.), *Altruism and helping behavior* (pp. 103–126). New York: Academic.

Aslin, R. N. (1987). Visual and auditory development in infancy. In J. D. Osofsky (Ed.), *Handbook of infant development* (pp. 5–97). New York: Wiley.

Baars, B. J. (1986). *The cognitive revolution in psychology.* New York: Guilford.

Bachrach, A. J. (1972). *Psychological research: An introduction* (3rd ed.). New York: Random House.

Baer, D. M. (1970). An age-irrelevant concept of development. *Merrill-Palmer Quarterly of Behavior and Development, 16,* 238–245.

Baer, D. M. (1976). The organism as host. *Human Development, 18,* 87–98.

Baer, D. M., & Deguchi, H. (1985). Generalized imitation from a radical–behavioral point of view. In S. Reiss & R. Bootzin (Eds.), *Theoretical issues in behavior therapy* (pp. 179–217). New York: Academic.

Baer, D. M., Peterson, R. F., & Sherman, J. A. (1967). The development of imitation by reinforcing behavioral similarity to a model. *Journal of the Experimental Analysis of Behavior, 10,* 405–416.

Baldwin, J. D., & Baldwin, J. I. (1988). *Behavior principles for everyday life.* Englewood Cliffs, NJ: Prentice-Hall.

Bandura, A. (1977). *Social learning theory.* Englewood Cliffs, NJ: Prentice-Hall.

Banks, M. S., & Salapatek, P. (1983). Infant visual perception. In J. J. Campos (Ed.), *Infancy and developmental psychobiology* (pp. 435–571). New York: Wiley.

Bar-Tal, D., Raviv, A., & Goldberg, M. (1982). Helping behavior among preschool children: An observational study. *Child Development, 53,* 396–402.

Barnett, M. A. (1987). Empathy and related responses in children. In N. Eisenberg & J. Strayer (Eds.), *Empathy and its development* (pp. 146–162). New York: Cambridge University Press.

Barrett, K. C., & Campos, J. J. (1987). Perspectives on emotional development II: A functionalist approach to emotions. In J. D. Osofsky (Ed.), *Handbook of infant development* (pp. 555–578). New York: Wiley.

Bates, E., Bretherton, I., Shore, C., & McNew, S. (1983). Names, gestures and objects: Symbolization in infancy and aphasia. In K. Nelson (Ed.), *Children's language* (Vol. 4, pp. 59–123). Hillsdale, NJ: Erlbaum.

Bates, E., O'Connell, B., & Shore, C. (1987). Language and communication in infancy. In J. D. Osofsky (Ed.), *Handbook of infant development* (pp. 149–203). New York: Wiley.

Bateson, P. P. G., & Reese, E. P. (1968). Reinforcing properties of conspicuous objects before imprinting has occurred. *Psychonomic Science, 10,* 379–380.

Bateson, P. P. G., & Reese, E. P. (1969). The reinforcing properties of conspicuous stimuli in the imprinting situation. *Animal Behavior, 17,* 692–699.

Bechtoldt, H. P., & Hutz, C. S. (1979). Stereopsis in young infants and stereopsis in infants with esotropia. *Journal of Pediatric Ophthalmology, 16,* 49–54.

Becker, J. A. (1982). Children's strategic use of requests to mark and manipulate social status. In S. A. Kuczaj (Ed.), *Language development: Language, thought and culture* (Vol. 2, pp. 1–35). Hillsdale, NJ: Erlbaum.

Bell, S. M., & Ainsworth, M. D. S. (1972). Infant crying and maternal responsiveness. *Child Development, 43,* 1171–1190.

Benson, J. B. (1990). The significance and development of crawling in human infancy. In J. E. Clark & J. H. Humphrey (Eds.), *Advances in motor development research* (Vol. 3, pp. 91–142). New York: AMS Press.

Benson, J. B., & Uzgiris, I. C. (1985). Effect of self-initiated locomotion on infant search activity. *Developmental Psychology, 21,* 923–931.

Berndt, T. J. (1992). *Child development.* Orlando, FL: Harcourt Brace Jovanovich.

Bijou, S. W. (1976). *Child development: The basic stage of early childhood.* Englewood Cliffs, NJ: Prentice-Hall.

Bijou, S. W. (1979). *Behavior analysis of the infantile stage of development.* Unpublished Manuscript.

Bijou, S. W., & Baer, D. M. (1961). *Child development: A systematic and empirical theory.* Englewood Cliffs, NJ: Prentice-Hall.

Bijou, S. W., & Baer, D. M. (1978). *Behavior analysis of child development.* Englewood Cliffs, NJ: Prentice-Hall.

Bloom, K., Russel, A., & Wassenberg, K. (1987). Turn taking affects the quality of infant vocalizations. *Journal of Child Language, 14,* 211–227.

Blough, D., & Blough, P. (1977). Animal psychophysics. In W. K. Honig & J. E. R. Staddon (Eds.), *Handbook of operant behavior* (pp. 514–539). Englewood Cliffs, NJ: Prentice-Hall.

Bohannon, J. N., & Stanowicz, L. (1988). The issue of negative evidence: Adult responses to children's language errors. *Developmental Psychology, 24,* 684–689.

Boller, K., Rovee-Collier, C., Borovsky, D., O'Connor, J., & Shyi, G. (1990). Development changes in the time-dependent nature of memory retrieval. *Developmental Psychology, 26,* 770–779.

Bornstein, M. H. (1976). Infants' recognition memory for hue. *Developmental Psychology, 12,* 185–191.

Bower, T. G. R. (1966). The visual world of infants. *Scientific American, 215,* 80–92.

Bower, T. G. R. (1979). *Human development*. San Francisco: Freeman.

Bowlby, J. (1969). *Attachment and loss: Vol. 1. Attachment*. New York: Basic.

Bowlby, J. (1973). *Attachment and loss: Vol. 2. Separation*. New York: Basic.

Brackbill, Y. (1958). Extinction of the smiling response in infants as a function of reinforcement schedule. *Child Development, 29*, 115–124.

Branch, M. N. (1977). On the role of "memory" in the analysis of behavior. *Journal of the Experimental Analysis of Behavior, 28*, 171–179.

Bremner, J. G. (1978). Egocentric versus allocentric spatial coding in 9-month-old infants: Factors influencing the choice of code. *Developmental Psychology, 14*, 346–355.

Bretherton, I. (1987). New perspectives on attachment relations: Security, communication and internal working models. In J. D. Osofsky (Ed.), *Handbook on infant development* (pp. 1061–1100). New York: Wiley.

Brown, R. W., & Bellugi, U. (1964). Three processes in the child's acquisition of syntax. *Harvard Educational Review, 34*, 133–151.

Bryant, P., Bradley, L., Maclean, M., & Crossland, J. (1989). Nursery rhymes, phonological skills, and reading. *Journal of Child Language, 16*, 407–428.

Bukatko, D., & Daehler, M. W. (1992). *Child development: A topical approach*. Boston: Houghton Mifflin.

Campos, J. J., & Langer, A. (1971). The visual cliff: Discriminative cardiac orienting responses with retinal size held constant. *Psychophysiology, 8*, 264–265.

Campos, J. J., Langer, A., & Krowitz, A. (1970). Cardiac responses on the visual cliff in prelocomotor human infants. *Science, 170*, 196–197.

Catania, A. C. (1973). The concept of the operant in the analysis of behavior. *Behaviorism, 1*, 103–115.

Catania, A. C. (1992). *Learning* (3rd ed.). Englewood Cliffs, NJ: Prentice-Hall.

Chalkley, M. A. (1982). The emergence of language as a social skill. In S. A. Kuczaj (Ed.), *Language development: Language, thought and culture* (Vol. 2, pp. 75–111). Hillsdale, NJ: Erlbaum.

Chance, P. (1993). *Learning and behavior* (3rd ed.). Belmont, CA: Wadsworth.

Chomsky, N. (1959). Review of verbal behavior. *Language, 35*, 26–58.

Chomsky, N. (1980). *Rules and representations*. New York: Columbia University Press.

Cohen, L. B., & Gelber, E. R. (1975). Infant visual memory: Basic visual processes. In L. B. Cohen & P. Salapatek (Eds.), *Infant perception: From sensation to cognition* (Vol. 1, pp. 347–403). New York: Academic.

Cohn, J. F., Campbell, S. B., Matias, R., & Hopkins, J. (1990). Face-to-face interactions of postpartum depressed and nondepressed mother–infant pairs at 2 months. *Developmental Psychology, 26*, 15–23.

Cohn, J. F., & Elmore, M. (1988). Effect of contingent changes in mothers' affective expression on the organization of behavior in 3-month-old infants. *Infant Behavior and Development, 11*, 493–505.

Cohn, J. F., & Tronick, E. Z. (1983). Three-month-old infants' reaction to simulated maternal depression. *Child Development, 54*, 184–193.

Collins, W. A., & Kuczaj, S. A. (1991). *Developmental psychology: Childhood and adolescence*. New York: Macmillan.

Commons, M. L., Church, R. M., Stellar, J. M., & Wagner, A. R. (1988). *Quantitative analyses of behavior: Biological determinants of reinforcement*. Hillsdale, NJ: Erlbaum.

Cornell, E. H. (1978). Learning to find things: A reinterpretation of object permanence studies. In L. Siegel & C. Brainerd (Eds.), *Alternatives to Piaget: Critical essays on the theory*. New York: Academic.

Day, R. H. (1987). Visual size constancy in infants. In B. E. McKenzie & R. H. Day (Eds.), *Perceptual development in early infancy: Problems and issues.* Hillsdale, NJ: Erlbaum.

Day, R. H., & McKenzie, B. E. (1981). Infant perception of the invariant size of approaching and receding objects. *Developmental Psychology, 17,* 670–677.

DeCasper, A. J., & Fifer, W. P. (1980). Of human bonding: Newborns prefer their mother's voices. *Science, 208,* 1174–1176.

DeCasper, A. J., & Prescott, P. A. (1984). Human newborn's perception of male voices: Preference, discrimination, and reinforcing value. *Developmental Psychobiology, 17,* 481–491.

DeCasper, A. J., & Sigafoos, A. D. (1983). The intrauterine heartbeat: A potent reinforcer for newborns. *Infant Behavior and Development, 6,* 19–25.

DeCasper, A. J., & Spence, M. J. (1986). Prenatal maternal speech influences on newborns' perception of speech sound. *Infant Behavior and Development, 9,* 133–150.

Dobzhansky, T., Ayala, F. J., Stebbins, G. L., & Valentine, J. W. (1977). *Evolution.* San Francisco: Freeman.

Donahoe, J. W., & Palmer, D. C. (1994). *Learning and complex behavior.* Boston: Allyn and Bacon.

Dunn, J., Bretherton, I., & Munn, P. (1987). Conversations about feeling states between mothers and their young children. *Developmental Psychology, 23,* 132–139.

Dworetzky, J. P. (1990). *Introduction to child development* (4th ed.). St. Paul, MN: West.

Dworetzky, J. P. (1993). *Introduction to child development* (5th ed.). Minneapolis/St. Paul: West.

Eckerman, C. O., Whatley, J. L., & Kutz, S. L. (1975). Growth of social play with peers during the second year of life. *Developmental Psychology, 11,* 42–49.

Eimas, P., Siqueland, E., Jusczyk, P., & Vigorito, J. (1971). Speech perception in infants. *Science, 171,* 303–306.

Eisenberg, N. (1982). Introduction. In N. Eisenberg (Ed.), *The development of prosocial behavior* (pp. 1–21). New York: Academic.

Eisenson, J., Auer, J. J., & Irwin, J. V. (1963). *The psychology of communication.* New York: Appleton-Century-Crofts.

Emde, R. N. (1987). Infant mental health: Clinical dilemmas, the expansion of meaning, and opportunities. In J. D. Osofsky (Ed.), *Handbook of infant development* (pp. 1297–1320). New York: Wiley.

Epstein, R. (1981). On pigeons and people: A preliminary look at the Columbian simulation project. *The Behavior Analyst, 4,* 43–55.

Epstein, R. (1983). Resurgence of previously reinforced behavior during extinction. *Behavior Analysis Letters, 3,* 391–397.

Epstein, R. (1985). Extinction-induced resurgence: Preliminary investigations and possible application. *Psychological Record, 35,* 143–153.

Etzel, B. C., & Gewirtz, J. L. (1967). Experimental modification of caretaker-maintained high-rate operant crying in a 6- and a 20-week-old infant (Infans tyrannotearus): Extinction of crying with reinforcement of eye contact and smiling. *Journal of Experimental Child Psychology, 5,* 303–317.

Fagan III, J. F. (1970). Memory in the infant. *Journal of Experimental Child Psychology, 9,* 217–226.

Fagen, J. W., & Rovee-Collier, C. (1983). Memory retrieval: A time-locked process in infancy. *Science, 222,* 1349–1351.

Fagen, J. W., Rovee, C. K., & Kaplan, M. G. (1976). Psychophysical scaling of stimulus similarity in 3-month-old infants and adults. *Journal of Experimental Child Psychology, 22,* 272–281.

Fantino, E., & Logan, C. A. (1979). *The experimental analysis of behavior: A biological perspective.* San Francisco: Freeman.

Fantz, R. (1961). The origin of form perception. *Scientific American, 204,* 66–72.

Fantz, R. L. (1964). Visual experience in infants: Decreased attention to familiar patterns relative to novel ones. *Science, 146,* 668–670.

Finkelstein, N. W., & Ramey, C. T. (1977). Learning to control the environment in infancy. *Child Development, 48,* 806–819.

Flannagan, O. (1991). *The science of the mind* (2nd ed.). Cambridge, MA: MIT Press.

Rogel, A. (1982). Affect dynamics in early infancy: Affective tolerance. In T. Field & A. Fogel (Eds.), *Emotion and early interaction* (pp. 25–56). Hillsdale, NJ: Erlbaum.

Frodi, A. M., Lamb, M. E., Leavitt, L. A., & Donovan, W. L. (1978). Father's and mother's responses to infant smiles and cries. *Infant Behavior and Development, 1,* 187–198.

Furrow, D., Nelson, K., & Benedict, H. (1979). Mothers' speech to children and syntactic development: Some simple relationships. *Journal of Child Language, 6,* 423–442.

Futuyma, D. J. (1979). *Evolutionary biology.* Sunderland, MA: Sinauer.

Gallahue, D. L. (1989). *Understanding motor development: Infants, children, adolescents* (2nd ed.). Indianapolis: Benchmark Press.

Gelfand, D. M., & Hartmann, D. P. (1982). Response consequences and attributions: Two contributors to prosocial behavior. In N. Eisenberg (Ed.), *The development of prosocial behavior* (pp. 167–196). New York: Academic.

Gelfand, D. M., Hartmann, D. P., Cromer, C. C., Smith, C. L., & Page, B. C. (1975). The effects of instructional prompts and praise on children's donation rates. *Child Development, 46,* 980–983.

Gentner, D. (1982). Why nouns are learned before verbs: Linguistic relativity versus natural partitioning. In S. A. Kuczaj (Ed.), *Language development: Language, thought and culture* (Vol. 2, pp. 301–334). Hillsdale, NJ: Erlbaum.

Geschwind, N. (1979). Specializations of the human brain. *Scientific American, 241,* 180–199.

Gewirtz, J. L. (1961). A learning analysis of the effects of normal stimulation, privation, and deprivation on the acquisition of social motivation and attachment. In B. M. Foss (Ed.), *Determinants of infant behaviour* (pp. 213–229). London: Methuen.

Gewirtz, J. L. (1972a). On the selection and use of attachment and dependence indices. In J. L. Gewirtz (Ed.), *Attachment and dependency* (pp. 179–215). Washington, DC: Winston.

Gewirtz, J. L. (1972b). Attachment, dependence, and a distinction in terms of stimulus control. In J. L. Gewirtz (Ed.), *Attachment and dependency* (pp. 139–177). Washington, DC: Winston.

Gewirtz, J. L. (1976). The attachment acquisition process as evidenced in the maternal conditioning of cued infant responding (particularly crying). *Human Development, 19,* 143–155.

Gewirtz, J. L. (1977). Maternal responding and the conditioning of crying: Directions of influence within the attachment-acquisition process. In B. C. Etzel, J. M. LeBlanc, & D. M. Baer (Eds.), *New developments in behavioral research: Theory, method, and application* (pp. 31–57). Hillsdale, NJ: Erlbaum.

Gewirtz, J. L., & Boyd, E. F. (1976). Mother–infant interaction and its study. In H. W. Reese (Ed.), *Advances in child development and behavior* (Vol. 2). New York: Academic.

Gewirtz, J. L., & Boyd, E. F. (1977). Does maternal responding imply reduced infant crying? A critique of the 1972 Bell and Ainsworth report. *Child Development, 48,* 1200–1207.

Gewirtz, J. L., & Pelaez-Nogueras, M. (1991a). The attachment metaphor and the conditioning of infant separation protests. In J. L. Gewirtz & W. M. Kurtines (Eds.), *Intersections with attachment* (pp. 123–144). Hillsdale, NJ: Erlbaum.

Gewirtz, J. L., & Pelaez-Nogueras, M. (1991b). Proximal mechanisms underlying the acquisition of moral behavior patterns. In W. M. Kurtines & J. L. Gewirtz (Eds.), *Handbook of moral behavior and development* (Vol. 1, pp. 153–182). Hillsdale, NJ: Erlbaum.

Gewirtz, J. L., & Pelaez-Nogueras, M. (1992a). Infants' separation difficulties and distress due to misplaced maternal contingencies. In T. M. Field & P. M. McCabe (Eds.), *Stress and coping in infancy and childhood* (pp. 19–46). Hillsdale, NJ: Erlbaum.

Gewirtz, J. L., & Pelaez-Nogueras, M. (1992b). Infants social referencing as a learned process. In S. Feinman (Ed.), *Social referencing and the social construction of reality in infancy* (pp. 151–173). New York: Plenum.

Gibson, E. J. (1977). The development of perception as an adaptive process. In I. L. Janis (Ed.), *Current trends in psychology* (pp. 111–120). Los Altos: William Kaufmann, Inc.

Gibson, E. J., & Spelke, E. S. (1983). The development of perception. In P. H. Mussen, J. H. Flavell, & E. M. Markman (Eds.), *Handbook of child psychology: Vol. 3. Cognitive development* (4th ed., pp. 1–76). New York: Wiley.

Gibson, E. J., & Walk, R. D. (1960). The "visual cliff." *Scientific American, 202,* 64–71.

Ginsburg, H. P., & Opper, S. (1988). *Piaget's theory of intellectual development* (3rd ed.). Englewood Cliffs, NJ: Prentice-Hall.

Gleitman, L. R., & Wanner, E. (1984). Current issues in language learning. In M. H. Bornstein & M. E. Lamb (Eds.), *Developmental psychology: An advanced textbook* (pp. 181–240). Hillsdale, NJ: Erlbaum.

Godman, A. (1982). *The Barnes & Noble thesaurus of chemistry.* New York: Barnes & Noble.

Gordon, F. R., & Yonas, A. (1976). Sensitivity to binocular depth information in infants. *Journal of Experimental Child Psychology, 22,* 413–422.

Granrud, C. E. (1986). Binocular vision and spatial perception in 4- and 5-month-old infants. *Journal of Experimental Psychology: Human Perception and Performance, 12,* 36–49.

Granrud, C. E., Haake, R., & Yonas, A. (1985). Infants' sensitivity to familiar size: The effect of memory on spatial perception. *Perception and Psychophysics, 37,* 457–466.

Granrud, C. E., & Yonas, A. (1984). Infants' perception of pictorially specified interposition. *Journal of Experimental Child Psychology, 37,* 500–511.

Granrud, C. E., Yonas, A., & Opland, E. A. (1985). Infants' sensitivity to the depth cue of shading. *Perception and Psychophysics, 37,* 415–419.

Granrud, C. E., Yonas, A., & Pettersen, L. (1984). A comparison of responsiveness to monocular and binocular depth information in 5- and 7-month-old infants. *Journal of Experimental Child Psychology, 38,* 19–32.

Granrud, C. E., Yonas, A., Smith, I. M., Arterberry, M. E., Glicksman, M. L., & Sorknes, A. C. (1984). Infants' sensitivity to accretion and deletion of texture as information for depth at an edge. *Child Development, 55,* 1630–1636.

Green, J. A., Gustafson, G. E., & West, M. J. (1980). Effects of infant development on mother–infant interactions. *Child Development, 51,* 199–207.

Green, M. (1989). *Theories of human development: A comparative approach.* Englewood Cliffs, NJ: Prentice-Hall.

Grusec, J. E., & Dix, T. (1986). The socialization of prosocial behavior: Theory and reality. In C. Zahn-Waxler, E. M. Cummings, & R. Iannotti (Eds.), *Altruism and aggression* (pp. 218–237). Cambridge, Cambridge University Press.

Grusec, J. E., & Redler, E. (1980). Attribution, reinforcement, and altruism: A developmental analysis. *Developmental Psychology, 16,* 525–534.

Gustafson, G. E. (1984). Effects of the ability to locomote on infants' social and exploratory behaviors: An experimental study. *Developmental Psychology, 20,* 397–405.

Hake, D. F., Olvera, D., & Bell, J. C. (1975). Switching from competition to sharing or cooperation at large response requirements: Competition requires more responding. *Journal of the Experimental Analysis of Behavior, 24,* 343–354.

Hake, D. F., & Vukelich, R. (1972). A classification and review of cooperation procedures. *Journal of the Experimental Analysis of Behavior, 18,* 333–343.

Hake, D. F., Vukelich, R., & Olvera, D. (1975). The measurement of sharing and cooperation as equity effects and some relationships between them. *Journal of the Experimental Analysis of Behavior, 23,* 63–79.

Harlow, H. F. (1967). Love in infant monkeys. In J. L. McGaugh, N. M. Weinberger, & R. E. Whalen (Eds.), *Psychobiology: The biological bases of behavior* (pp. 100–106). San Francisco: Freeman.

Harlow, H. F., & Zimmerman, R. R. (1959). Affectional responses in the infant monkey. *Science, 130,* 421–432.

Harris, P. L. (1987). The development of search. In P. Salapatek & L. Cohen (Eds.), *Handbook of infant perception* (Vol. 2, pp. 155–207). Orlando, FL: Academic.

Hart, B. M., Allen, K. E., Buel, J. S., Harris, F. R., & Wolf, M. M. (1964). Effects of social reinforcement on operant crying. *Journal of Experimental Child Psychology, 1,* 145–153.

Haviland, J. M., & Lelwica, M. (1987). The induced affect response: 10-week-old infants' responses to three emotional expressions. *Developmental Psychology, 23,* 97–104.

Hay, D. F. (1979). Cooperative interactions and sharing between very young children and their parents. *Developmental Psychology, 15,* 647–653.

Hay, D. F. Caplan, M., Castle, J., & Stimson, C. A. (1991). Does sharing become increasingly "rational" in the second year of life? *Developmental Psychology, 27,* 987–993.

Hay, D. F., & Murray, P. (1982). Giving and requesting: Social facilitation of infants' offers to adults. *Infant Behavior and Development, 5,* 301–310.

Hempel, C. G. (1966). *Philosophy of natural science.* Englewood Cliffs, NJ: Prentice-Hall.

Hepper, P. G. (1989). Foetal learning: Implications for psychiatry? *British Journal of Psychiatry, 155,* 289–293.

Hess, E. H. (1973). *Imprinting: Early experience and the developmental psychobiology of attachment.* New York: Van Nostrand.

Hetherington, E. M., & Parke, R. D. (1986). *Child psychology: A contemporary viewpoint* (3rd ed.). New York: McGraw Hill.

Hill, W. J., Borovsky, D., & Rovee-Collier, C. (1988). Continuities in infant memory development. *Developmental Psychology, 21,* 43–62.

Hineline, P. N. (1990). The origins of environment-based psychological theory. *Journal of the Experimental Analysis of Behavior, 53,* 305–320.

Hingtgen, J. N., Sanders, B. J., & DeMeyer, M. K. (1965). Shaping cooperative responses in early childhood schizophrenics. In L. P. Ullmann & L. Krasner (Eds.), *Case studies in behavior modification* (pp. 130–138). New York: Holt, Rinehart and Winston.

Hingtgen, J. N., & Trose, J. F. C. (1966). Shaping cooperative responses in early childhood schizophrenics: II. Reinforcement of mutual physical contact and vocal responses. In R. Ulrich, T. Stachnik, & J. Mabry (Eds.), *Control of human behavior* (pp. 110–113). Atlanta, GA: Scott, Foresman.

Hirsch, H. V. B., & Spinelli, D. N. (1971). Modification of the distribution of receptive field orientation in cats by selective visual exposure during development. *Experimental Brain Research, 13,* 509–527.

Hoff-Ginsberg, E. (1990). Maternal speech and the child's development of syntax. *Journal of Child Language, 17,* 85–99.

Hoffman, H. S., & Ratner, A. M. (1973). A reinforcement model of imprinting: Implications for socialization in monkeys and men. *Psychological Review, 30,* 527–544.

Hoffman, H. S., Searle, J. L., Toffey, S., & Kozma, F. (1966). Behavioral control by an imprinted stimulus. *Journal of the Experimental Analysis of Behavior, 9,* 177–189.

Hoffman, H. S., Stratton, J. W., & Newby, V. (1969). Punishment by response-contingent withdrawal of an imprinting stimulus. *Science, 163,* 702–704.

Hoffman, M. L. (1982). Development of prosocial motivation: Empathy and guilt. In N.

Eisenberg (Ed.), *The development of prosocial behavior* (pp. 281–313). New York: Academic.

Horowitz, F. D. (1987). *Exploring developmental theories: Toward a structural/behavioral model of development.* Hillsdale, NJ: Erlbaum.

Jeung, E. H. L., & Rheingold, H. L. (1981). Development of pointing as a social gesture. *Developmental Psychology, 17,* 215–220.

Johnson, D. F., & Cumming, W. W. (1968). Some determiners of attention. *Journal of the Experimental Analysis of Behavior, 11,* 157–166.

Jusczyk, P. W., Pisoni, D. B., Walley, A., & Murray, J. (1980). Discrimination of relative onset time of two-component tones by infants. *Journal of the Acoustical Society of America, 67,* 262–270.

Kalnins, I. V., & Bruner, J. S. (1973). The coordination of visual observation and instrumental behavior in early infancy. *Perception, 2,* 307–314.

Kandel, E. R. (1975). Nerve cells and behavior. In R. F. Thompson (Ed.), *Progress in psychobiology.* San Francisco: Freeman.

Karniol, R. (1989). The role of manual manipulative stages in the infant's acquisition of perceived control over objects. *Developmental Review, 9,* 205–233.

Kaufmann, R., Maland, J., & Yonas, A. (1981). Sensitivity of 5- and 7-month-old infants to pictorial depth information. *Journal of Experimental Child Psychology, 32,* 162–168.

Keogh, J., & Sugden, D. (1985). *Movement skill development.* New York: Macmillan.

Knapp, T. J. (1987). Perception and action. In S. Modgil & C. Modgil (Eds.), *B. F. Skinner: Consensus and controversy* (pp. 283–294). New York: Falmer.

Knapp, T. J. (1992). *Verbal Behavior:* The other reviews. *The Analysis of Verbal Behavior, 10,* 87–95.

Kopp, C. B. (1979). Perspectives on infant motor system development. In M. H. Bornstein & W. Kessen (Eds.), *Psychological development from infancy: Image to intention* (pp. 9–35). Hillsdale, NJ: Erlbaum.

Kuchuk, A., Vibbert, M., & Bornstein, M. H. (1986). The perception of smiling and its experiential correlates in three-month-old infants. *Child Development, 57,* 1054–1061.

Kuhl, P. K., & Miller, J. D. (1975). Speech perception by the chinchilla: Voiced-voiceless distinction in alveolar plosive consonants. *Science, 190,* 69–72.

Kuhl, P. K., & Miller, J. D. (1978). Speech perception by the chinchilla: Identification functions for synthetic VOT stimuli. *Journal of the Acoustical Society of America, 63,* 905–917.

Kymissis, E., & Poulson, C. L. (1990). The history of imitation in learning theory: The language acquisition process. *Journal of the Experimental Analysis of Behavior, 54,* 113–127.

Lamb, M. E., & Bornstein, M. H. (1987). *Development in infancy: An introduction* (2nd ed.). New York: Random House.

Lamb, S. (1991). First moral sense: Aspects of and contributors to a beginning morality in the second year of life. In W. M. Kurtines & J. L. Gewirtz (Eds.), *Handbook of moral behavior and development: Vol. 2. Research* (pp. 171–189). Hillsdale, NJ: Erlbaum.

Lenneberg, E. H. (1970). Speech as a motor skill with special reference to nonaphasic disorders. In R. Brown (Ed.), *Cognitive development in children: Five monographs of the society for research in child development* (pp. 393–405). Chicago: University of Chicago Press.

Lenneberg, E. H., Rebelsky, F. G., & Nichols, I. A. (1965). The vocalizations of infants born to deaf and hearing parents. *Human Development, 8,* 23–37.

Lester, B. M., & Zeskind, P. S. (1982). A biobehavioral perspective on crying in early infancy. In Fitzgerald, B. M. Lester, & Yogman (Eds.), *Theory and research in behavioral pediatrics* (Vol. 1, pp. 133–180). New York: Plenum.

Lewis, M. (1987). Social development in infancy and early childhood. In J. D. Osofsky (Ed.), *Handbook of infant development* (pp. 419–493). New York: Wiley.

Lewis, M., & Rosenblum, L. H. (1974). *The effect of the infant on its caregiver*. New York: Wiley.

Lieberman, P., Crelin, E. S., & Klatt, D. H. (1972). Phonetic ability and related anatomy of the newborn and adult human, Neanderthal man, and the chimpanzee. *American Anthropologist, 74*, 287–307.

Lindsley, O. R. (1966). Experimental analysis of cooperation and competition. In T. Verhave (Ed.), *The experimental analysis of behavior* (pp. 470–501). New York: Appleton-Century-Crofts.

Lipsitt, L. P. (1981). Sensorimotor development: What infants do and how we think about what they do. In D. M. Brodzinsky, I. E. Sigel, & R. M. Golinkoff (Eds.), *New directions in Piagetian research and theory* (pp. 29–37). Hillsdale, NJ: Erlbaum.

Littenberg, R., Tulkin, S., & Kagan, J. (1971). Cognitive components of separation anxiety. *Developmental Psychology, 4*, 387–388.

Lockman, J. J., & Hazen, N. L. (1989). *Action in social context: Perspectives on early development*. New York: Plenum.

Lorenz, K. (1935). Der Kumpan in der Umvelt des Vogels. *Journal für Ornithologie, 83*, 137–213.

Lovaas, O. I., Freitas, K., Nelson, K., & Whalen, C. (1967). The establishment of imitation and its use for the development of complex behavior in schizophrenic children. *Behavior Research and Therapy, 5*, 171–182.

Maccoby, E. E. (1986). Social groupings in childhood: Theory relationship to prosocial and antisocial behavior in boys and girls. In D. Olweus, J. Block, & M. Radke-Yarrow (Eds.), *Development of antisocial and prosocial behavior: Research, theories, and issues* (pp. 263–284). Orlando, FL: Academic.

MacCorquodale, K. (1970). On Chomsky's review of Skinner's Verbal Behavior. *Journal of the Experimental Analysis of Behavior, 13*, 83–99.

Malott, R. W., & Whaley, D. L. (1981). *Psychology*. Kalamazoo, MI: Behaviordelia.

Masur, E. F. (1988). Infants' imitation of novel and familiar behaviors. In T. R. Zentall & B. G. Galef (Eds.), *Social learning: Psychological and biological perspectives* (pp. 301–318). Hillsdale, NJ: Erlbaum.

Mazur, J. E. (1990). *Learning and behavior*. Hillsdale, NJ: Prentice-Hall.

McCain, G., & Segal, E. M. (1988). *The game of science* (5th ed.). Pacific Grove, CA: Brooks/Cole.

McKenzie, B. E., Tootell, H. E., & Day, R. H. (1980). Development of visual size constancy during the 1st year of human infancy. *Developmental Psychology, 16*, 163–174.

McKirdy, L. S., & Rovee, C. K. (1978). The reinforcing efficacy of visual and auditory components in infant conjugate conditioning. *Journal of Experimental Child Psychology, 25*, 80–89.

Meltzoff, A. N. (1985). Immediate and deferred imitation in fourteen- and twenty-four month-old infants. *Child Development, 56*, 62–72.

Meltzoff, A. N. (1988). The human infant as homo imitans. In T. R. Zentall & B. G. Galef (Eds.), *Social learning: Psychological and biological perspectives* (pp. 319–341). Hillsdale, NJ: Erlbaum.

Meltzoff, A. N., & Moore, M. K. (1977). Imitation of facial and manual gestures by human neonates. *Science, 198*, 75–78.

Meltzoff, A. N., & Moore, M. K. (1983). Newborn infants imitate adult facial gestures. *Child Development, 54*, 702–709.

Michael, J. L. (1975). Positive and negative reinforcement, a distinction that is no longer necessary; or a better way to talk about bad things. *Behaviorism, 3*, 33–44.

Michael, J. (1980). The discriminative stimulus or SD. *The Behavior Analyst, 3*, 47–49.

Michael, J. (1982). Distinguishing between discriminative and motivational functions of stimuli. *Journal of the Experimental Analysis of Behavior, 37*, 149–155.

Michael, J. (1983). Evocative and repertoire-altering effects of an environmental event. *The Analysis of Verbal Behavior, 2*, 19–21.

Michael, J. (1984). Verbal behavior. *Journal of the Experimental Analysis of Behavior, 42*, 363–376.

Michael, J. (1986). Repertoire-altering effects of remote contingencies. *The Analysis of Verbal Behavior, 4*, 10–18.

Michael, J. (1993a). *Concepts and principles in behavior analysis.* Kalamazoo, MI: Society for the Analysis of Behavior.

Michael, J. (1993b). Establishing operations. *The Behavior Analyst, 16*, 191–206.

Milewski, A. E., & Siqueland, E. R. (1975). Discrimination of color and pattern novelty in one-month human infants. *Journal of Experimental Child Psychology, 19*, 122–136.

Miranda, S. B., & Fantz, R. L. (1974). Recognition memory in Down's Syndrome and normal infants. *Child Development, 45*, 651–660.

Morek, E. L. (1983). *The mother of Eve: As a first language teacher.* Norwood, NJ: Ablex.

Murphy, C. M., & Messer, D. J. (1977). Mothers, infants, and pointing: A study of a gesture. In H. R. Schaffer (Ed.), *Studies in mother–infant interaction* (pp. 325–354). London: Academic.

Murray, F. B. (1981). The conservation paradigm: The conservation of conservation research. In D. M. Brodzinsky, I. E. Sigel, & R. M. Golinkoff (Eds.), *New directions in Piagetian research and theory* (pp. 143–173). Hillsdale, NJ: Erlbaum.

Mussen, P., & Eisenberg-Berg, N. (1977). *Roots of caring, sharing, and helping.* San Francisco: Freeman.

Neuringer, A. J. (1970). Superstitious key pecking after three peck-produced reinforcements. *Journal of the Experimental Analysis of Behavior, 13*, 127–134.

Nevin, J. A. (1973). Stimulus control. In J. A. Nevin (Ed.), *The study of behavior: Learning, motivation, emotion, and instinct* (pp. 114–152). Glenview, IL: Scott Foreman.

Oxford English Dictionary (2nd ed.) (1989). Oxford, U.K.: Oxford University Press.

Palmer, D. C. (1986). Chomsky's nativism: A critical review. In L. J. Hayes & P. N. Chase (Eds.), *Psychological aspects of language.* Springfield, IL: Thomas.

Palmer, D. C. (1991). A behavioral interpretation of memory. In L. J. Hayes & P. N. Chase (Eds.), *Dialogues on verbal behavior* (pp. 261–279). Reno, NV: Context.

Palmer, D. C., & Donahoe, J. W. (1992). Essentialism and selectionism is cognitive science and behavior analysis. *American Psychologist, 47*, 1344–1358.

Parsley, N. J., & Rabinowitz, F. M. (1975). Crying in the first year: An operant interpretation of the Bell and Ainsworth (1972) findings. *Child Study Journal, 5*, 83–89.

Penner, S. G. (1987). Parental responses to grammatical and ungrammatical child utterances. *Child Development, 58*, 376–384.

Peterson, N. (1960). Control of behavior by presentation of an imprinted stimulus. *Science, 132*, 1395–1396.

Petrovich, S. B., & Gewirtz, J. L. (1991). Imprinting and attachment: Proximate and ultimate considerations. In J. L. Gewirtz & W. M. Kurtines (Eds.), *Intersections with attachment* (pp. 69–93). Hillsdale, NJ: Erlbaum.

Petterson, L., Yonas, A., & Fisch, R. O. (1980). The development of blinking in response to impending collision with preterm, full-term, and postterm infants. *Infant Behavior and Development, 3*, 155–165.

Piaget, J. (1952). *The origins of intelligence in children.* New York: Norton.

Piaget, J. (1964). Development and learning. In R. E. Ripple & V. N. Rockcastle (Eds.), *Piaget rediscovered.* Ithaca, NY: Cornell University Press.

Pisoni, D. B. (1977). Identification and discrimination of the relative onset of two component tones: Implications for voicing perception in stops. *Journal of the Acoustical Society of America, 61*, 1352–1361.

Poling, A., Schlinger, H., Starin, S., & Blakely, E. (1990). *Psychology: A behavioral overview*. New York: Plenum.

Poulson, C. L. (1983). Differential reinforcement of other-than-vocalization as a control procedure in the conditioning of infant vocalization rate. *Journal of Experimental Child Psychology, 36*, 471–489.

Poulson, C. L. (1988). Operant conditioning of vocalization rate of infants with Down Syndrome. *American Journal on Mental Retardation, 93*, 57–63.

Poulson, C. L., & Kymissis, E. (1988). Generalized imitation in infants. *Journal of Experimental Child Psychology, 46*, 324–336.

Poulson, C. L., Nunes, L. R. P., & Warren, S. F. (1989). Imitation in infancy: A critical review. In H. W. Reese (Ed.), *Advances in child development and behavior* (Vol. 22, pp. 271–298). San Diego, CA: Academic.

Premack, D. (1965). Reinforcement theory. In D. Levine (Ed.), *Nebraska symposium on motivation*. Lincoln: University of Nebraska Press.

Rader, N., Bausano, M., & Richards, J. E. (1980). On the nature of the visual-cliff avoidance response in human infants. *Child Development, 51*, 61–68.

Radke-Yarrow, M., Cummings, M., Kuczynski, L., & Chapman, M. (1985). Patterns of attachment in two and three year olds in normal families and families with parental depression. *Child Development, 56*, 884–893.

Reynolds, G. S. (1961). Attention in the pigeon. *Journal of the Experimental Analysis of Behavior, 4*, 203–208.

Reynolds, G. S. (1975). *A primer of operant conditioning* (Rev. ed.). Glenview, IL: Scott Foresman.

Rheingold, H. L. (1977). Sharing at an early age. In B. C. Etzel, J. M. LeBlank, & D. M. Baer (Eds.), *New developments in behavioral research: Theory, method, and application* (pp. 498–502). Hillsdale, NJ: Erlbaum.

Rheingold, H. L. (1982). Little children's participation in the work of adults, a nascent prosocial behavior. *Child Development, 53*, 114–125.

Rheingold, H. L., & Eckerman, C. D. (1973). Fear of the stranger: A critical examination. In H. W. Reese (Ed.), *Advances in child development and behavior* (Vol. 8, pp. 185–222). Orlando, FL: Academic.

Rheingold, H. L., & Emery, G. N. (1986). The nurturant acts of very young children. In D. Olweus, J. Block, & M. Radke-Yarrow (Eds.), *Development of antisocial and prosocial behavior* (pp. 75–96). Orlando, FL: Academic.

Rheingold, H. L., Gewirtz, J. L., & Ross, H. W. (1959). Social conditioning of vocalizations in the infant. *Journal of Consulting and Clinical Psychology, 52*, 67–73.

Rheingold, H. L., & Hay, D. F. (1980). Prosocial behavior of the very young. In G. S. Stent (Ed.), *Morality as a biological phenomenon* (pp. 93–108). Berkeley: University of California Press.

Rheingold, H. L., Hay, D. F., & West, M. J. (1976). Sharing in the second year of life. *Child Development, 47*, 1148–1158.

Richards, J. E., & Radar, N. (1981). Crawling-onset age predicts visual cliff avoidance in infants. *Journal of Experimental Psychology: Human Perception and Performance, 7*, 382–387.

Rovee, C. K., & Fagen, J. W. (1976). Extended conditioning and 24-hour retention in infants. *Journal of Experimental Child Psychology, 21*, 1–11.

Rovee-Collier, C. K., & Capatides, J. B. (1979). Positive behavioral contrast in 3-month-old infants on multiple conjugate reinforcement schedules. *Journal of the Experimental Analysis of Behavior, 32*, 15–27.

Rovee-Collier, C. K., & Gekoski, M. J. (1979). The economics of infancy: A review of conjugate reinforcement. In H. W. Reese & L. P. Lipsitt (Eds.), *Advances in child development and behavior* (Vol. 13, pp. 195–255). New York: Academic.

Rovee-Collier, C., Griesler, P. C., & Earley, L. A. (1985). Contextual determinants of retrieval in three-month-old infants. *Learning and Motivation, 16,* 139–157.

Rovee-Collier, C. K., Morrongiello, B. A., Aron, M., & Kupersmidt, J. (1978). Topographical response differentiation and reversal in 3-month-old infants. *Infant Behavior and Development, 1,* 323–333.

Rovee-Collier, C. K., Sullivan, M. W., Enright, M., Lucas, D., & Fagen, J. W. (1980). Reactivation of infant memory. *Science, 208,* 1159–1161.

Rovee-Collier, C. K., & Sullivan, M. W. (1980). Organization of infant memory. *Journal of Experimental Psychology, 6,* 798–807.

Sagi, A., & Hoffman, M. L. (1976). Empathic distress in the newborn. *Developmental Psychology, 2,* 175–176.

Santrock, J. W. (1988). *Children* (2nd ed.). Dubuque: Brown.

Scarr, S., Weinberg, R. A., & Levine, A. (1986). *Understanding development.* San Diego, CA: Harcourt, Brace Jovanovich.

Schaffer, H. R., & Emerson, P. E. (1964). The development of social attachments in infancy. *Monographs of the Society for Research in Child Development, 29* (3, Serial No. 94).

Schlinger, H. D. (1992). Theory in behavior analysis: An application to child development. *American Psychologist, 47,* 1396–1410.

Schlinger, H. D. (1993). Learned expectancies are not adequate scientific explanations. *American Psychologist, 48,* 1155–1156.

Schlinger, H. D., & Blakely, E. (1987). Function-altering effects of contingency-specifying stimuli. *The Behavior Analyst, 10,* 41–46.

Schlinger, H. D., & Blakely, E. Q. (1994). A descriptive taxonomy of environmental operations and its implications for behavior analysis. *The Behavior Analyst, 17,* 43–57.

Schmitt, D. R., & Marwell, G. (1968). Stimulus control in the experimental study of cooperation. *Journal of the Experimental Analysis of Behavior, 11,* 571–574.

Schoenfeld, W. N., & Cumming, W. W. (1963). Behavior and perception. In S. Koch (Ed.), *Psychology: A study of a science* (pp. 213–252). New York: McGraw-Hill.

Schwartz, A. N., Campos, J. J., & Baisel, E. J. (1973). The visual cliff: Cardiac and behavioral response on the deep and shallow sides at five and nine months of age. *Journal of Experimental Child Psychology, 15,* 86–99.

Schwartz, B. (1989). *Psychology of learning and behavior.* New York: Norton.

Shaffer, D. R. (1988). *Social and personality development* (2nd ed.). Pacific Grove, CA: Brooks/Cole.

Shaffer, D. R. (1994). *Social and personality development* (3rd ed.). Pacific Grove, CA: Brooks/Cole.

Sheppard, W. (1969). Operant control of infant vocal and motor behavior. *Journal of Experimental Child Psychology, 7,* 36–51.

Sherman, J. A. (1965). Use of reinforcement and imitation to reinstate verbal behavior in mute psychotics. *Journal of Abnormal Psychology, 70,* 155–164.

Sidman, M. (1960). *Tactics of scientific research.* New York: Basic Books.

Sidman, M. (1986). Functional analysis of emergent verbal classes. In T. Thompson & M. Zeiler (Eds.), *Analysis and integration of behavioral units* (pp. 213–245). Hillsdale, NJ: Erlbaum.

Siqueland, E. R., & DeLucia, C. A. (1969). Visual reinforcement of nonnutritive sucking in human infants. *Science, 165,* 1144–1146.

Skinner, B. F. (1935). The generic nature of the concepts of stimulus and response. *Journal of General Psychology, 12,* 40–65.

Skinner, B. F. (1938). *The behavior of organisms.* Englewood Cliffs, NJ: Prentice-Hall.

Skinner, B. F. (1947). Experimental psychology. In W. Dennis (Ed.), *Current trends in psychology*. Pittsburgh: University of Pittsburgh Press.

Skinner, B. F. (1950). Are theories of learning necessary? *Psychological Review, 57*, 193–216.

Skinner, B. F. (1956). A case history in scientific method. *American Psychologist, 11*, 221–233.

Skinner, B. F. (1957). *Verbal behavior*. Englewood Cliffs, NJ: Prentice-Hall.

Skinner, B. F. (1972). A lecture on having a poem. *Cumulative Record* (3rd ed.) (pp. 345–355). New York: Appleton-Century-Crofts.

Skinner, B. F. (1974). *About behaviorism*. New York: Knopf.

Skinner, B. F. (1989). *Recent issues in the analysis of behavior*. Columbus, OH: Merrill.

Slater, P. J. B. (1985). *An introduction to ethology*. Cambridge, U.K.: Cambridge University Press.

Sluckin, W. (1965). *Imprinting and early learning*. London: Methuen.

Sorce, J. F., Emde, R. N., Campos, J., & Klinnert, M. D. (1985). Maternal emotional signaling: Its effect on the visual cliff behavior of 1-year-olds. *Developmental Psychology, 21*, 195–200.

Stevenson, H. W. (1970). Piaget, behavior theory, and intelligence. In R. Brown (Ed.), *Cognitive development in children* (pp. 95–108). Chicago: University of Chicago Press.

Stoller, S. A., & Field, T. (1982). Alteration of mother and infant behavior and heart rate during a still-face perturbation of face-to-face interaction. In T. Field & A. Fogel (Eds.), *Emotion and early interaction* (pp. 57–82). Hillsdale, NJ: Erlbaum.

Sullivan, M. W., Rovee-Collier, C. K., & Tynes, D. M. (1979). A conditioning analysis of infant long-term memory. *Child Development, 50*, 152–162.

Thelen, E. (1979). Rhythmic stereotypies in normal human infants. *Animal Behavior, 27*, 699–715.

Thelen, E. (1983). Learning to walk is still an "old" problem: A reply to Zelazo (1983). *Journal of Motor Behavior, 15*, 139–161.

Thelen, E., Kelso, J. A. S., & Fogel, A. (1987). Self-organizing systems and infant motor development. *Developmental Review, 7*, 39–65.

Thompson, R. A. (1987). Empathy and emotional understanding: The early development of empathy. In N. Eisenberg & J. Strayer (Eds.), *Empathy and its development* (pp. 119–145). New York: Cambridge University Press.

Thompson, T., & Lubinski, D. (1986). Units of analysis and kinetic structure of behavioral repertoires. *Journal of the Experimental Analysis of Behavior, 46*, 219–242.

Timberlake, W., & Allison, J. (1974). Response deprivation: An empirical approach to instrumental performance. *Psychological Review, 81*, 146–164.

Todd, G. A., & Palmer, B. (1968). Social reinforcement of infant babbling. *Child Development, 39*, 591–596.

Trevarthen, C. (1977). Descriptive analyses of infant communicative behaviour. In H. R. Schaffer (Ed.), *Studies in mother–infant interaction* (pp. 227–270). London: Academic.

Tronick, E. Z., Ricks, M., & Cohn, J. F. (1982). Maternal and infant affective exchange: Patterns of adaptation. In T. Field & A. Fogel (Eds.), *Emotion and early interaction* (pp. 83–100). Hillsdale, NJ: Erlbaum.

Vasta, R., Haith, M. M., & Miller, S. A. (1992). *Child psychology: The modern science*. New York: Wiley.

Vaughan, M. E., & Michael, J. L. (1982). Automatic reinforcement: An importance but ignored concept. *Behaviorism, 10*, 217–227.

Wahler, R. G. (1967). Infant social attachments: A reinforcement theory interpretation and investigation. *Child Development, 38*, 1079–1088.

Waters, E., Hay, D. F., & Richters, J. E. (1986). Infant–parent attachment and the origins of prosocial and antisocial behavior. In D. Olweus, J. Block, & M. Radke-Yarrow (Eds.),

Development of antisocial and prosocial behavior: Research, theories, and issues (pp. 97–125). Orlando, FL: Academic.

Watson, J. S. (1967). Memory and contingency analysis in infant learning. *Merrill-Palmer Quarterly, 13,* 55–76.

Watson, J. S., & Ramey, C. T. (1972). Reactions to response-contingent stimulation in early infancy. *Merrill-Palmer Quarterly, 18,* 219–227.

Webster's Seventh New Collegiate Dictionary (1965). Springfield, MA: Merriam.

Webster's New World Dictionary (1984). Springfield, MA: Merriam.

Werner, J. S., & Siqueland, E. R. (1978). Visual recognition memory in the preterm infant. *Infant Behavior and Development, 1,* 79–98.

West, M. J., & Rheingold, H. L. (1978). Infant stimulation of maternal instruction. *Infant Behavior and Development, 1,* 205–215.

Whaley, D. L., & Malott, R. W. (1973). *Elementary principles of behavior.* New York: Appleton-Century-Crofts.

White, B. L. (1967). An experimental approach to the effects of experience on early human behavior. In J. P. Hill (Ed.), *Minnesota symposium on child psychology* (pp. 201–225). Minneapolis: University of Minnesota.

White, B. L. (1971). *Human infants: Experience and psychological development.* Englewood Cliffs, NJ: Prentice-Hall.

White, B., Castle, R., & Held, R. (1964). Observations on the development of visually directed reaching. *Child Development, 35,* 349–364.

White, B. L., & Held, R. (1966). Plasticity of sensorimotor development in the human infant. In J. Rosenblith & E. Allinsmith (Eds.), *The causes of behavior: Readings in child development and educational psychology* (pp. 60–70). Boston: Allyn & Bacon.

White, T. G. (1982). Naming practices, typicality, and underextension in child language. *Journal of Experimental Child Psychology, 33,* 324–346.

Whitehurst, G. J. (1972). Production of novel and grammatical utterances by young children. *Journal of Experimental Child Psychology, 13,* 502–515.

Whitehurst, G. J., Falco, F. L., Lonigan, C. J., Fischel, J. E., DeBaryshe, B., Valdez-Menchaca, M. C., & Caufield, M. (1988). Accelerating language development through picture book reading. *Developmental Psychology, 24,* 552–559.

Whitehurst, G. J., & Valdez-Menchaca, M. C. (1988). What is the role of reinforcement in language acquisition. *Child Development, 59,* 430–440.

Wiesel, T. N. (1982). Postnatal development of the visual cortex and the influence of environment. *Nature, 299,* 583–592.

Wolff, P. H. (1969). The natural history of crying and other vocalizations in early infancy. In B. H. Foss (Eds.), *Determinants of infant behavior.* London: Methuen.

Yonas, A., Cleaves, W., & Petterson, L. (1978). Development of sensitivity to pictorial depth. *Science, 200,* 77–79.

Yonas, A., Granrud, C. E., & Petterson, L. (1985). Infant's sensitivity to relative size information for distance. *Developmental Psychology, 21,* 161–167.

Yonas, A., Oberg, C., & Norcia, A. (1978). Development of sensitivity to binocular information for the approach of an object. *Developmental Psychology, 14,* 147–152.

Yonas, A., & Owsley, C. (1987). Development of visual space perception. In P. Salapatek & L. Cohen (Eds.), *Handbook of infant perception* (Vol. 2, pp. 79–122). Orlando, FL: Academic.

Yonas, A., Pettersen, L., & Granrud, C. E. (1982). Infant's sensitivity to familiar size as information for distance. *Child Development, 53,* 1285–1290.

Zahn-Waxler, C., & Radke-Yarrow, M. (1979). Child rearing and children's prosocial initiations toward victims of distress. *Child Development, 50,* 319–330.

Zahn-Waxler, C., & Radke-Yarrow, M. (1982). The development of altruism: Alternative research strategies. In N. Eisenberg (Ed.), *The development of prosocial behavior* (pp. 109–137). New York: Academic.

Zahn-Waxler, C., Radke-Yarrow, M., Wagner, E., & Chapman, M. (1992). Development of concern for others. *Developmental Psychology, 28,* 126–136.

Zeiler, M. D. (1986). Behavioral units: A historical introduction. In T. Thompson & M. D. Zeiler (Eds.), *Analysis and integration of behavioral units* (pp. 1–12). Hillsdale, NJ: Erlbaum.

Zelazo, P. R., Zelazo, N. A., & Kolb, S. (1972). "Walking" in the newborn. *Science, 176,* 314–315.

Zeskind, P. S., & Marshall, T. R. (1988). The relation between variations in pitch and maternal perceptions of infant crying. *Child Development, 59,* 193–196.

Zuriff, G. E. (1985). *Behaviorism: A conceptual reconstruction.* New York: Columbia University Press.

Index

Active vs. passive learner, 128, 181–182
Adaptive behavior, 34–35, 66, 108, 123
Affective synchrony. *See* Empathy, types of
Altruism, 218–219
American Sign Language, 160
Ames trapezoidal window, 107
Aplysia, habituation in, 53
Approach behavior, 196
   proximity-establishing and proximity-
      maintaining behaviors, 196–200
   types of, 189
Attachment
   in altricial animals, 199–200
   behaviors, 189–200
      approach, 196; *see also* Approach be-
         havior
      signaling, 190; *see also* Signaling behavior
   figures, 188
   as metaphor, 186
   in precocial animals, 197–199
   relations, 16, 19–20, 185–213
   system, 188
Automatic reinforcement, 90
   of babbling, 160
   as ecological reinforcers in motor behav-
      ior, 90
   of helping, 226
   of language, 181
   of perceptual behavior, 108

Behavior analysis, 31–47
   compared to natural selection, 43, 108, 123
   of infant crying, 193
   of locomotor control, 82
   of postural control, 79
   of rhythmical stereotypies, 73–74
   units of analysis, 33–35
Behavioral contrast, 60
Behavioral plasticity, 42–43

Binocular disparity. *See* Depth perception
Binocular stimulus control. *See* Depth perception
Biology
   in motor behavior, 67
   role of in behavior analysis, 35, 38
Bonding, 28
Bowlby, John, 186, 194, 196–197
   theory of attachment, 187–189

Categorical perception, 153
Causes of behavior, 43–44
   proximate and ultimate, 44
Cephalocaudal development, 68
Chomsky, Noam, 154, 170, 176, 177–179
   theory of language and criticisms of, 177–
      178
Circular explanation, 19–20
Circular reasoning, 18
Classical conditioning, 128, 129, 239
   as a function altering operation, 40
Cognition, 121
Cognitive development, 121–149
   egocentrism, 125
   sensorimotor period of, 125–136
      primary circular reactions, 127–128
      primitive anticipations, 128–129, 133
      secondary circular reactions, 129–132
      tertiary circular reactions, 134–135
Compound stimuli, 65
Conditioned reinforcer. *See* Reinforcement
Conjugate reinforcement schedule, 56–57,
   58, 71, 131
Conservation of volume, 23
Contingency, 34
Control; *see also* Science, goals of
   behavior analytic view of, 76
   in motor development, 76; *see also* Pos-
      tural control, Manual control

Cooperative behavior. *See* Prosocial behavior, types of
Correlational research methods, 6, 20–24
    age-correlated research, 21
    value of, 22
Crawling, 81
Crying
    Bell and Ainsworth (1972) study, 191
        criticisms of, 191–193
    behavior analysis of, 193
    form vs. function, 156–157, 190–191
    maternal responding to, 191
    as a motivational variable, 191; *see also*
        Establishing operation
    in newborns, 187
    as signaling behavior, 190–194; *see also*
        Signaling behavior, types of
    types of, 191
    undifferentiated vs. differentiated, 157

Da Vinci, Leonardo, 105
Dependent variable, 6
    in prediction, 10
Depth perception, 97–109
    behavior analytic view of, 108–109
    binocular cues of, 97–99
        disparity, 98
    kinetic cues of, 98, 99–104
        motion parallax, 98, 99, 101, 102, 106
        accretion-deletion of texture, 103–104
        optical expansion, 98, 99
    static (monocular) cues of, 98, 104–108
        familiar size, 106–108
        interposition, 107–108
        shading, 108
        linear perspective, 106
        pictorial cues of, 105
    stereopsis, 98
    visual cliff experiment, 99–101
Development, concept of, 41–42
    behavior analytic view of, 42
    traditional view of, 41
Differential reinforcement. *See* Reinforcement
Discrimination. *See* Operant discrimination
Discriminative stimulus (SD), 34
    for children's verbal responses, 180
    for grasping, 123
    for infant protests, 202, 203
    pointing as, 223
    for size constancy, 118

Discriminative stimulus (SD) (*cont.*)
    social, 208–209
    verbal, 164
    Dr. Seuss, 208

Ecological reinforcers. *See* Reinforcement
Emotional sharing, 237–239
Empathy, 230–242
    behavior analytic interpretation of, 239–242
    defined, 231
    types of, 232–239
        affective synchrony in mother–infant play, 232–236
        interpreting facial cues of emotion, 236
        reactive crying in newborns, 232
Environment, 35
    behavior analytic view of, 36–37
    locus of control in, 37–38
    traditional view of, 35–36
Essentialistic view, 219
    of altruism, 218
    of language, 151
    of morality, 216
Establishing operations (EO), 33, 41, 56
    infant crying as, 191
    for sympathetic behavior, 240
Evolutionary-ethological theories (of attachment), 187–190
Extension, 167–168
    overextension, 167
    underextension, 167
Extinction. *See* Operant extinction

Facial recognition, 194
Familiar size. *See* Depth perception, static (monocular) cues of
Fetal learning. *See* Prenatal learning
Forgetting, 61–64
    decay hypothesis of, 62
Form of behavior. *See* Structural approaches
Freud, 9, 11, 18, 38, 188–189
Function altering operations, 40–41; *see also* Reinforcement
    classical conditioning, 40
    imprinting as, 41
    modeling as, 41
    operant conditioning, 40

Functional classification system in behavior analysis, 39–41
Function of behavior, 17–18, 35
Functional relations, 2, 4, 33–34
Functional units of analysis, 33

Generalization
in cognitive development, 126–127
response, 130, 173
stimulus, 119, 126–127, 167–168
defined, 167
in Vervet monkeys, 168
Genes, role of
in behavior analysis, 35, 38, 42–43, 108
in motor behavior, 67
Gestalt psychology, 176
Grammar, 169, 171–176
branches of,
morphology, 169
syntax, 169

Habituation procedures
in size constancy experiments, 112
in visual recognition memory experiments, 51–56
Hand regard. See Manual control
Harlow, Harry, 199–201
Helping. See Prosocial behavior
Holophrase, 170

Imitation, 136–142
generalized, 140–141
experiments on, 141–142
genetic explanations of, 140
Piagetian view of, 137–138
as reflexive behavior, 139
role of learning in, 140
Imprinting, 73, 197–199
as a function altering operation, 41
reinforcement models of, 198
Independent variable, 6, 21
in prediction, 10
Infant protests. See Stranger anxiety
Infant walkers, 84
Inference, cognitive and behavior analytic, 38
Internal events, 37

Kinetic stimulus control. See Depth perception
Knowledge (of environment) as a cognitive explanation, 92

Language. See Verbal behavior
Language development, 151–183
behavior analytic view presented in textbooks, 179
essentialist approach to, 151
role of reinforcement in, 180
Language universals, 175–176
Law of Effect, 4, 5
Law, scientific, 4, 8
Linear perspective. See Depth perception, static (monocular) cues of
Locomotor control, 80–85
behavior analysis of, 82
motivational variables in, 83
reinforcers in, 84
unconditioned reinforcers in, 83
Long-term memory, 61–64
Lorenz, Konrad, 197

Mand. See Verbal behavior, functional units of
Manual control, 85–90
hand regard, 86, 88
pincer grasp, 89
reaching and grasping, 86, 88
visually guided reaching, 86; see also Visually guided reaching
Maturation, 67
accounts of motor development, 69
defined, 68
role of in motor development, 68
Memory, 45, 49–66
behavior analytic view of, 45
as a circular explanation, 50, 51
cognitive view of, 45, 50
operant conditioning procedures, 57–61
research on, 51–65
Modeling, as a function altering operation, 41
Moral behavior (development), 215–242
behavior analytic view of, 216–217, 218
cognitive view of, 216, 217
essentialist view, 216, 218, 219; see also Essentialistic view
Morphology. See Grammar, branches of
Mother–infant play,
affective synchrony, 232–236
face-to-face interactions, 233–236
behavior analytic interpretation of, 235–236
cognitive models of, 234
Motion parallax. See Depth perception, kinetic cues of

Motivational operations, 4, 165; *see also* Motivational variables, Establishing operations
Motivational variables, 33, 41, 162; *see also* Establishing operations, Motivational operations
    crying as, 191
    in locomotor control, 83
    and mands, 162
Motor development, 67–94
    behavior analytic view of, 93–94
    cognitive view of, 92–93

Naming, development of, 163–168
Natural selection. *See* Behavior analysis, compared to natural selection
Normative data, 6, 42

Object perception, 109–120
    behavior analytic view of, 115–120
Object permanence, 18–19, 23, 42, 142–148
    as example of circular reasoning, 19 , 148
    as theoretical construct, 142
    in sensorimotor development, 125, 144
Operant conditioning, 108
    cognitive interpretation of, 65–66
    of cooperative behavior, 229
    of crying, 193
    as a function altering operation,, 40
    of head turning, 102
    of smiling, 195
Operant discrimination, 40
    interpretation of anticipation in infants, 134
    interpretation of memory experiments, 62
Operant extinction, 3, 133, 236; *see also* Reinforcement, visual
    in Stage 4 of Piaget's sensorimotor period, 133
Optical expansion. *See* Depth perception, kinetic cues of
Overextension. *See* Extension
Overgeneralization (of verb use). *See* Overregularization
Overregularization (of verb use), 172, 173

Passive learner. *See* Active vs. passive learner
Pavlovian conditioning. *See* Classical conditioning
Piaget, 10, 18, 23, 27, 28, 93, 121–139, 142, 144–148; *see also* Piagetian concepts

Piagetian concepts, 122–125; *see also* Cognitive development
    accommodation, 122
    assimilation, 122
    behavior analytic view of, 123–124
    functional assimilation, 126
    organization and adaptation, 122–124
    psychological structures, 124–125; *see also* Schemes
    recognitory assimilation, 127
Perception
    defined behaviorally, 96
    defined cognitively, 95–96
Perceptual development, 95–120
    reinforcers for, 108
Pointing. *See* Prosocial behavior
Postural control, 76–80
    behavior analysis of, 79
    description of, 76
Prehension, 68
Prediction, scientific. *See* Science, goals of
Prenatal learning, 207–208
Prespeech, development of, 155–160
    babbling, stage of, 158–160
        automatic reinforcement of, 160
        canonical, 158
        conditioned reinforcement of, 159–160
        in deaf children and children of deaf parents, 160
        environmental influences on, 158–159
        manual, 160
    crying, 156–157; *see also* Crying
    phonation stage of, 157
Pre-walking, 80–81
Prosocial behavior, 218–242; *see also* Altruism, Empathy
    cooperating, 227–230
    essentialist view of, 218
    helping, 225–227
    sharing, 220–224
        experiments in, 220–222
        pointing, 222–224
Prosocial motivation, 237–239
Proximodistal development, 68

Reactive crying. *See* Empathy, types of
Recall memory, 51
Recognition memory. *See* Visual recognition memory
Reflexes, 74
    postural, 75–76
    rooting, 74

Reflexes (*cont.*)
  sucking, 126
  unconditioned (unconditional), 74
  walking, 69
Reification, 25
Reinforcement, 3, 59, 207
  automatic. *See* Automatic reinforcement
  conditioned, 41, 159–160
  differential, 174,
    of other behavior (DRO), 203
    in Stage 4 of Piaget's sensorimotor period, 133
  ecological 89–90
  as a function altering operation, 59, 207;
    see also Function altering operations
  of hand regard, 88–89
  intrauterine heartbeat as, 208
  law of, 2
  in perceptual development, 108
  of rhythmical stereotypies, 73
  of sympathetic behavior, 240–242
  theory of, 5
  visual, 56
    operant extinction of, 56
    satiation effects of, 56
  of walking, 84
Reinforcers. *See* Reinforcement
Respondent conditioning. *See* Classical conditioning
Response, 34
Response differentiation, 60
Response induction. *See* Generalization, response
Rhythmical stereotypies, 70–74
  reinforcement of, 73
  role of environment in development of, 71, 73
Rooting reflex. *See* Reflexes
Rule-governed morphology, 172

S-delta, 118
Science, 1–13
  goals of, 5–7
    control, 6
    prediction, 5–7
    understanding, 8, 12–13
Scientific interpretation, 7–8
Scientific understanding. *See* Science, goals of
SD. *See* Discriminative stimulus
Search behavior, 144–148
  AB search error, 145–148

Sensation, 95–96
Separation anxiety, 201–204
  behavior analytic interpretation of, 202–204
  theories of, 202
Scaffolding, 180
Schemes, 124–125; *see also* Piagetian concepts
Sharing. *See* Prosocial behavior
Signaling behavior; *see also* Attachment
  types of, 190–195
    crying, 190–194
    smiling, 194–195
Size constancy
  behavior analytic view of, 115–117
  cognitive view of, 111
  description of, 110
  experiments on, 102, 111–114
  reification of, 110–111
Skinner, B.F., 34, 38, 62, 73
  on imprinting, 199
  on scientific explanation, 35
  on theory, 31–33
  on verbal behavior, 152, 162, 164, 176
Smiling, 194–195
  operant conditioning of, 195
  as signaling behavior, 194; *see also* Attachment
  as social behavior, 194
Social and emotional development, 185–242; *see also* Attachment, Moral behavior
  behavior analytic view of, 206–212
  described, 186
Social behavior, 185
Social environment, 185
Social referencing, 209–212, 236, 237
  behavior analytic interpretation of, 210–212
  traditional description of, 209
  visual cliff experiments in, 209–210, 236

Social reinforcement, 207–208
Social stimuli, 185
Spatial referencing system, 147
Speech, development of, 161–171
  behavior analytic approach to, 161–162
  structural approaches to, 161
Speech perception, 152–155
  categorical perception, 153–155
Stage theories of development, 23
Static (monocular) stimulus control. *See* Depth perception

Stereopsis. *See* Depth perception
Stimulus, 34
  evocative functions of, 39–40
  functions of, 39
  generalization. *See* Generalization
Stimulus-change decrement, 63
Stranger anxiety, 204–206
Structural approaches to behavior, 16–20,
    35
  problems of, 17–20, 24–26
Sucking reflex, 126
Superstitious responding, 64
Syntax. *See* Grammar, branches of

Tact. *See* Verbal behavior, functional units
    of
Telegraphic speech, 171

Theory, scientific, 1–13
  criteria for evaluating, 8–11
    applied to developmental theory, 26–
      29
    external validity, 10
    generality, 9, 60
    parsimony, 11
    testability, 9–10
    utility, 10–11, 229
  defined, 4–5
  empirical support for, 10
  facts and, 2–4
  logical support for, 10
Three bears rule, 166–167

Unconditional (or unconditioned) reflexes.
    See Reflexes
Underextension. *See* Extension

Verbal behavior, 152
  controlled by depth cues, 119
  creativity in, 182
  functional units of, 162, 164
    echoic, 164
    intraverbal, 164
    mand, 162
    tact, 119, 164, 167, 170, 174
Verbal Behavior, 162
  Chomsky's review of, 177
  other reviews of, 177
Vervet monkeys, 168
Visual cliff apparatus, 100
  in depth perception experiments, 99–101
  in social referencing experiments, 209–
    210, 236
Visual fixation in infants, 51, 55
  cognitive and behavior analytic views
    of, 55–56
  operant stimulus control of, 53
Visual recognition memory
  habituation procedures in, 51–56
    paired comparison (novelty prefer-
      ence), 54–56
    single-stimulus, 51–54
    novelty discrimination procedures in, 56–
      57
Visually guided reaching, 117–120; *see also*
    Manual control of
Voluntary control of behavior, 67, 90–92
  free will and, 91
  vs. involuntary, 74

Walking, 82
  reinforcement of, 84
Walking reflex, 69